SOMOS XICANAS

ADVANCE PRAISE FOR *SOMOS XICANAS*

A beautiful and inspiring anthology that celebrates the Chicana woman in all her power. Keep it on your nightstand permanently for daily inspiration.

— **Reyna Grande**, author of *The Distance Between Us*

A brilliant gathering of poetic voices from all corners of our Xicana world! In *Somos Xicanas*, we find established elders, Castillo, Villanueva, Cervantes, Cisneros, alongside new voices from the Rio Grande Valley in Texas to the Midwest, to California. This inspiring collection is expertly curated into three sections — 'Somos Seeds,' 'Somos Stems & Branches,' and 'Somos Fruits & Flowers' — each offering variety in structure by intermingling prose pieces with poetry, allowing the voices to move between spoken word, freestyle, formal lyrical poetry, memoir and personal essays full of affirmations of what it is to be Xicana. The linguistic performance in Spanish, English, Spanglish, and even Nahuatl found in the contributions offers readers a journey across our Chicanidades. Read this collection to glean the extraordinary experiences of Xicanas by a fine-tuned choir of poetic voices!

— **Norma E. Cantú**, Murchison Distinguished Professor in Humanities, Trinity University, San Antonio, Texas

An essential text and instant classic, *Somos Xicanas* gathers in lyrical solidarity the voices of a wide range of Chicana identities, all fearlessly exploring the Anzalduan nepantla and its roots in once-repressed indigeneity. Powerful poems and prose by established and emerging voices alike become, in the editors' deft hands, brilliant threads woven together into a multi-hued rebozo that, through its beauty and utility, leave the reader wiser and more prepared for la lucha, as the words of women — in cihuatlahtolli — have always done for those willing to listen.

— **David Bowles**, award-winning author of *They Call Her Fregona* and *The Prince & the Coyote*

This is one SPIRITUALLY MOVING language bouquet of nopal thorns, marigolds and cuetlaxochitls (poinsettias). What an accomplished array of multigenerational women and geographically diverse short story writers, essayists and poets all profoundly in touch with their ancestral and contemporary herstories; told not just in English, Spanish, but also in Nahuatl and Caló. Its power resides in actual lives de las mujeres Xicanas. You'll savor the affirmations, reminisces and unconquerable love that permeates these pages.

— **Carlos Cumpián**, Board Member of the Chicago Literary Hall of Fame, author of *Human Cicada* (Prickly Pear Publishing)

This impressive collection of contemporary Chicana writers presents an artistically and philosophically mature aspect of American literature. This anthology is arranged as if it were a plant whose seeds lay in a wasteland but, against great odds, sprout and grow into a tree. It proclaims the journey of the human spirit is not just to survive but to thrive, to assert itself, "To Be."

Chicanas historically were not only pushed to the margins of invisibility in U.S. society but oppressed by the patriarchy of Hispanic traditional culture. The artists herein first recover the seeds — the origins — of their repressed identity in the dark layers of the imagination. From there, the works advance into the growth of consciousness, and finally individual and collective self-assertion. These eloquent poems, fiction, and non-fiction are a testimonial to Chicana identity and the triumph of the human spirit are highly recommended for scholars and the intellectually curious.

— **Rosa Martha Villarreal**, author of the critically acclaimed novels *Doctor Magdalena*, *Chronicles of Air and Dreams*, and *The Stillness of Love and Exile*

SOMOS XICANAS

An all Xicana anthology illuminating
both the enduring and new Xicana
identity, presence and culture

Edited by

LUZ SCHWEIG

with

SCOTT RUSSELL DUNCAN, JENNY IRIZARY & ARMANDO B. RENDÓN

RIOT OF ROSES
PUBLISHING HOUSE
SEJATNGA
UNCEDED TONGVA TERRITORY
SOUTH WHITTIER, CALIFORNIA

SOMOS XICANAS
First Edition Copyright © 2024
Published by Riot of Roses Publishing House
Sejatnga, South Whittier, CA
www.riotofrosespublishinghouse.com

Copyright © 2024 by Luz Schweig
Library of Congress Cataloging-in-Publication Data
ISBN Softcover: 978-1-961717-23-7
Ebook: 978-1-961717-24-4
Hardcover: 978-1-961717-25-1

Typeset in Adobe Garamond Pro

Riot of Roses Publishing House is a Xicana-owned, independent establishment founded to amplify the stories of historically silenced voices

For any inquiries, write to Riot of Roses Publishing House

Riotofrosesllc@gmail.com

Editor-in-Chief: Luz Schweig
Assistant Editors:
Jenny Irizary, Scott Russell Duncan, Armando B. Rendón, Carolyn Chilton Casas
Cover design: Luz Schweig
Interior Layout: Emily Anne Evans

I dedicate this labor of love to my two sisters,
Eréndira and Elisabeth
con mucho amor y cariño

And to all my other hermanas, near and far,
across the Xicana Nation!

CONTENTS

CONTENTS

II SOMOS STEMS & LEAVES

CONTENTS

CONTENTS

FOREWORD

My first instinct when imagining the Foreword for *Somos Xicanas* was to draw on my newly acquired academic language and Westernized analytical framing. However, as a third-year PhD student navigating the often-turbulent waters of academic theory and methodologies, while remaining committed to decolonizing my academic spaces and maintaining my commitment to Indigenizing my theory, pedagogy, and praxis, I began to feel the systems of erasure tugging at me, threatening to limit how I represent the collective wisdom within this anthology in the most authentic and vulnerable way possible.

In academia, I can sometimes feel heaviness in my chest, like I'm balancing on the edge of breath and submersion, where the pull beneath the surface feels relentless. My limbs push forward, exhausted but determined, with each breath I steal gasps from a tide that constantly swells to drag me under. Yet, there is a rhythm to this struggle, an ache within survival, like a lover both tender and cruel. The sea tells me it could claim me at any moment, but here I remain, alive and ever-transforming in my Xicana identity and evolving positionality in the academy. Through this unceasing ebb and flow, I've realized this anthology, our collective writings, belong in all spaces, even those that feel alien or hostile. Our voices, histories, and stories are necessary, and they are integral to reshaping the tides and reclaiming spaces that have long sought to silence them.

Through my studies, I've come to understand my Xicana reality as a living extension of my ancestors, whose legacies I liberate through poetics. Our past, present, and future Indigenous and AfroIndigenous bloodlines cry out for poetry and prose unbound from the colonizer DNA manifesting in every system born from genocide that continues to distort and silence us. The authors of *Somos Xicanas* carry the sacred bloodline that holds our knowledge and ignites resistance, recovering spaces where our voices, experiences, and cultural truths are acknowledged and exalted. Together, we engage in an act of rescription by writing and rewriting the narratives imposed upon us, untangling ourselves from oppressive forces that attempt to fragment and diminish our identities.

Through our words, we reclaim the right to define ourselves, challenging the structures that seek to contain us. In this collective process of poetic testimonio, we celebrate by refusing the confines of imposed narratives. We carve out spaces where our stories, bodies, and identities are transformative, expansive, and powerful, allowing us to reimagine and reaffirm our place in the world. As contributors to *Somos Xicanas*, we know what we are doing and why it matters. When our creativity and activism as scholars, writers, educators, artists, community organizers, and curanderas transcend time and space, it is to declare that we are present, undeniable, and ever-creating new futures in our fully enfleshed realities.

I think I speak for all contributors when I say we are not here to perpetuate oppressive narratives or recolonize one another, nor do we dictate how one should identify on their journey toward self-affirmation. Use this anthology to align with your own Xicanisma, or to understand the diverse positionalities and possibilities of Xicana realities across various intersectionalities, race and ethnicity, gender and sexuality, class and socioeconomic status, migration and citizenship, language and translingual practices, ancestry and Indigenous heritage, spirituality and religion, as well as disability and accessibility. Xicana identity is shaped by place, acknowledging that identity is fluid and influenced by the landscapes we inhabit. This anthology offers readers a lens to reflect on how these intersectionalities forge their own journeys and contribute to a broader narrative of resistance, reclamation, and cultural affirmation.

Like apostolic petitions, the authors of *Somos Xicanas* present their poetry and prose as spiritual and intellectual offerings, sacred texts grounded in the experiences of Xicana women, enriched by ancestral knowledge and decolonial thought. These meditations, prayers, and psalms echo the wisdom of the past while reimagining it, breathing new life into ancient teachings through voices long silenced. The authority to pass these along in our own words is an act of agency, of power in the hands of the women and communities from which it was once taken.

Through these reimagined poetics, we construct a body of work that forges paths forward and acknowledges our multiplicity, complexity, and interconnectedness. We honor the tradition of storytelling while rejecting the structures that have silenced Xicanas since our inception, as

I believe it to be, at the point of Spanish contact. The distorted narratives surrounding historic figures like Malintzin, also known as La Malinche, were told through the oppressive lenses of Bernal Díaz del Castillo, Hernán Cortés, and Francisco López de Gómara. This perpetuated harmful misconceptions and reduced her to a symbol of betrayal bleeding into the violent ascription of chingada, rather than acknowledging her complexity as a survivor in a colonial world. In recovering our stories, we disrupt the colonial gaze, restoring agency and depth to our ancestral women.

The *Seeds* section of the *Somos Xicanas* anthology serves as a representation of genesis, symbolizing creation, beginnings, and the foundational narratives that shape the Xicana self. Each poem acts as a seed planted in fertile literary soil, destined to grow into adaptable expressions of hybrid-identity resistance. These poems explore origins on multiple levels, personal, collective, historical, spiritual, magical, and mythological.

In "We Would Like You to Know," Ana Castillo boldly asserts the bearing and complexity of Xicana identity in the face of stereotypes, refusing simplistic narratives. Lines such as "We do not all pick lettuce, run assembly lines, clean restaurant tables, even if someone has to do it" push back against the monolithic depictions often imposed on Xicanas, emphasizing the vast distinctions within the community. Castillo's poem further highlights how Xicanas navigate a world that tries to pin them to a single, reductive image: "We never claimed to be a homogenous race." By declaring, "we are going forward. There is no going back," the poem captures a collective sense of determination, anchoring Xicana identity in both insistence and refusal to be defined by external forces.

The poem "I am an Aztec Dance" by Briana Muñoz defines the Xicana as a continuous ceremony, a dance of life shaped by ancestral rhythms, connecting her to the heartbeat of huehuetl, to the four sacred directions, and to her own hybrid identities of child, woman, warrior, and ancestor. Her verses invoke a personal origin story connected to mythological symbols like Tezcatlipoca and Coatlicue. Her dance becomes a metaphor for the cyclical nature of existence, where the body becomes a vessel of knowledge, much like the pre-Columbian pictograms that fade with time yet continue to exist through her DNA. Muñoz's lines, "I am sweat, water / I am dancing through the pain," evoke physical and spiritual sacrifices embedded in self-discipline and continuity. The Aztec dance is meditative, an ongoing process of becoming, where inherited remembrance guides us, and the dance itself is a testament to regeneration.

Sonia Gutiérrez's "Cosmos" connects female archetypes such as Wind Woman, Tree Woman, and Blood Woman to natural elements, demonstrating how these figures embody aspects of the world's creation. These archetypes born from and existing in the Earth, mirror how Xicanas are both creators and products of their environments. The poem reflects Indigenous epistemologies, positioning nature as central to identity and knowledge. In these poems, female characters and archetypes resist patriarchal and colonial definitions of identity. They become embodiments of various origins, cultural, personal, and cosmic, building and rebuilding the architectures of their existence. These writings assert that Xicana identity is ever-present, fluid, and deserving of recognition in every space. Xicanisma, much like Mother Earth herself, is constantly being (re)created, always evolving.

The *Stems and Leaves* section represents growth, expansion, and the ongoing process of becoming in the Xicana experience. Building upon the origins laid out in *Seeds*, the imagery of stems and leaves suggests stamina, steadfastness, and durability, the capacity to stretch outward toward light while remaining firmly grounded. These poems reflect how Xicana identity is continuously nourished and transformed in response to adversity, similar to how stems and leaves seek out and grow toward the sun as survival while remaining anchored in the earth.

In "Nopalera" by Marissa Cueva, the nopal symbolizes generational continuity within the Xicana experience. The poem connects memory with ancestral significance, highlighting the intimacy between the speaker, her Tita, and the traditions that shape their lives. Through the act of peeling nopales, the poem metaphorically conveys the intergenerational transfer of knowledge and healing. Tita's request for the speaker to remove the thorns, "Quítame las espinas," represents the passing down of wisdom and pain, as well as the speaker's role in continuing traditions while carrying the burdens of past generations.

The nopal, with its vibrant green leaves, grows from an aged trunk showing how the younger generation takes root in the strength and struggles of their ancestors while progressing in their own constancy. The female archetypes in this section are portrayed as caretakers of memory rather than passive figures; they are active participants in their own growth, representing the nurturing and protective forces that sustain refusal. These archetypes drawn from spirit, flesh, and nature reflect the ongoing process of regenerating and reimagining one's place in the cosmos, always grounded in personal and communal legacies.

The *Flowers and Fruits* section signals the culmination of growth, where the writings depict a fruition toward identity, with the act of bearing fruit symbolizing the production of new forms of knowledge, creativity, and expressions that nourish both individuals and the collective. In "Con Poesía" by Xánath Caraza, poetry takes on a transformative role in the digital and cyber context where words sustain. The imagery of "cybernetic clouds" and "artificial pulsations like flowers tattooed across the screen" draws a connection between traditional expressions of poetry and the modern digital landscape. In this context, poetry and prose serve as a bridge, offering solace during times of isolation, especially in a world where interactions are increasingly mediated through digital platforms, a reality amplified by the cultural shift brought on by COVID.

The poem illustrates how poetry disperses "times of darkness," suggesting that even in the digital realm, words continue to bring light to those affected, disconnected, or alienated as we witness global injustices across our screens. The imagery, the "tattooed flowers," "pulsations," and "music that bathes us," conveys how the rhythm of poetry transcends the physical world, entering the cybernetic sphere to reach. Poetry as an artistic endeavor represents a critical force that contributes to sustainability and continuity. This reflects the notion of poetry as both theory and practice, where writing becomes a means of embodying knowledge.

In "Poema de Fuego," Diana Pando explores the potent metaphor of fire to signify both destruction and renewal. Fire becomes a force that consumes, purifies, and creates space for regeneration, reflecting the complex nature of the Xicana experience as I understand it. The act of eating fire conveys both power and pain, as it becomes a part of the speaker's being, reshaping her from within. This suggests a reclamation of control over destruction, turning them into something transformative. The image of the "candle cracked by heat" further emphasizes how the intensity of fire can damage, yet the cracks it leaves behind can be seen as marks of endurance and rebirth.

The paradox of fire as both violent and empowering is essential to understanding the bruja Pando's poem. The bruja is historically demonized, whispered about as "mala bruja" and targeted for destruction as others cry "¡quema la bruja!" Yet, within Xicana culture, for many, the bruja has been reclaimed as a symbol of authority and revitalization. The tension between being seen as a curse or a blessing reflects the broader struggle for Xicanas to define themselves against colonial imprints and patriarchal narratives that seek to suppress their autonomy and power. Fire, in this context, becomes the means through which Xicanas reassert themselves, transforming the words and accusations of others into flames that fuel their reclamation. The duality of fire, dangerous yet empowering, speaks to the complex hybridity of identity, where the struggle for autonomy and voice is accompanied by transformative potential.

As I reflect on the narrative arc of the *Somos Xicanas* anthology, I return to the metaphor of harsh water at the beginning of this forward. While I initially discussed water as turbulent and threatening, it now symbolizes healing and renewal. Like the relentless waves I often face in academia, the waters of our history can be overwhelming, pulling us under. As the poems in *Somos Xicanas* offer a narrative of flourishing, so too does water sustain that flourishing, nourishing the seeds, stems, leaves, flowers, and fruit of our writings.

The contributors of *Somos Xicanas* recover these healing waters, revolutionizing often tempestuous histories into a source of transformation and regeneration. Through the water and with our words, we baptize future generations, ensuring that the stories of Xicanas will continue to thrive in all spaces. Our poetics flow through time, connecting us to our past, grounding us in the present, and creating new futures.

As prophets and storytellers speaking truths that sustain our histories and communities, *Somos Xicanas* focalizes us as creators, nurturers, and sustainers. Through our poems, prose, prayers, and meditations, we establish authority to pass along teachings in our own words, much like an apostolic lineage of Xicanisma, spreading truths and experiences to all who read and listen. This anthology ultimately asserts that the works of Xicanas belong within the rhetoric of academic spaces, in all educational spaces, in community centers, in medical waiting rooms, in public libraries, in cultural festivals, on stages where poetry and performance come alive, in the hands of youth as they explore their identities, in social justice movements, in digital forums, and in the hearts of those seeking understanding of the Xicana.

Jen Yáñez-Alaniz
Chicana [Mestiza] poet activist, scholar, educator
October 24, 2024

INTRODUCTION

"The only way I can write, is to give voice to that which I know,
to that which is underrepresented."

Ana Castillo

There was a time when women's voices were held sacred, and our palabras — delivered in songs — accompanied us in life, as there were songs for birthing, for menstruating, for weddings, for harvesting, for dying, etc. Our palabras were celebrated for holding meaning and might, waxing and waning in natural phases, like the moon. But after invasion and oppression, our voices were subjugated, and pushed underground, much like the 45 ancestral rivers that once ran though México-Tenochtitlan and are now covered with pavement.

The invisibility of the underground rivers reminds me of underrepresented voices, including the voices of our abuelitas and tatarabuelitas: though apparently eclipsed to some, they've always been available to us, their granddaughters and great granddaughters. And just as the right of rivers to flow is now gradually being restored,[1] ancestral voices have been flowing anew through us, into public spaces, especially over the last few decades. As part of this new era, a significant body of Xicana literature has emerged against all odds, like rushing rivers breaking through pavement. In these books we carry forth life itself— our palabras delivering vital nourishment and medicina to those who need it most, as sure as blood flows through veins.

Had I come across such literary medicina when I was a thirteen-year-old immigrant, I may not have wilted as I did in new terrain. As a young woman, I experienced unbearable invalidation and loneliness in an estadounidense, euro-centric, public school system that obscured our culture and contributions. I became confused as to why the curriculum — completely bereft of our Indigenous voices —

---

1 In January 2017, Mexico City incorporated Article 13 into its constitution, (the Carta Magna), which proclaims: "The right to the preservation and protection of nature will be guaranteed by Mexico City authorities . . .", followed by a campaign by the Earth Law Center to secure the legal rights of the Río Magdalena Atlitic, the last free-flowing river in Mexico-Tenochtitlan.

either seriously misrepresented our history (as I knew it to be from my schooling in Mexico), or completely erased it. And though well meaning, I perceived my parents as contributing to this erasure, by encouraging us to assimilate. Even the Spanish language disappeared from our home. Like a germinating seed that had been uprooted and tossed upon pavement, I found nothing north of el Río Bravo to dig myself into: no yielding soil to help me grow. An overwhelming culture shock ensued.

I have no doubt that if someone had introduced my teenage self to a book written by a Xicana, it would have made a world of difference to me! Instead, I fell into a deep depression and dropped out of high school. One of my inspirations in curating this anthology is for it to find its way into the hearts of the youth that need it most. My hope is that the powerful Xicana voices in this book crack someone's pavement and release the rivers trapped underneath. Like the mighty river Huitzilopochco waiting to be freed — whose waters once flowed where Avenida Río Churubusco now lays, just around the corner from my old childhood neighborhood — there are many voices just waiting to be liberated.

I will never forget the first time I was taught to throw my voice into the wind: "échale tu canto al viento, pa' que llegue mas lejos." I loved picturing my voice swept into the sky like a violet jacaranda flower on a windy day, twirling all the way to the plaza down the street. Although I grew up in Mexico City, as a child, I was apapachada on the Oaxacan laps of women with long braids. And before my short, curly hair had grown into a long braid of my own, I asked my mother if she would make me a braid of yarn, which I proudly wore until I turned five. By then, I thought, people would be able to see that I belonged to the gentle ways of those Indigenous mujeres who sat for long stretches sorting beans, filled the garden with laughter and knew to sing in the same direction the wind was blowing.

Later, I learned that our ancestral representation of the wind, or the element of ether, was the red mask of Ehecatl — red, like blood, to signify life, transporting songs and seeds vital to our survival. For both the rivers and the wind connect us, carrying nourishment across great distances. I like to think of the book in your hands as the fragrant wind into which 80 Xicanas have thrown their voices, traveling in all directions, far and wide, to reach you — a warm exhalation capable of reviving what's long been dormant, or of feeding with validation what's already been awakened. Just as our antepasados' sophisticated understanding of architectural acoustics made it possible for voices in Teotihuacan to carry across great distances, this literary breath connects and enlivens us. We breathe life into each other with our cantos.

As these writings reveal, Xicana consciousness naturally encompasses the experience of such interdependence with each other, with the natural world around us, and with our ancestral roots. We thrive as a result of cultivating connections with all three. Our wellness is, in and of itself, a testament to our own resilience and the strength of our ancestry. In the title of this book I have chosen to use the "X" spelling in "Xicana"[2] as a way to emphasize this wellness. Though some have argued that the Roman letter "X" originated with the alphabet of the invaders, letters themselves have a neutral value until we ascribe one to them. While I am not able to write what you are currently reading in pictograms — one of the ways our ancestors so beautifully expressed themselves — I am still able to make this valuable distinction.

The "X" symbolically harkens back to Indigenous times, before the Spanish invasion, before our human right to wellness was turned into a privilege for which we had to fight. Personally, the "X" reminds me of the ancient Xochimilca people known for their ability to make chinampa gardens flourish, under the leadership of a female tlahtoāni. Had such intelligent farming methods not been barbarically ravaged by Cortés,[3] Raza would surely be leading the world in sustainable agriculture today, and much more! Therefore, the "X" may also be viewed as a symbol for all the valuable contributions we have yet to make to the world: all the ancient knowledge we aim to revive.

Later in this Introduction, I also use the "x" at the end of the

---

2 Consistent with the pronunciation of "Xochimilco" and "Mexicana" in classical Nahuatl, the term "Xicana" is pronounced "Shee-can-na." However, Xicana inclusivity paradigms embrace self-identifying Xicanas who still use the "Chicana" (chee-can-na) pronunciation, as we recognize and respect that language and the written word evolves gradually when emerging from the complex history of the people generating it.

3 In 1521, Cortés sent his cavalry into Xochimilco, resulting in a fierce battle that brutally massacred most of the Xochimilca people.

word, as in "Xicanx," to recognize the very nuanced and sophisticated views our ancestors had of gender, and to respect those in our community who align with those views, as part of greater decolonizing efforts to restore these valuable perspectives. The Xicana perspective naturally rejects narrow either/or binaries, as it assumes and honors greater complex diversity within groups, such as the existence of multiple or evolving languages and gender lived experiences.

I specifically entered into this project with the intention of illuminating the Xicana perspective, with the premise that the introspective Xicana voice has an internally generated, intuitive hermeneutic through which it asserts and understands itself. I respectfully sought to set aside any preconceptions of my own about what it meant to be a Xicana and, rather than guiding the themes in the book, allowed my hermanas to speak for themselves, careful to honor the ways in which they did. I called on my hermanas to shine a light on the diverse ways they view themselves and the world. Almost overnight, the submissions began pouring in! Many stories, poems, and essays later, I am awed at the ways these Xicana writers showed up and courageously bled words onto pages, like ancestral ritualistic offerings of Tenochca priestesses.

In carefully curating the voices for this anthology, I was moved by the way its 80 individual Xicana contributors echo one another, moving seamlessly between shared themes, waxing poetically about Xicana life. And the lens through which Xicanas perceive reality is undeniably multifaceted, acknowledging the presence of diverse, individual Xicana experiences and expressions while simultaneously recognizing and participating in the essential collective to which we all belong.

One of my temachtianis once told me that rivers flow from Mother Chalchiuhtlicue's quechquemitl, like unraveling threads, and that we are like the loosened threads she weaves back into the fabric that is life; together, we make a giant shawl. The writings in this volume are like the intricate patterns woven onto its surface, weaving complex stories of intersecting historical ideologies. "For multiple histories could hardly have done other than breed complex people and equally complex families" (Octavio I. Romano).[4]

---

4 "The Historical and Intellectual Presence of Mexican-Americans," *El Grito*, Vol. II, No.2.

Like a validation of the "complexities" all Xicanas are made of, the diverse offerings and aesthetic tendencies represented in this collection also reflect the inevitability of fusing cultures and writing styles. The Xicana voice breaks away from the dominant framework others put around us, and reclaims its own narrative. Through carefully unfolding the complex, pluralistic philosophical landscape that saturates the Xicana experience — and into which only Xicanas have the necessary nuanced insights — we exercise our unique responsibility to express our voice as an act of resistance, thereby countering the appropriation of opportunities and resources by the dominant, settler society.

As such, our Xicana literature participates in what Tlazoltiani Jessica Zamarripa calls the "grand despertar." It's a time in which spaces for awakening and nourishing our cultural and Indigenous roots are popping up all over the place, both online and off. We are increasingly starting to feel seen, heard, and supported, and with this flourishing comes a natural flow of cultural production. Especially now, a time in which book bans disproportionately target brown women authors,[5] there is an overwhelming need for Xicana literature.

Such privileged power imbalances in literature availability and distribution are, in part, what inspired me to create an "all-Xicana anthology," and publish it at a Xicana-owned and operated press. When I first made the call for submissions for Somos Xicanas, the "Latino/ Mexican" representation in the publishing industry only weighed in at 6%.[6] Despite recent nationwide protests over racial inequality, the inspired #DignidadLiteraria campaign of 2019, and subsequent promises made by culpable major trade publishers, little significant progress has been made in prioritizing racial diversity within the mainstream publishing industry.

When attempts to change the establishment from within meet with resistance — true to the spirit of the Chicano Movement of the '60s — it gives rise to revolutionary actions. Such is the new alternative

---

5   "Book Bans in Political Context: Evidence from U.S. Schools," Marcelo S.O Goncalves, Isabelle Langrock, Jack LaViolette & Katie Spoon, *PNAS Nexus*, June 2024, Volume 3, Issue 6

6   Lee & Low, "The Lee & Low Diversity Baseline Survey 3.0," Lee & Low Books, 2023, www.leeandlow.com

literary landscape that burgeons with independent Xicana/o/x presses eager to facilitate the Xicana/o/x voice. Together, these efforts — employing technology that was unavailable to our elders, such as building networks via social media — represent a new wave of organized resistance countering hegemonic publishing. In doing so, we offer an alternative literary culture — one that authentically reflects nuestra gente Xicana/o/x, because we are the ones generating it. We are the ones writing and publishing our own stories.

There are no better stories than those presented to us through the lenses and voices of la gente who lived them. Storytelling that flows from lived experience benefits all parts of a community, just as sure as the heart pumps blood to all extremities of the body, or ancestral rivers flow out of Lake Texcocco. Such authentic narratives have a certain integrity that is irreplaceable, for they contain the views held by the community itself, and not the views that outside agendas superimpose on them. As one of our contributors, Angela M. Sánchez, writes "dignity means getting to be represented as how you see yourself."

Somos Xicanas is part of the greater movement to legitimately claim our Xicana/o/x voices, and create new literary spaces in which to express ourselves, outside restrictive establishments. In response to the literary spaces where our presence has been historically misrepresented or denied, the Xicana voices in this volume proudly contribute to a greater conversation in which the Xicana/o/x community at large imagines the kind of changes it would like to see enacted, and works towards securing them in each of our own unique, innovative, non-conforming ways. The Xicana voices in this volume have an unmistakable activist component to them that forwards the politics of liberation and, in solidarity, enters into conversations with other liberation movements around the world.

My Mexican father was a lover of justice. The genesis of this book rests in his death. In preparing my ofrenda for Día de Muertos tomorrow, mi querido papá is on my mind: how he grew up in a family of little means, worked his way up from a janitor position, and made many sacrifices so that we could have privileges that he never did. As I worried that I hadn't done enough to make him proud in the way of contributing to our heritage, the seed to this anthology appeared en mi corazón. My heart stirred with so many emotions while grieving him.

In the course of curating this anthology, I realized that running parallel to the experience of belonging is one of feeling isolated. For many, part of the Xicana experience means having a personal history of never feeling Xicana enough — questioning where one belongs. If this is you, Querida Reader, I hope you find yourself somewhere in the pages of this book, and know that you too represent the fluid multitudes found in the greater Xicana community. Your voice is valuable and, like the 80 Xicana voices in this book, also legitimately belongs to the great tapestry of our rich culture and history.

Feel free to claim the Xicana reality with conviction! As Ana Castillo says: "labels are often signifiers. It's important to know how you're being labeled, but the most important is the one you give yourself."[7] Thanks to Castillo's groundbreaking work — and that of other respected mujeres grandes del movimiento, generously appearing in this book and elsewhere — Xicana voices are now thriving. This book is a mere hint of the endless narratives that Xicanas have to offer, voluminous as the songs of the cenzontle! And the underlying threads linking both the poetry and prose in this collection are ones of unmistakable Xicana pride: the harvest of trailblazing Xicanas that came before us. Together, we water each other's lyrical flores, flood the dry riverbeds with our palabras, inhabit the pages of the books we author.

Luz Schweig
Día de los muetrtos, 2024

"The pulse of existence, the heart of the universe, is fluid.
Identity, like a river, is always changing, always in transition,
always in nepantla. Like the river downstream,
you're not the same person you were upstream.
You begin to define yourself in terms of
who you are becoming, not who you have been."

Gloria E. Anzaldúa[8]

---

7 Originally published in the printed program of the Chicago Literary Hall of Fame Fuller Award for Lifetime Achievement, March 2022, in an interview with Christine Maul Rice.

8 *this bridge we call home: radical visions for transformation*, Gloria E. Anzaldúa, Routledge, November 20, 2002.

I
SOMOS
SEEDS

"I feel that I never stop crossing borders when it comes to writing. I write in every form that I can create, or invent... Our voice is our power. It's how we speak up about what we want, who we want to vote for, what laws we want to live by, what we think is fair or not fair, and what resources and opportunities we deserve. I tell people *make sure that your voice is heard.*"

Carmen Tafolla

We Would Like You to Know

Ana Castillo

We would like you to know
we are not all
docile
not revolutionaries
but we are all survivors.
We do not all carry
zip guns, hot pistols,
steal cars.
We do know how
to defend ourselves.

We do not all have
slicked-back hair
distasteful apparel
unpolished shoes
although the economy
doesn't allow everyone
a Macy's charge card.

We do not all pick
lettuce, run
assembly lines, clean
restaurant tables, even
if someone has to do it.

We do not all sneak
under barbed wire
or wade the Rio Grande.

These are the facts.

We would like you to know
we are not all brown.
Genetic history has made
some of us blue-eyed as any
German immigrant
and as black as a descendent
of an African slave.
We never claimed to be
a homogenous race.

We are not all victims,
all loyal to one cause,
all perfect; it is a
psychological dilemma
no one has resolved.

We would like to give
a thousand excuses
as to why we all find
ourselves in a predicament
residence of a controversial
power
how we were all caught
with our pants down
and how petroleum was going
to change all that but
you've heard it all before and
with a wink and a snicker
left us babbling amongst
ourselves.

We would like you to know
guilt or apologetic gestures
won't revive the dead
redistribute the land
or natural resources.
We are left
with one final resolution
in our own predestined way,
we are going forward.
There is no going back.

From *My Father Was a Toltec and Selected Poems*, Ana Castillo, Anchor Books,
April 2004, p. 81

Serpiente de primavera
Xánath Caraza

Soy hija de la luz con lágrimas de luciérnagas verdiazules en las mejillas. La espuma de mar sigue mis pasos en la playa, los borra, no deja huella, quiere esconderlos en sus entrañas. El mar me satura de diminutos caracoles y azules cangrejos, pero mi cuerpo engaña a la espuma y los deja deslizarse lentamente por cada centímetro de mi bronceada piel, dejando un haz de criaturas marinas sobre la arena. Soy hija de la luz y del canto de las aves en la húmeda selva. Llevo la esencia de las flores en el corazón. El canto del cenzontle late en mi vientre, se mezcla con las citlalis en el cielo de la noche. Soy hija de las lenguas perdidas, de los fonemas ocultos en la garganta de la selva. No hay caminos que no escuchen mis pasos y en los senderos que aún no he llegado, ya se presienten mis versos. Palabras encadenadas con sílabas de huehuetl. Soy hija de los latidos de congas y teponaxtlis, hija de la luz con el canto del cenzontle atravesado en el pecho. El mar azul me persigue los pasos cada día. Las resplandecientes luciérnagas ya han tatuado sus poemas en mi piel. Mi padre es el tornado que se mezcla con la ensortijada serpiente turquesa de primavera.

(Granada, Andalucía, España, junio de 2013)

Serpent of Spring

I am a daughter of the light with tears of blue-green fireflies on my cheeks. Sea foam follows my steps on the beach, erases them, leaves no trace, attempts to hide them in its bowels. The sea soaks me with diminutive snails and blue crabs, but my body fools the foam and leaves them slipping slowly along every inch of my bronze skin, leaving a mound of marine creatures on the sand. I am a daughter of the light and of the song of the birds in the damp jungle. I carry the essence of flowers in my heart. The song of the cenzontle beats in my belly, it mixes with the citlalis in the night sky. I am a daughter of the languages lost in the tones hidden in the throat of the jungle. There are no paths that do not hear my steps, and on trails where I have yet to appear, premonitions of my verses hold sway. Words link to syllables of huehuetl. I am a daughter of the beating of congas and teponaxtlis, daughter of the light with the song of the cenzontle falling across my chest. The blue sea pursues my steps every day. Brilliant fireflies have already tattooed their poems on my skin. My father is the tornado and mingles with the plumed turquoise serpent of spring.

(Granada, Andalusia, Spain, June 2013)

Koatl Xochitlipoal

Najaya ikonej tlauili ika ichokilis tlen xoxokazultik kokimej ipan xayaknejchikilis. Iposontli ueyi atl ki tokilia no nejnemilistli ipan ueyiatentli, kipoliltia, axtlen mokaua, ki neki ipan ijtiko kintlatis. Ueyi atl nech temitia ika pilkuetlaxkomej uan kin kauilia tlajmatsi ma mo alaxokaj ipan no tlatlatok kuetlaxkoli, kajkaua se tsontli pilatltekuanimej ipan xali. Najaya ikonej tlauili uan iuikalis totomej ipan xolontok kuatitlamik. Ipan no yolo niuika iauiyalis totomej ipan xolontok kuatitlamik. Ipan no yolo niuika iauiyalis xochimej. Iuikalis setsontlitototl uitoni ipan no ijtiko, momaneloa ika youalsitlalimej tlen ijluikatl. Najaya ikone tlajtolmej tlen polijkenjinin kakilis ipan ikecholoyo kuatitlamitl. Ax onkaj ojtli tlen ax ki kakij no nemilis uan kampa ayi ni nejnentok, mo machiliaya nouikalis. Tlajtolsasali ika piltlatolmej tlen ueuetl. Najaya ikonej iuitontli tlatejtsontli uan teponaxtli, taluili ikonej ika stsontlitototl ipan no yolixpa. Asultikueyiatl nech tokilia mojmostla. Petlani kokimej kitlatskiltijkejya inin xochitlajtol ipan no kuetlaxkotl. No tata ejekatl tlen momaneloa ika ilaktskoatl xoxoktik xochitlipoal.

(Granada, Andalucía, España, junio de 2013)

Cosmos
—After María Sabina
Sonia Gutiérrez

I am a Wind Woman from the whirlwind of memory.
I am a Tree Woman with perfectly imperfect knots.
I am a Fruit Woman from the ripe mango and avocado trees.
I am a Bird Woman fluttering through time.
I am a Water Woman who drips between her legs.
I am a Blood Woman who flows to and from rivers and oceans.
I am a Moon Woman who rides high tides.
I am a Fish Woman tattooed with the palette of rainbows.
I am an Earth Woman from the depths of sacredness.
I am a Corn Woman from the harvest of my ancestors.
I am a Fire Woman who evaporates Holy Water.
I am a Spider Woman who stealthily weaves herself.
And one day I will be a Bone Woman who will return dressed
as the cosmos. And, *you*, who are you?

"Cosmos." KPFA Radio, 18 April 2020.

Cosmos
—al estilo de María Sabina

Soy Mujer Viento del remolino de la memoria.
Soy Mujer Árbol con nudillos perfectamente imperfectos.
Soy Mujer Fruta de los árboles del mango y aguacate maduro.
Soy Mujer Pájaro que revolotea a través del tiempo.
Soy Mujer Agua que se escurre entre sus piernas.
Soy Mujer Sangre que fluye al mar y al río.
Soy Mujer Pez tatuada con la paleta de los arco iris.
Soy Mujer Luna que pasea las mareas altas.
Soy Mujer Tierra de la profundidad sagrada.
Soy Mujer Maíz de la cosecha de mis antepasados.
Soy Mujer Fuego que evapora el Agua Bendita.
Soy Mujer Araña que se teje sigilosamente.
Y un día seré Mujer Hueso que retoñará vestida del cosmos.
¿Y, *tú*, quién eres?

"Cosmos" first appeared in the author's *Paper Birds: Feather by Feather / Pájaros de papel: Pluma por pluma*, El Martillo Press, April, 2024

"Yo soy divina energía, piel de la tierra; I am My Mother's Daughter"
Lorna Dee Cervantes

I am not my mother's daughter.
I am my grandmother's dirt.
Her broken nails unhooked me
from my latch. The brown spoons
of her sturdy arms and hands
holding her strength, her sharp
nails flicking my ears for my sass.
I was not my mother's violin
she never learned to play
or her father's xylophone
she loved but couldn't have.
I am not the mandolin
or the mandolineros seducing
my grandmother's capable
dancing body from her garden.
I am the flor at the Paseo
de las Flores, a brown
stem of a girl among the
roses — always too brown
for my mother. I am not
the Shirley Temple
my mother hoped
to birth. I am The Earth,
piel de la tierra, pura
energía divina.

I am an Aztec Dance
Briana Muñoz

My existence is ceremony
        in the way that I am huehuetl
heart beat
rapid,   as embryo
slower,   with age

I am an Aztec dance
        dedicated to the four directions
I am child, and woman, warrior, and the ancestors
who live through my DNA

I am venado
cautious   light on their feet
antlers   direct line to Creator

My existence is fire dance
        self discipline
and sacrifice

I am Tezcatlipoca
        obsidian tongued
        jaguar shapeshifter
as I am
Coatlicue, Huitzilopochtli, as I am Xochipilli

I am an Aztec dance
my fingerprints, pre-Columbian pictograms
fading with time, like my grandmother's
erased

I am sweat
        water
I am dancing through the pain
        meditation

Acocoxochitl

Dahlia Aguilar

When your grandmother was first named
for the mystic author of spiritual writings and poems,
then named for Jesus

Teresa Jesusa
Teresa Jesusa

It was not for you to wonder
if you would end up on the page
or the cross.

Nails or pens
Nails or pens

Your father would have neither,
named you for no one in the blood who came before
named you for the favorite gardening flower of the Mexica
the national flower of Méjico
To map your way home, Acocoxochitl.

Affirmation of an Indigenous Xicana

Dulciana Rosario Corral

I am a small seed,
That was carried in an
Eagle's claws,
Dropped right where I was meant to be,
  I honor you cuauhtli
I am a forest of purple trees,
A home for many living relatives,
Where time is irrelevant,
Where we live circularly,
  I honor our protective chimalli
I am a dancing spirit,
With no shame,
In movement, like everything around me,
  I honor you ollin
I am moving along
To the song of Tonantzin,
Weaving in and out of time,
space, and energy.
I am a shapeshifting being,
The essence of ollin,
That can speak volumes through silence,
That loves itself deeply.
I am the rage birthed from flames,
I am the words that roll off the
Tongues of those
Speaking in the wind,
I am the moisture
In the air,
Always present
To embrace our collective truths,
I am guided by the roots of this earth,
Bridging my ancestors known and unknown to me,
I am in my truth.

I Am From El Indio

Liz Coronado Castillo

I am from West Texas
a dot off of I-10
actually, a smaller dot outside of that dot
I am from Brogado. . . known to some as El Indio. . .
I am from El Indio
I am from mountains and majestic night skies
From surreal sunsets only our Creator could paint
From the smell of guame letting us know the rain is coming
The relief to the hot dry summers
I am from the land of fresh water miraculously pouring out of the desert
The water that sustains the crops
The crops my grandparents tended to in the blistering heat while the
patrones sat in their trucks
I am from calloused hands and full hearts
I am from "¿Qué water park?"
"Ahí está la sequía"
I am from cooking from a feeling
"Échale poquito"
"¿Qué tanto"
"Échale!"
I am from cuartitos and gallineros
I am from "No salgas descalza porque te vas a enfermar"
and you have to protect pregnant women during an eclipse
no sé por qué and you don't ask why
I am from Christmas meant the men were outside making the asado
and I yearned to be outside
I am from you have to be healed from ojo and empacho
I am from "Yo tengo un remedio para eso"
I am from my ancestors' dreams
I am from El Indio

En Movimiento

Rosanna Alvarez

I was born of resistance, a terremoto, cracking concrete
        Cabrona, calzonuda y resongona
        at the intersections of disappointment and possibility
        del campo in the Valley of Heart's Delight
        in an orchard on land tended to by brown bodies
        as they shared stories of their travels,
        picking at their calluses while laughing in the sun

I was born of resistance, a terremoto, cracking concrete
        Buried under a cemented maze mixed by calloused hands
        under the direction of those that attempted to sever
        my ombligo from las tres hermanas,
        even though I was the first-born of nine,
        Choking out the maíz, frijol, and calabaza.

I was born of resistance, a terremoto, cracking concrete
        rumblings of disruptions, murmured histories, whispered secrets
        swallowed tears, hazy realities, vivid dreams, and
        prayers held in front yard nichos dedicated to female saints.

I was born of resistance, a terremoto, cracking concrete
        Hungry with a curiosity for these stories
        with a longing   to dig
        into the dirt   and know more.

Gilberto y Orfelinda
Erika Vallejo

I remember the hot dirt burning my bare feet.
The Texas sun could be so mean.
That didn't stop me from running.
"Ponte unos zapatos," Ama yelled.
I can hear my 6-year-old self…
Reading the Bible to my tío Juan at the instruction of my apa.
He was so proud of my English skills.
For all the miles he had to walk to get to school…
He knew it had been worth
it if his nieta could read and speak the language of those who once
oppressed him.
"No Mexicans, no dogs," Apa said.
That's what the barber shop across the railroad tracks in Río Grande read.
Yet, racism is not quite dead.
Although here I am:
Future *doctora y más*!
Learning to read paid off.
My heart lies in the imposter palm trees of the Río Grande Valley.
The RGV will always be home to me.
Las tortillas de maíz y barbacoa smell divine.
One day I'll be back.
Porque yo,
Soy una Tejana por life.

Corn Husk Girl
Angela Acosta

We never got the recipe right:
standard American cheese,
Maseca flour from the bottom shelf
of Publix, where shopping is a pleasure.

I always linked being Mexican (American) with tamales,
that the corn husks would wrap around my skin
and I, too, would become the product of warm nights,
Spanish cuentos, and deserts teeming with life.

I yearned for a family recipe,
a pin on the map to show where we belonged.
Part of me is wrapped up in a colorful sarape
snacking on sweet dessert tamales made by someone else's grandma.

Tamales are my imagined Christmas tradition,
a tribute to the times we made them,
to the frozen ones from Trader Joe's, and the promise
I'll learn more from ancestral histories wrapped in corn husk.

I Dream of Nixtamal

Elisa A. Garza

because I can no longer
stomach corn, my gut
ravaged beyond the challenge
of those unsoaked yellow beads
bred in uniform fields,
genetically identical maize
submitting to the colonizer,
a need for cheap grain and sugar
that will grow disease free,
insect resistant, and barren.

I dream of heirloom kernels,
uneven lines of red and blue
drying in husks, waiting
for the acidic bath,
for a soaking in cal, lime
that will transform them
into the nutrient-rich staple
my ancestors ate as hominy
or ground daily into masa
for tortillas and atole,
the seasonal tamales,
for fermenting tejuino.

I dream of comida mexicana
as I remember the slow desert
summers of my youth,
when we baked under the sun
like a tortilla on the comal,
toasting brown like the crispy
tostadas we spread with beans
and topped with shredded lettuce
for dinner. Now ready-made in bulk,
brittle tostadas from the store
conveniently are not steeped,
not nixtamal, barely maize,
corn for the masses,
just another grain, assimilated.

Still, I dream of nixtamal,
from the nahuatl —
nextli, lime burned to ashes
that will bathe among maize —
nextamalli, swollen kernals to eat
or grind into dough —
tamalli, a meal wrapped
like an embrace —
the sustenance
we remember
only in our dreams.

Guardian

—After Leonora Carrington's "The Giantess (The Guardian of the Egg)"
Erika Ayón

I was born with blonde hair.
My grandfather called me "gallinita."
As fear crept in, the gold faded.
With it, perhaps the ability to hold eggs
between my hands,
allow birds to fly inside my coat,
ballerinas to dance on my skin.

Is this why my favorite color is red,
because I want to catch fire,
tame a wild horse,
stop tsunamis.
If only in nightmares.

I am one of ten sisters,
forgotten under rubble.
In my hands I carry stones
to throw between the giant's eyes.
Collect arrows in my mouth.
Build nests in my hair.

My history with eggs follows.
At five, I used the whites to piece together paper.
At fourteen, I dropped my "baby" egg
over a ledge while waiting for the school bus.
Cartons of eggs slip from my fingers in grocery aisles.

I question if I am a guardian
of them, anything, anyone.
I desire to be
a giant guardian
of at least one.

I am the writer
Laura Díaz Tovar

. . . but have no words;
today is a day for grounding myself,
my thoughts, my damaged pieces.

Colonized pieces of turquoise
left in my sepulcro vacio
sprinkled like seeds across dirt fields,
sinking into the earth's exhale when the great dying begins,
only to be discovered by hands seeking to erase my life.

Long after I've left this place, remember the mangled pieces.

Today is the day to look at calendars and count the years
it takes for someone else's cells — coded, ancient DNA —
to be completely expunged from me, from us as a people.

I am the writer, but couldn't find the word for *NO*.

I kept inviting the sad inside to hold my hand,
witness the depths of scarred dreams and broken bones.
I kneel before the altar I created in my soul — in the darkness of the night.
Slowly, I begin to excavate healing words
from the quiet and wounded chambers
of my decaying heart.

The words remind me that I am café con leche,
pink conchas, y birotes con frijoles, de tortas pero no ahogadas.

I am jazz de Miles and Coltrane, Son Jarocho, de los blues de Billie
Holiday and rap — intricate beats — deep desde Tupac to Kendrick,
de Mariachi en la plaza, y los toros en carnaval where my tio Chaly
would buy us all la botana y cervecitas. (I never liked the taste of beer,
pero those memories of all of us together are flowing together into
sentences.)

I remember I am Agustín Lara, whispered late at night, Sade, purple
like Prince, y serenatas en mi venta under lucid moons.

I am Guadalajara de la tierra de los Tecuexe y de San José de Muwekma
Ohlone land.
I am de Rio Medellin, Autlán de Navaro donde nacio el Tio Carlos
Santana, de South 7th street with its big backyard full of corn and
chiles, gallinas and stray gatitos, de Marta y Reed Streets, in the heart
of downtown.

I am liberation like a roar of thunder in the murmurs of cicadas at sunset
and in every brown pajarito at sunrise, holding the promise of freedom —
because sometimes those sounds are all the music I need to keep going.

And I remember what words we've had to repeat to exhaustion:
that it is not about bad apples when death comes disguised as Blue
Lives Matter,
that it is easier to ignore the roots of that tree than the filth it was
planted in.
That it is not apples that cause the destruction of land, and of brown
and black bodies,
but that it is the farmer seeped in colonial shit, poisoning water, and air,
and how we love, and how we heal — selling crates of rotten fruit
as retribution for demanding we be free.

So, we dig deep into the earth and find that we are connected by roots —
like the secret language of trees with words.
I hear them in the wind.
And in a flash, the words come to me like lightning,
filling me with power and light, arriving like cuicatl.
I use them to write poems across my heart — our hearts.
I became the veracious witness.
I am the writer.

Boxing Nun — 1966
Juliana Aragón Fatula

My older brother teaches me how to box in our backyard.
He warns me never to curl my thumb inside my hand.
"That's how you break it." He tells me. "Balance, bounce, quick. Light
on your feet."
He dances around like a boxer and punches at the air. We box until dark.
Years later when we are in our thirties, he tells me,
"I always thought you'd grow up and become a nun."
I almost fall off my barstool laughing.
"We're not even Catholic, pendejo!
Pero, if I think about it a minute. I do act like a nun.
I spend time cloistered behind my walls, but I'm writing. Not praying.
I'm more like the cigar smoking, whiskey-drinking nun
in the movie *Two Mules for Sister Sara*.
Maybe my bro senses my Divine Love: an essence, tangible like
magnetism.
My electric current inside me, makes clocks, computers, and
microwaves go haywire.
I see loved ones who have gone to the spirit world.
I've spoken in tongues when praying.
Maybe my bro thinks since I was such a tomboy,
that I didn't like boys and that I'd live a life of celibacy.
Funny, he never once thought I'd grow up to be a lesbian like our cuz.
If given the choice between the two, nun, or lezzy,
I'd rather be a lesbian. A lipstick lesbian.

From the author's unpublished manuscript *Chingona Corn Mother: A Spiritual
Memoir*

Latino Queer Night at Pulse
Melinda Palacio

When we dance, we both lead.
My tía laughs when I tell her
I don't know how to dance.

Not every song's a cumbia.
We feel the sas-sas beat
in our bellies, but our

four left feet tangle, swivel in
too close because that's where our
hearts long to be.

Who cares that we both lead,
that our pant legs meet
at the same crease.

Our shoes don't care
whose foot takes the first
awkward step.

Music slows smooth,
our feet find peace.
Prince rains purple a toda mácquina.

The next tune is faster.
Something from two decades ago.
We know that dance, our dance.

We tilt back our heads and moon walk.
Eyes closed our slick chests, his hairy,
mine a slippery mop of sweat, find each other.

In this light, music pounding, hands uplifted,
no one cares that two fine mariposas and
four left feet spread wings and dance.

First appeared online in Latinopia.com

Love Scenes
Blanca Torres

It all started the day Enriqueta's father came home from work and told her he had a surprise for her in the back of his truck. The skin between his fingers still had clumps of soil from landscaping lawns all day. He led her outside with his hands over her eyes and didn't remove them until they were standing in the driveway. Sitting on the truck's bed was a 13-inch television with a built-in VCR player.

"What do you think, mija, do you like it?"

Enriqueta was twelve years old and wearing a baggy sweatshirt despite the warm June air to hide her budding breasts and balance the increasing width of her hips. She could tell by the way her father's eyebrows arched and his mouth was slightly agape that he was genuinely excited. Her first reaction was "VCR? Everyone at school has a DVD player." It was 2002 after all. She kept that thought in her head, remembering that her father rarely brought home gifts and didn't know much about technology. Instead, she jumped up to swing her arms around her father's neck and said, "I love it, Papi!"

When Octavio, Enriqueta's father, looked at her and the way her thick brown hair stopped just above her shoulders, he felt like his heart might burst. It reminded him of the time his own father had returned from a long trip to the capital and brought him his first pair of shoes. He was eight years old.

Enriqueta's mother, Marcela, stood in the doorway as Octavio lifted the set from the truck and walked toward the house. She was still wearing the gray sweatpants and old T-shirt she had worn to work except now she wore her gingham apron her mother had sent her from Mexico. It was the kind that had embroidered flowers on the bust and front pockets. She crossed her arms and shook her head as her husband carried the television into her daughter's room. Beads of sweat began to roll down the sides of his tan face. He was still wearing his work shirt with the words "Johnson Landscaping" embroidered on one breast pocket and his name in italic letters on the other.

Marcela didn't believe children should be allowed to have their own televisions or spend too much time alone in their rooms. "People are going to think we can't stand to be around our kids," she told him. He reasoned that it was free, his boss was going to throw it out and how could he let a functioning electronic go to waste? How could he stand by and watch such a sin take place? "You're right," she said, nodding her head. "Wastefulness is a sin." So the television VCR combo settled in on top of Enriqueta's dresser.

The next time Enriqueta went on her weekly trip to the library, her intention was to check out the books on the summer reading list her English teacher had passed out on the last day of school. Most of the time, she walked by the movie section without taking notice, but on this day, she turned back and zeroed in on the hundreds of movies sitting on the shelves. She felt as if someone had handed her the key to her own car. She had never checked out a movie before because her parents only allowed family videos and Disney films for her younger brothers, Ruben and Eduardo. And, her parents never wanted to watch anything in English.

"Why waste time on American television when we can watch Univision or Telemundo?" her mother had always asked when Enriqueta wanted to watch *Friends* or *Saturday Night Live* or *Total Request Live*. She felt left out at the lunch table on Mondays when her group of friends recounted the jokes and scenes from sitcoms or movies they watched over the weekend. The movies were what she most envied because most of the time someone had hosted a sleep-over and watched several films while eating pizza and Ben & Jerry's ice cream. Enriqueta's parents banned sleepovers. "You have a house, why would you want to sleep anywhere else?" her father had said many times.

Now, standing in front of all those rows of movies, she felt her shoulders tingle. *I can watch whatever I want.* She began running her index finger along the titles trying to remember the ones her friends had mentioned most. *I must start with the classics*, she thought. She quickly amassed a tall pile of titles including *Pretty Woman, My Best Friend's Wedding, While You Were Sleeping,* and *Sleepless in Seattle.* She left the library with her backpack stuffed with the tapes and not a single book.

Because she had turned twelve that spring, Enriqueta's parents sat her down at the beginning of the summer and explained her new responsibilities. She would be in charge of watching the boys while her mother was at work. That meant hours of sitting in the backyard while they chased each other or kicked around a soccer ball and then putting them down for a nap at 3 p.m.

Enriqueta's summer afternoons consisted of lying down on her bed while another library movie played on the TV/VCR combo. Her favorites were the ones where an unlikely romance blossoms and everyone is okay and happy at the end. She was enamored with those women who seemed to have complete lives — good job, funny friends, and always the sunny apartment. The only thing missing was a guy whose life was also just as neat except for his convenient lack of a girlfriend. Enriqueta began to believe that love functioned the way it did in those movies. Two attractive people just had to find each other, pretend they don't like each other, then realize they did like each other and finally, after a series of humorous misunderstandings, end up embracing in a final scene topped off with a kiss. Love meant finding out the other person's favorite song or pizza toppings and doing something nice like going to an opera or a concert in the park. She began writing everything down in a notebook so she would know what to do later on in her life.

1. Stay in shape so you will always look good in a swimsuit or caught changing clothes (*My Best Friend's Wedding*)
2. Pick a favorite candy, something quirky is best (*The Wedding Planner*)
3. Learn to use uncommon words in everyday dialogue like "geography." (*Pretty Woman*)
4. Assemble a crew of friends who will always be around to cheer you up (*Bridget Jones's Diary*)

She wanted to look like the leading ladies whose hair always fell into the right place and whose outfits always looked crisp like freshly washed sheets on a bed. Enriqueta wanted that kind of life where the character's problems centered on things like not having a date for a friend's wedding or realizing that the cute guy who lives next door has a girlfriend. She pictured herself falling in love in a bistro or on a scenic mountain hike. She wanted it to be neat and graceful like a ball gown.

Before the TV/VCR combo arrived, Enriqueta had spent every evening watching Mexican soap operas with her mother. From the time she was in kindergarten, she had curled up next to her mother on the couch after dinner and the dishes were washed. This started back before the boys were born and they lived in the one-bedroom apartment with a dull, beige carpet and the kitchen cabinets were made of particleboard. It took years to save up enough for a house with a yard and a living room big enough for a sectional sofa, which had been Enriqueta's mother's dream since moving to the United States from Mexico. When Marcela wanted to think of home, she just turned the channel to a Spanish language network. Telenovelas were on most times of the day only broken up by news shows in the morning and evening. The characters always had two-part names like Maria Alicia, Marta Susana, Juan Sebastian or Jose Ricardo — names that were supposed to communicate passion and distinction. Enriqueta had trouble understanding the women in those stories with their darkly lined eyes, fake eyelashes, and bold shades of lipstick. She learned that a scene where a female protagonist was alone staring out a window, repeating a man's name and wiping tears from her eyes meant she was in love. It was usually an impossible love where the man is rich and she's poor or the man's mother wants him to marry someone else or his former girlfriend confesses she's carrying his child.

The series always featured twisted side plots involving someone finding out they were really adopted at birth or suddenly woke up blind one morning. Telenovelas provided the love scenes Enriqueta watched for years that made her think she never wanted to fall in love. Her mother, however, loved watching novelas. She loved the final wedding scenes when, after a long struggle, the two lead characters ended up together and when villains would end up paying for their evil ways by being buried alive or interned in a sanatorium. Despite the plot extremities, the evening was the only time of day Enriqueta's mother could relax and sit in one place for an entire hour, watching her novela, and stroking her daughter's hair.

The boys would spend that time pushing each other on the swing set in the back yard or inspecting their father's toolbox while he repaired some neighbor's car in the driveway. That meant those hours, after a long day of work and before sleep weighed everyone down, were their time — mother and daughter.

Marcela began noticing how quickly Enriqueta would rush through washing the dishes after dinner. She tried talking to her about what was happening that night on *Chains of Bitterness* or *Angels Without Paradise*, but Enriqueta simply nodded and continued putting dishes away in the cabinets. An hour later, Marcela walked past Enriqueta's room during a bathroom break and saw her daughter's face bathed in that blanching blue hue of the television.

"Enriqueta what are you watching?"

"A movie, duh."

Enriqueta's eyes stayed focused on the screen.

"What does that mean, 'duh'?"

It was a word Marcela had never heard in any of the dozens of night school classes she took in her early years in the U.S. Enriqueta rolled her eyes.

"It means you should already know the answer, duh."

Had Marcela been her mother at that moment, she would have walked over to Enriqueta, slapped her in the face and given her one of those speeches along the lines of, "Now listen here, I am your mother!" But instead, she stood in the hallway feeling her chest tighten.

The word "duh" stuck in Marcela's mind while she lay in bed that night trying to fall asleep. It reminded her of a time when Enriqueta was in second grade and was invited to a slumber party for a friend's birthday. Octavio and Marcela agreed she could only stay until 10 p.m. After they arrived at home, Marcela followed Enriqueta to her room so she could help her daughter undress and put on her pajamas the way she did every night. That night, Enriqueta told her mother to leave. "I can change myself," she told her. "Oh come on," Marcela said. "Let me help you so I can tuck you in." Enriqueta crossed her arms. "No." Marcela walked over to Enriqueta and tried to pull her daughter's arm. Enriqueta relented and then Marcela noticed that her daughter was wearing at least two layers of clothing. She rolled the top sleeve back and saw what was underneath.

"You're wearing your pajamas underneath your clothes, aren't you? Enriqueta, we told you that you could not sleep over, why did you take pajamas? Why did you hide your pajamas from me?"

Marcela looked down at her eight-year-old daughter, who had put her hands on her hips and pursed her lips.

"I thought you might change your mind and let me stay."

"Your father said 'no' several times, why would he change his mind?"

"Come on, all the other parents do it, why can't you?"

"We've been over this Enriqueta. Your father says no and that means no. I won't tell him what you did tonight, but don't think I'm going to forget."

What she didn't forget was the way Enriqueta's eyes looked that night, unmoving, impenetrable, and stern, something she had not seen before.

The next morning, Marcela turned over in her bed to look at her husband who was snoring even though the alarm clock blared near his head. She massaged his shoulder to rouse him and when he finally opened his eyes, she smiled.

"Amor," she said. "I want you to take the TV out of Enriqueta's room…today."

She only used the term "amor" with him when she wanted to ask for something she didn't absolutely need like a new Sunday dress or dinner at a restaurant.

"She doesn't go back to school for another two months," he said, rubbing his eyes. "It serves as entertainment."

"Entertainment! Sitting in her room alone while she could be spending time with the family, how can you call that entertainment?"

"*Most* parents would be glad to give their daughter her own television," he said. "*Most* parents would rather not take things away from their children. It's okay for the kids to have fun sometimes."

Marcela couldn't think of a valid response to challenge him. She folded her arms across her chest and stared at the floor.

"Marcela, I never had my own anything growing up. Don't you want Enriqueta to have things?"

"I want her to grow up in a loving family," she said firmly while she put on her robe and headed to the bathroom.

Marcela looked at her face in the mirror and then down at her hands that were always dry from cleaning floors and machines at the laundromat. She remembered when she was a teenager and her mother frequently telling her to take care of her hands because they were a dead giveaway for a woman's age. She scoffed whenever her mother tried to share some wisdom. It was easy to brush her mother's words off because she heard them every day until she married Octavio. The main reason he had brought her to the U.S. was so that their children could "have more and have better lives." The last time Marcela saw her mother was the day she made the trip from Michoacán when she was twenty years old and three months pregnant with Enriqueta. She didn't realize that from then on, she would only hear her mother's voice over faint and brief phone calls.

Marcela didn't tell her husband about the baby. She liked to think of Enriqueta as the one possession she was able to bring from Mexico. He might have left her at home to have the baby to keep her from crossing through the desert. But they had been lucky in finding a smuggler who gave them stolen passports with names and birthdates they memorized. They crossed in a car like visitors on a shopping trip. It took three days to finally arrive in that small, dusty town in Washington where his cousin Martin lived. Marcela was like all the other young wives who believed it was just a phase — in a year or two they'd take their savings and go home. But there was always a chance to earn more, find a better job, work harder. So, they stayed. And there she was, after all she and Octavio had given their daughter, wanting to take some of it back.

Later that evening after dinner, Marcela's youngest sister Lupe came over with black streaks running down from her eyes to her chin.

"You could wipe that off, you know," Marcela said to her when she answered the door. "Did you drive all the way over here like that?"

"I'm sorry I didn't have time to freshen up while Jose shattered my heart."

She was beginning to choke up, so Marcela hugged her quickly and pushed some loose strands of hair behind her sister's ears. She knew her sister just needed someone to say, "It's okay, he was a jerk anyway, you're too good for him, you'll find someone else…" It was a role she had played for years since Lupe decided to move north and "find a man." She had found many, but kept none. Lupe always had someone to take her out dancing on Saturday nights and then invite to family parties on

Sundays. She never showed up alone. The breakups steadily seemed less and less tragic to Marcela — wasn't Lupe used to the cycle by now? She decided that for this time, she would resist rambling through her litany of condolences.

Lupe dabbed her eyes with a tissue as if she was about to stop, but then another heavy sob came on.

"Okay, listen, Lupe, you're 27 years old and still pretty. Women in this country get married when they're 35 and have kids when they're 40 as if they were spring chickens. You can be just like that."

Lupe burst into an even louder sob and buried her head in her hands while shaking her head. The weeping went on for a few more minutes. Enriqueta walked into the kitchen and headed to the refrigerator for some apple juice.

"What was his name this time?" Enriqueta asked. She, too, knew the drill. "Oscar, Renato…Ramon?"

"Jose, his name is Jose."

The three of them sat down at the kitchen table and Lupe began her story.

"We went out for dinner, everything was great. I ordered the enchiladas, he had the chiles rellenos. Then he got mad because the waiter was extra nice to me and stared at me when I got up to go to the bathroom. I smiled back at him…once. That's it. Then he asked me if I really wanted to be with him or if I was just waiting for something better. Something better? Like a waiter? Please. But, he was angry and finally he told me it was over. I told him he was making a mistake, that I do care about him. He wouldn't listen."

"Wait, wait," Enriqueta said, sitting up straight in her chair. "Don't you see? This is the time for your montage — you know, like in the movies. This is the part where a song plays and both of you do things to keep busy like taking a cooking class or walking the dog and then one day you are leaving a coffee shop and he is just getting there and you see each other and realize how much you missed each other and then you get back together. See? Do you get it? You need some hobbies, then he'll be back."

Enriqueta was out of breath and nodding her head. She felt as if she had just solved the difficult word problem on a math test. Her mother and aunt looked at her with their heads slightly tilted to the side.

"Hobbies?" Lupe said. Her gaze shifted toward the window. "A cooking class is not a bad idea."

"What are either of you talking about?" Marcela asked. Her voice became louder. "Enriqueta, what do you know about boyfriends and girlfriends? What do you mean by 'hobbies'?"

"Mom, come on. It's so obvious."

Enriqueta looked over at Lupe, who was still staring out the window.

"So, Tía, what are you going to do?…You should buy some new clothes…Can I come with you?"

"Of course! This is great. I'm not going to cry over Jose, I'm going to get him back."

"Lupe, don't listen to Enriqueta. She's a child. You know better than to go crawling back to a man who has pushed you away."

"I know what I'm talking about…" Enriqueta began. Her cheeks felt hot. She glared at her mother.

"Marcela, you don't get it," Lupe said. "I'm not the one who's going to crawl back. He is."

She grabbed her purse from the back of her chair and stood up.

"Well, I'm off. Las veo, adios," she said as she planted kisses on each of their cheeks.

They walked Lupe out the front door. Marcela sat down on one end of the sofa and picked up the remote control. *Distilling Love*, a drama that took place on a Tequila plantation, was about to start.

"Wait, Mom," Enriqueta said before her mother could click the power button. "I want to ask you a question. Why did you marry Dad?"

"Oh well, it was simple. That's how it was back then in our pueblito. I had seen him a few times in the plaza and then … he gave me the look."

"The look?" Enriqueta asked.

"Yes, the look. It was how a young woman knew if a man liked her."

"Just by looking?"

"Yes, looking. And so we passed each other a few more times in the plaza and one day he asked me my name. A few weeks later, he came to my house with his parents. My mother told me to bring chairs into the living room. Turns out our fathers knew each other. He asked my parents if he could marry me and they accepted. That's how it happened."

Marcela was blushing and smiling like a young girl in the doll section of a toy store.

"So he just asked? That's all he did? He didn't take you on dates and tell you funny stories?"

"Enriqueta, when have you ever heard your father tell a funny story? And what do you mean by 'date?' What purpose does that serve? We both came from decent families, we had seen each other in the plaza and so we got married."

Enriqueta felt like a balloon had just popped inside her stomach. She had expected a grand story full of intrigues and complications or at least something heart-warming and cute. But her parents did not fit either bill. She began thinking of her father who was for sure at that moment covered in grease from his elbows to his fingertips. She thought of how every year, he offered his daughter a dollar to remind him of his wife's birthday. As far as their wedding anniversary, all he knew was that it was sometime in September. She realized she had never seen him come home with a bouquet of roses or a heart-shaped box of chocolates. She never heard him complete her mother's sentences or kiss her unexpectedly while she folded laundry or did some other menial task. *My poor mother*, Enriqueta thought, *she is married to the most unromantic man in the world.*

Before she could step into the hallway, Enriqueta shouted, "Stop! Mom, do you even know what true love is?"

"And, do you want to know what love is?" Marcela asked. "Okay, well I'll tell you what it is. Love is work. Love is knowing that when you get married, you will have to take care of yourself and your husband and your children, and you say yes, I will do it. I will cook and I will clean and take you to church and teach you to be a decent person. Love is getting up every day, going to work, coming home and doing that again and again and again."

For Enriqueta, her mother's words felt dull like having to take the granola bar instead of the brownie.

"Your Tía Lupe is single because she doesn't want do the work, she only wants to be told she's pretty and for someone to bring her flowers," Marcela said. "But flowers die, Enriqueta. They dry up and you throw them in the trash and life goes on."

Enriqueta shook her head. Her mother's explanation seemed all wrong. She pictured the scenes of a woman blushing at something a man said to her like, "Your eyes are beautiful like the sunset. I've never seen someone as beautiful as you." She thought of the way the women seemed caught off guard as if they had never considered they were beautiful. She wondered if her mother had ever felt that way – and therefore, if she ever would. Was it wrong for Tía Lupe to chase that kind of love?

"I'm tired," she told her mother. "Can I go to bed now?"

"Yes, mija, go to bed. I'm tired, too.

Those thoughts percolated in Enriqueta's mind the rest of the night. At first she was just a little irritated, then angry and by the time she woke up from tossing and turning all night, she was furious. It was a Saturday, so she knew her father would be in the garage pouring gasoline in the lawn mower to start the day. She marched in there with her fists balled up and lips pressed together.

"Good morning, mija," he said while putting screwdrivers into a drawer.

"Dad," she said sternly. "I can't believe you…Do you even love Mom?"

A screwdriver fell from his hand.

"You think I don't love your mother?"

"You…you never do anything nice for her. You never try to make her feel special."

"Why are you saying these things? Where is this coming from?"

She began citing examples of the type of man he wasn't. He didn't wear suits like the men on the telenovelas or had never bought his wife a personalized photo frame or T-shirt like men in romantic comedies.

"I've never even seen you kiss her on the lips!"

"You want to see me kiss her on the lips!" his voice then changed from confused to severe. "Enriqueta, what's wrong with you? I'm taking away your television. You will never again watch an American movie in this house!"

Enriqueta tried to argue with her father as he walked toward her room.

"Stay right here," he told her as he pointed to the kitchen. Her hands curled into tight fists and she pursed her lips until they hurt, but she stood in the spot where her father had pointed.

"I hate you and so should Mom!" she yelled while he pulled the TV/VCR's cord out of its socket.

Neither of them said anything when Octavio returned a few minutes later with the appliance in his arms on his way to the garage. Enriqueta walked back to her room and stared at the empty space above her dresser. She locked the door and lay down on the bed. Two hours passed before her mother knocked on the door and asked her to come out.

"Leave me alone. I'm fine all by myself."

Enriqueta heard the jingling of keys and then the doorknob clicked. Her mother opened the door and walked over to her bed.

"Your father says you fought."

"He took away my TV."

Marcela pulled on Enriqueta's arm until her daughter sat up and then hugged her. She kissed her daughter's cheek and began tucking stray strands of hair behind Enriqueta's ears. For a moment, Enriqueta thought her mother might be able to convince her father to bring it back.

"I told him to take it away."

"Why? That's not fair!"

"You don't need your own TV."

"That doesn't mean you should take it away!"

"Enriqueta, you shouldn't get attached to things. You need to realize things are just things."

"You don't understand," Enriqueta said, pulling away from her mother and burying her face in her pillow. Marcela stood up and walked toward the door of Enriqueta's room.

"I know what's good for you."

The TV VCR combo was given a new home on a shelf in the garage where it began to collect dust. For weeks, Enriqueta had moped around the house refusing to watch novelas with her mother, but still went straight to her room after dinner. A stack of books replaced the movie tapes from her library visits. By September, she had crossed out each of the titles on the summer reading list.

One day, a man who came over for an oil change spied the console and asked why it went unused.

"Oh that," Octavio said. "I need to get rid of it."

"Is it broken?" the man asked.

"No, it works just fine."

"I'll give you forty bucks for it."

The man handed Octavio three twenty bills; one was for the oil change. He started thinking of what bill he could pay with the extra cash. Then he left the garage, walked into Enriqueta's room where she was lying on her bed reading.

"Grab a jacket," he said. "We're going shopping."

"Where are we going?" she asked.

"Wherever you want," he said. "After we make a stop at Rojas' Floral Shop."

Enriqueta ran to her father, swung her arms around his neck and grinned at him for the first time in weeks.

I Grew Up Going to la Pulga
—After Daniel Garcia Ordaz
Briana Muñoz

I grew up going to la pulga
every Sunday,
where my grandparents sold
planchas y escobas,
cantaritos y vestidos de ballet folklórico,

sewn by fingers
that pushed colorful fabric
across a 32- stitch machine.

My grandma's foot
pressed lightly against the pedal,
in intervals.

In Mexico, my grandmother was a nurse.

I grew up going to la pulga
and sitting on buckets flipped over
while tapping my feet to the music
blaring from neighboring vendor booths
that sold bootleg NB Ridaz CDs.

I grew up going to la pulga
where one could find a pair of fresh botines
or first communion gifts,
fruta picada, or caged birds for sale.

When us kids wanted spending money,
our parents would send us to la pulga
to help our grandparents.
All the primos were first introduced
to business, in this manner,

or perhaps, survival.

I grew up going to la pulga
observing men cologned
and suited in tejanas,
wearing their ladies on their arm.
Later, they'd dance a quebradita
at the Friday night baile.

My grandma had nicknames
for every regular, here.
El Gordito
Doña Piojos
La Señora de los Raspados

It was at la pulga,
when attending to my grandparents' customers,
where I learned that my Spanish skills
were at a level of someone
considered to be Pocha.

I grew up going to la pulga
where my "domingo,"
a term for allowance,
would be spent at the toy vendor booth
once earned, after a long day's hard work.

The Privilege of Pre-Ripped Jeans
Amalia Ortiz

I entered college in 1990, when glossy new wave and synth pop dictated my fashion choices. In the mainstream, glam rock seemed to have no end, and Guns N' Roses, Mötley Crüe and the rest of the boys' clubs seemed to only have room for the femininity of Lita Ford.

My freshman year, I looked to thrift stores to provide what I could not sew. A year later with the release of *Smells Like Teen Spirit*, the grunge tsunami smacked youth with a distinct sound and fashion. The gloss of the 80s was instantaneously passé. They called the music "grunge" and the models were "heroin chic."

But the tecatos I knew growing up were far from chic. I remember one scrawny, dark-skinned indio-looking dude with missing teeth who would ask to sweep our sidewalk for spare change.

Load up on guns and bring your friends.
It's fun to lose and to pretend.[1]

My 9th grade year in the mid-80s, I begged my gramma to buy me a pair of pre-ripped jeans. She hissed and spat an angry, "No." In those days, my back-to-school clothes came from Kmart, and this was not (yet) a point of shame for me. I attended school in a rural school district of mostly poor, brown children of farm workers. The "rich" kids I knew were only safely middle class. I dreamed of one day being middle class when I grew up, like something out of a John Hughes film.

All business in our tiny border town was related to agriculture in one way or another. Otherwise, you worked for the city, the school district, or the church. We were about 95% Mexican, and our lineages were pretty clear. If you were white, you came from a family that had power, or at least land and privilege. Most white students descended from the land owners and bosses. The rest of us were destined for labor. This truth was all around me, but I still somehow didn't fully grasp this dynamic at the time.

1 Nirvana. "Smells Like Teen Spirit." *Nevermind*, Butch Vig, DGC Records, California, May 1991.

When my brand new acid-wash Kmart jeans caught on a desk and ripped at the knee, my grandma grew furious. The fabric wasn't real, heavy-duty denim: the fabric of labor. No, this denim was threadbear and lower quality, made even more brittle by the acid treatment.

"Why would anyone buy jeans meant to look like they were damaged?" Gramma snapped. "Es la moda!" I reassured her.

Outside of society, they're waitin' for me.
Outside of society, that's where I want to be.[2]

The rip at the knee transformed the jeans into something more exciting. Jeans stained like a laundromat accident! Knees exposed like Sid Vicious or The Ramones! Gramma hated those jeans which ripped too easily. At the time, I didn't understand the insult of wasting her hard-earned money on clothing that made me look poor. They became my favorite pair, ripping more and more over the following school year. By the time I was accepted into college, they were shorts with strands of thread knotted and dangling. Gramma commanded me to throw them away, but it was too late. I was already gone.

Ain't nobody dope as me. I'm dressed so fresh, so clean.
(So fresh and so clean clean)[3]

I grew up without air conditioning, so the front door to my childhood home always gaped open for the world to peer through the screen door to our living room. The South Texas heat conditioned me to live on display. We waved at the faces passing by on the way to my grampa's shoe repair shop next door.

One year when I was in junior high, a white lady from church appeared at the dusty screen with a box full of clothes. Her family owned a farm and her husband and two boys had grown out of the flannel shirts she handed to my grandmother. "A gift" she said, for my older brother.

2 Smith, Patti. "Rock N Roll N***." *Easter*, Jimmy Iovine, Arista, New York City, New York, 1978.
3 Outkast. "So Fresh, So Clean." *Stankonia*, Organized Noize, LaFace Records, Arista, Atlanta, Georgia, Los Angeles, California, 2000.

Gramma graciously thanked her, but as soon as the white church lady walked away, Gramma snapped at me to store the box in the closet for our next trip to Mexico.

See, I grew up without a clothes dryer, so we had to line dry. And we had a cement shower and cement floor for years. And then there was the week my junior year when we could only afford to eat a bag of potatoes, so I made potato flautas, mashed potatoes, potato salad, potato soup, papas con huevo… you get the picture.

But no matter how bad our poverty, I always had a sense that we were not as poor as cousins in Mexico, who we gave all our old clothing to. We were not as poor as it could get.

When I asked Gramma what was wrong with the clothes the church lady brought, she barked that the flannel would make my brother look like a campesino (a Mexican farm worker). She'd be damned if she let that happen.

Don't you think I'm so sexy? I'm dressed so fresh, so clean.
(So fresh and so clean clean)[4]

My birthday is December 24, which meant when I was growing up I never had a birthday party my real friends could attend. Almost every Christmas Eve, we would cross the Rio Grande to visit our cousins in Matamoros, Mexico. Eight kids and two parents somehow lived in a tiny two-bedroom house. There was always a bed or two in the living room, and the smell of open sewers in the colonia littered by oil from the car repair shop next door. The hot water seldom worked, and the plumbing often overflowed.

But I loved visiting, in winter, because when it was cold, we all huddled under blankets in the living room and everyone would drink coffee to stay warm — even the kids.

The whole colonia came out when my Tia would break out my birthday cake covered with candles she had baked or brought from the U.S. Barefoot neighborhood kids I had never met before would come out of the woodwork and sing "Las Mañanitas" and wolf down cake and ice

---

4 Outkast. "So Fresh, So Clean." *Stankonia*, Organized Noize, LaFace Records, Arista, Atlanta, Georgia, Los Angeles, California, 2000.

cream. They would line up to hit the piñata filled with U.S. candies, and I would recognize my hand-me-downs on these children, which made me flush with shame at the brand-new dress Gramma insisted on me wearing every year.

In the US, we were a charity case — the working poor — but in Mexico, I was the rich girl.

> *You'll never live like common people,*
> *You'll never do whatever common people do,*
> *You'll never fail like common people,*
> *You'll never watch your life slide out of view,*[5]

The first time I went to a thrift store, I was on a date. I remembered the Matamoros street children dressed in my clothing. I felt that same flash of shame, but hid it from my white college boyfriend who assured me we could find some really funky treasures in other people's trash. The feeling quickly subsided at the rush of fitting in. The irony of the ripped jeans and flannel shirts we picked out that day went temporarily unnoticed. I pulled on my first flannel and thought it impractical for South Texas heat, unless you wanted to shield your skin from hours in the sun. I tied a bandana on my head, but it made me look too much like a chola — or even worse, like a cleaning lady.

> *I feel stupid and contagious.*
> *Here we are now, entertain us.*[6]

A year out of college, I am hired to design costumes for *The Grapes of Wrath*. I buy dozens of items from thrift stores which later I tea-dye to look dirty and old. Then, I distress everything (I pause today to consider that technical term "distress"). I scrape fabric threadbear with sandpaper and a cheese grater to match Dorothea

---

5 Pulp. "Common People." *Different Class*, Chris Thomas, Island Records, London, England, 1995.
6 Nirvana. "Smells Like Teen Spirit." *Nevermind*, Butch Vig, DGC Records, California, May 1991.

Lange's classic photographs of the Great Depression. I focus on the knees bent in imaginary subjugation. The underarms, I stain brown and yellow to create fake sweat stains. There is an art to making things look authentically distressed.

> *Outside of society, they're waitin' for me.*
> *Outside of society, that's where I want to be.*[7]

In the memoir *Just Kids*,[8] Patti Smith obsessively describes her tattered and frayed second hand clothing with proud nostalgia. I get it. Punk is supposed to be anti-corporate and repurposed trash. But I can't take how she romanticizes "the fraternity of the artist; the hunger, their manner of dress." (Smith, 12) She was excited to join by "wearing long coats in July, the brotherhood of La Boheme."(29)

Her suffering to me seems more like an obvious choice in fashion as she ignored the new and pressed waitress uniform her mother gave her — a goodbye present to utilize when she moved out on her own to New York City. She writes, "I had a loving family and could have returned home. They would have understood, but I didn't want to go back with my head bowed." Patti never chose to don the uniform, but despite her neglect of it, it still existed — another choice. A backup plan. A way out of poverty.

She writes of her partner Robert Mapplethorpe, "There was no sense of culture or bohemian disorder in his parents' house. It was neat and clean and a model of postwar middle-class sensibilities, the magazines in the magazine rack, jewelry in the jewelry box."

(So fresh and so clean, clean.)[9]

It is *these* hints of privilege and fetish that make it clearer to me how Patti was able to write the lyrics to her song, "Rock and Roll

---

7   Smith, Patti. "Rock N Roll N***." *Easter*, Jimmy Iovine, Arista, New York City, New York, 1978.

8   Smith, Patti. *Just Kids*. New York, Ecco, 2010.

9   Outkast. "So Fresh, So Clean." *Stankonia*, Organized Noize, LaFace Records, Arista, Atlanta, Georgia, Los Angeles, California, 2000.

N*** and fool herself into believing she was entitled to use that word, because she really believed she had suffered. "Those who have suffered, understand suffering."[10] Forgetting that for her and Mapplethorpe suffering was a choice.

My mind races to the Non-Native punk rocker who can choose to ditch the mohawk at any time and return to respectable society, while the Pawnee can no more erase the mohawk from their cultural heritage than they can scrub away the brown from their skin.

> *Laugh along with the common people,*
> *Laugh along even though they're laughing at you,*
> *And the stupid things that you do.*
> *Because you think that poor is cool.*[11]

I earned my Masters' degree in 2016, and for the first time in my life, I felt securely middle class. These days, I buy secondhand clothing on Ebay, but I read descriptions thoroughly and examine photos for limited signs of wear. I understand my Gramma a little bit better now, and can't imagine paying for worn or tattered clothing.

> *Started from the bottom, now we here!*[12]

I also understand why hip-hop values mint condition snapbacks, unscuffed sneakers, and blinding bling. Assumptions are made about brown bodies in distressed clothing. The same assumptions aren't necessarily made about their white counterparts.

I feel my gramma's rage writing these words — her india spirit, more authentically punk than anything else I have known, though she never donned a punk costume. Her brown-skinned righteous anger

---

10 Smith, Patti. "Rock N Roll N***." *Easter,* Jimmy Iovine, Arista, New York City, New York, 1978.

11 Pulp. "Common People." *Different Class,* Chris Thomas, Island Records, London, England, 1995.

12 Drake. "Started from the Bottom." *Nothing Was the Same,* Mike Zombie, Noah Shebib, OVO Sound, Young Money Entertainment, Cash Money Records, and Republic Records, Noble Street Studios, Toronto, ON, Canada, 2013.

understood all too well what it meant to be born outside of society. And although she lived and died there, she would have laughed her ass off at the thought of willingly wanting to live life on the margins if she had any other choice.

People who have really struggled don't look at real signs of distress lovingly. Just like, you'll never know what it feels like to be a second-class citizen if you have an out. Or you can't blame the subjugated for wanting to prove they are worth more. Or you can't applaud the privileged for play-acting at their own subjugation.

> *Load up on guns and bring your friends.*
> *It's fun to lose and to pretend.*[13]

13 Nirvana. "Smells Like Teen Spirit." *Nevermind*, Butch Vig, DGC Records, California, May 1991.

Prince of the Rosemead Swap Meet
Victoria Ballesteros Ramírez

The Greatest Most Noble Child, born to Valentina and Jìanpíng — she of Compton and he of Pico-Union — has been bestowed the title of Prince of the Rosemead Swap Meet. The child is his NaiNai's first and only grandson and accompanies her to the swap where she sells bargain housewares and old knick-knacks revitalized with a few coats of spray paint. A small boy of husky build, he roams the corridors unattended, fingers coated with Mexican sugar, lips glossy with Choco Milk. He is quick with a smile and dispenses hugs with generosity, delighting the Señoras and NaiNais with his dimples and curly hair as he peruses their wares with neither intent nor means to buy anything as he does not yet understand the concept. He touches that which looks interesting, blessing it with his sticky fingerprints. The Swap elders clasp their hands and fawn over the child, watching him toddle from vendor to vendor. In him they see hope for the future, prosperity, a generation that will live unencumbered by the crushing despair of poverty and other things they left behind in their home countries.

The Prince of the Rosemead Swap reigns over the hordes of used toys, bicycle and car parts, Mexican barro figurines and pottery, cigarettes, Chinese herbs, inexpensive clothing, bonsai plants, deluxe sets of narcocorrido CDs, tattered paperbacks and erotic novels, rusty tools, San Marcos blankets, Spaderman and Ninja Turtle action figures, and a never-ending supply of housewares, everything priced to sell.

The prince sits on his ceremonial throne — the open bed of NaiNai's golden-yellow, 1982 Toyota pickup truck — shielded from the Santa Ana winds by a blue, industrial plastic tarp. His father Jìanpíng was put to work at his age, tossed into MacArthur Park dumpsters by NaiNai to retrieve good, sellable junk. The prince, however, is not allowed to lift a finger. He is spared NaiNai's sharp tongue and demands for obedience and free labor. This chubby brown boy is unaware of the austerity, minimalism, and hunger of his parents' upbringing. His pudgy, soft fingers won't know the kind of labor that has brought him his stature and title.

On a cool April morning, the Prince of the Rosemead Swap goes missing. He was last seen lingering by the toothless gardener's booth, admiring chili plants and the nopales with their bright red tunas. Word of the missing prince is shared across the rows and columns of wares and goods, rising to a panic that overtakes the vendors and spreads like ice milk melting on hot asphalt. An announcement is made by Janeth in the snack bar stating that the little boy is lost, and vigilance is needed. Chuey, the security guard who often gives the prince rides on his shoulders for an endless stream of giggles and squeals, crosses his arms and places his burly body in front of the chain-link exit. No one will be allowed to pass until he is assured of the prince's safe return.

Soon, the chota arrive. They make their way to NaiNai, who is frantic and yelling at an unfortunate woman who, unaware of the circumstances, is attempting to haggle over an old toaster. There is a crisis at hand, she tells law enforcement. Someone has taken the prince. More sheriffs arrive and the Rosemead Swap is crawling with uniformed deputies who walk the aisles in pairs, one scanning the landscape to the left, the other to the right, their radios buzzing with static and monotoned inquisitions and commands. A helicopter is circling overhead. The cigarette vendors hide their illicit wares and replace them with boxes of incense and small buddha statues. Julio, who sells homemade aromatic oils and colorful fabrics, joins the search for his little friend, calling out across the rows of booths, more alarmed with each passing minute.

Doña Eva, vendor of wooden rosaries, bibles, and religious accessories kneels to pray for the boy after lighting a candle to the Virgen de Guadalupe. Eva knows that Jesus is the Son of God Who Died for Our Sins, but when a miracle is needed, the Virgen always delivers. Doña Eva is joined by Don Sebio and Doña Pancha, who sell small, refurbished appliances, salvaged from yard sales and sometimes the trash, given new life and a bit of polish. The three are on their knees praying when a cry is heard across the swap, reminiscent of those coming from the El Monte VFW Hall on bingo night.

"He's here! I've found him!" someone is yelling.

Sheriff's deputies, customers, and vendors clamor to reach the voice. It is Encarnacíon, the paletera who pushes her refrigerated cart up and down the streets selling frozen treats. She is standing near the San Marcos blankets, pointing down to a small mound. A crowd gathers.

Two deputies approach as Encarnacío backs away. NaiNai is behind them running and shoving people aside. Everyone stands together, heads down as if in prayer, looking at the ground. At their feet, tucked beneath a thick purple blanket emblazoned with a tiger, is the little prince, his eyes closed, mouth open. He is still, like a porcelain doll. NaiNai kneels beside the boy. She places her hand under his shirt and rubs his squishy belly. The corners of his mouth curve upward, dimples flashing as he opens his eyes and smiles.

"Hi, NaiNai," he says as he yawns and rubs his eyes with tiny fists. He refocuses his gaze on his NaiNai.

"I dreamed I was a king!" he declares, laughing.

The crowd breaks into cries of joy, relief, and delight at the prince's words, as the elders of the Swap slap each other on the back, rejoicing that all is well again. Eva blesses herself and thanks the Virgen for keeping the prince safe while NaiNai scoops him up into her arms. Encarnacío hands out celebratory paletas as the boy yawns at all the fuss and rests his head against NaiNai's shoulder, his sticky cheek clinging to her t-shirt.

1950

Esther Garcia

Up and down the paths of downtown Albuquerque.

My mom grew up in what is known as Martinez Town, where everything is connected in grid-like formations, including the communities. North to South and East to West.

The sawmill tracks nestled along the neighborhood, everything within proximity to a young, healthy person who could simply walk.

At that time, it was considered the poorest part of town; today, it is filled with bougie gentrified gelato shops and breweries serving IPAs to tourists.

Bad decisions and gang rivalry seem to be the youngster's fate, or at least for these young women.

My mom recounts how her older sister resentfully fought alone on those tracks, beaten down and angry, while my mom dodged chingasos. Fighting for honor, fighting for family, they were seemingly untouchable.

For over fifty years, we have taunted my mother and aunts about their thuggish lives and the eternal images storytelling has etched in our contemporary minds.

They were the *Sawmill Gang*.

We often reflect on the one friend who tatted the web of mom's hand with a cactus needle, a homemade placa barely legible through the wrinkles and spots.

My tough aunt has been gone for about ten years; she battled cancer until her last day.

But as we watch Mom reluctantly say goodbye to a moment in time with each loss, we also see less of the spirit and less of the fight.

There were other members here and there keeping contact, still maintaining that solidarity. Each had a life and a family that didn't impede the bond of the women. But each left the sawmill way of life behind them.

It wasn't until that recent day in 2023 that Mom received a call. Another passing, from a heart attack, in a moment none of us saw coming, from another destroyed daughter.

My mom, in her mid-eighties, is legally blind and riddled with arthritis
that has rendered her immobile. A devastated woman, now mourning
with her unwavering loyalty to the memory of the sawmill beauty.
And today, my mom stood as the last
Pachuca.

Shoulders

Elena Dolores Solano

I was born in Detroit, in a neighborhood called the barrio, by the "Latinos" who came from distant parts of the United States, Mexico and Puerto Rico. In the 1920's Mexican families from the South and Southwest moved to Detroit for factory jobs which were plentiful. Puerto Rican families also came for the factory jobs. General Motors, Fisher Body, and various steel mills dotted the Detroit river. My parents, Rosa and Juan Solano, were part of that migration al norte. Eventually other goods made their way north, soon stores and churches that catered to the growing Mexican population filled our little barrio. Detroit was a booming car town.

Our bursting community was undone when blind and mindless urban planning, designed a thousand miles away, decided Detroit needed freeways. Those freeways ran through multiple minority communities. Thousands upon thousands of houses were destroyed. Entire neighborhoods were flattened. Our neighborhood was ripped in two, as if someone had broken its bones, hoping it would shrivel up, or die.

But the freeway also made a bridge necessary. It joined the southeast part of the neighborhood with the southwest section. We collectively became known as Southwest Detroit. The community was anchored by churches and parks on each end of it. But the concrete bridge was the primary artery for bikes, walking, driving, going to school, going to mass and shopping at the meat market that served the Mexican community. The bridge was never properly named. There were days it felt like the bridge to everywhere, while other days it felt like the bridge to nowhere.

The bridge was on the same avenue as the library I walked to at least twice a week. There was little fear in our barrio. We all seemed to know each other, so walking from our ramshackle house on 17th Street to the library a mile from our home was long, but lovely.

I passed casitas bursting with roses, Virgencitas adorned front yards, and flowerpots of red geraniums hung from porches. My eyes filled with color. I meandered past the only Mexican restaurant that seemed to exist at the time, several Mexican specialty shops, a family-owned tamale shop, the tortilla factory, and the local Mexican bakery.

Eventually I made my way to the library, La Biblioteca de La Gente, and pushed open the large oak door. There was a hush in the ancient building, so different from my home, which bustled with never-ending energy and movement. My mother cooked, my sister played with her dolls, while my brother Francisco played electric guitar downstairs with his friends. Our mama inevitably yelled, "Turn it down." Meanwhile, my father pounded away furiously on his typewriter, determined to master the English language. Our house was a living organism unto itself.

But the quiet of the library lulled me in. The smell of endless ages of fingerprints and dust-embedded the books. I sat at an old round table, smoothened by age and use. My skinny legs draped over the stained chair. I often feigned reading. Like everything in my life, I was ever curious, and the library was no exception. I stared at the people coming and going, but mostly I stared at Angelita. The librarian.

Angelita was young and hip, beautiful and sophisticated, and college educated. Most of all, she was Mexican American. Her halo of dark curls embraced her wide smile, and she wore clothes that were bright and flowered. She was the highlight of my walks to the library. She was also one of the first Mexican American women I met who had a college degree. In my young mind, I put together that she had an education and had moved across the country to work in our community — alone—by herself.

My heart filled with dreams as I watched Angelita month after month. She was independent. She was educated. She moved away from her family in Arizona. It seemed like she did what she wanted. I watched her talk to people at the desk. Her laughter was infectious. I watched as she shelved books, checked books out, and smiled effortlessly at each person who pushed open those big heavy doors.

I was nine years old, but I was determined to be like Angelita when I grew up. I decided I would go to college, move away from home, be independent and do what I wanted, all the while not knowing what any of that meant. I struggled for many years over being Mexican American, the child of migrant workers, a Chicana born in the 1960's, raised in a home filled with *Time* and *Life* magazine, newspapers, and *National Geographic*, and a father who loved politics.

Confusion often filled my head. My identity was wrapped up in trying to figure out how to be American. I knew en mi corazón, in my heart, that's not who I was. I was the cliché, "no soy de aqui, ni de aya." I am not from here, and not from there.

I was caught in the middle. Mexican, but not Mexican enough. American, but not enough to be defined as such. I felt like I was in a compression chamber, being asked to change into something I was not. I never fit the American model I saw so clearly on television. I knew I would never be a blond-haired child on *The Brady Bunch*.

Being Mexican American in a Northern state in the 1970's was difficult for many reasons. There was no "Hispanic Heritage Month" to celebrate all things Latinx. There were few books of any type on being Mexican or Mexican American, fiction or otherwise. There was no classic *The House on Mango Street*. It felt like there was nothing.

The vacuum left room for racism and classism. There was the litany that Mexicans were dirty and poor, uneducated, lazy, and always had the dreaded lice. There was the belief that we would not amount to much of anything. We were destined to be uneducated, married at a young age, and have babies. We would be employed at menial labor jobs or work at the car factories. The Chicano/a movement was just being birthed across the country. But in Detroit, there was no brown and proud.

For years I carried a deep, burning shame that consumed me. Much of it came because I was ashamed of being Mexican from such a large family. We lived in a ramshackle house, in a city that had been condemned. I was both ashamed and proud of my parents, with their proper clothing, their reserved politeness in public, and their high behavioral expectations. We were considered poor, underserved, a minority within a minority city. I felt ashamed because I didn't know who I was or where I fit in. There were days I could have scratched the shame off, like an itch that refused to be soothed.

My parents clung tightly to their mother-tongue, their culture, food, traditions, music and faith. They lived a dual-life, but I could see it wasn't easy for them. They faced deep poverty, racism, and classism. They held their heads high and kept their dignity intact with a work ethic and faith that carried them through many rough patches.

My calm, demure, sweet mama carried her own shame. The shame of being asked countless times, "You're pregnant again?" And yet, when I look at a picture of her early in her 12th pregnancy, she is smiling, she is playing. She told me stories of being asked to move her seat, or sit somewhere else because she wasn't white or because she was poor. She carried those indignities quietly, just as she carried the scars that covered her body from being burned by the Texas sun.

My parents came al norte to escape the toil of being farmworkers. They picked cotton for years and followed the migrant trail to California. My father, Juan Colmeno Solano had dark skin and a thick accent that could not be hidden. My mother, Rosa Castillo-Diaz Solano began working in the fields when she was four, following her mother around. She left school in third grade to work the fields. I don't know that my father ever had a formal education. After years of pouring smelt, liquid iron, working at various steel mills, he went to night school and became an electrician.

They were proud people, but there was also a certain shame they carried around. Shame and pride are opposite sides of the same coin. It came out in how my parents dressed and presented themselves inside and outside our home. My mother dressed in a conservative manner, she only wore dresses in muted colors of brown, beige, or soft blue with flowers. Her long, black hair was always pulled tightly into her signature chongo. I can still smell the Tres Flores she used. She never wore make-up, but she always looked beautiful.

My father kept his coal-black hair slicked back with Pinaud's Hair Tonic. He wore suit jackets, with crisp, starched white shirts and a bow-tie whenever he went out. His pants were ironed with a fine crease in each leg. To my chagrin, people asked me if he was a waiter in one of those fancy restaurants downtown, where Mexicans served, cooked and cleaned, but did not eat.

We, too, had to iron our clothes before we left the house. Our clothing had to match and be pristine. Our hair had to be done. My mother insisted that we always behave, that as girls we had to be lady-like. My father demanded that we never, ever get out of line. I loved how my parents dressed, how they looked and smelled, and how they made us dress and take care of ourselves. They were proper and polite, and almost demure whenever they were in public. But there were times it felt like we represented every Mexican in the United States.

There were also many times my parents were harsh, strict and punitive. My mother's parenting ebbed and flowed and changed over the years. She could be icy, cold, and punitive, but she could also be warm and affectionate. Over the years, she changed and became the mama we desperately needed, making up for my father's faults.

My father was the complete opposite of my mother. His thundering rage came and went on a daily basis. He raged at the Detroit Tigers on television, he raged at politicians and at meetings in the community. I asked my mother why my father was so angry. She told me he was, "Luz en la calle, y oscura en la casa." He was light in the streets and a shadow in our home.

Far too often he raged at the people we are called to love the most in this life — our families. His lashings, verbal and physical, seemed to come from some part of him that was deeply broken. His anger was raw and untamed. It had no bounds.

As siblings, we had no mercy for each other, at least not at first. It took us years to unlearn and learn another way of being with each other. Love and forgiveness came slowly. We are still learning. We are still healing.

But we were also strong, with other currents that carried us. My parents loved music, Texas conjuntos and Mexican rancheros were always blasting on our record players. While my mother loved planting seeds and watching them grow, and tending to her rose bushes, my father loved baseball and banging away on his typewriter. But more so, there was a part of them that lived for helping other people. They loathed injustice and discrimination against Mexicans and poor people.

My father was a political leader in our community, and throughout Detroit. He fought for unions, health care and education. He fought for the rights of Mexicans to be heard and recognized. He fought for Mexicans like himself. He demanded we be treated with dignity by the political and educational system. He became well known for his passionate fist-raising against the injustices perpetrated against Mexicans and other Latinos in Detroit.

Two of my brothers, Francisco and Daniel, were protesting against unfair immigration policies long before it was vogue. There is a picture of them standing in front of the Detroit Field Office of Immigration and Customs Enforcement. Fearless and brave and protesting.

My father had a massive stroke when I was sixteen. His name and picture still grace many local social service agencies in Southwest Detroit. In his activism, he taught my siblings and me to stand and fight for the rights of all people, but especially for Mexicans. As a family, we loved reading and politics. We believed in the power of unions and hard work, of having fun and faith, and of being loyal to our community and one another.

My mother was the quintessential mamacita, I called her that for as long as I can remember. There are no perfect mothers. There were times she was quick to anger, or used her stick too freely. She was demanding about our behavior. But there was another side of her that was gentle and generous. There was a part of me that felt entirely safe with her.

It was a warm April day and I left my white school sweater at home. A nun approached me at recess, she bent over me, and screamed, "Where is your sweater?" I didn't understand why she was screaming at me. I wasn't cold. I was sitting in the sun, soaking up the warmth of the spring day. We lived across the street from the school and I ran to our house, sobbing into my mother's arms, into the folds of her apron. I was home. I was safe.

My sweet mama visited the same library I haunted and checked out book after book. She read voraciously, as if those books lit a fire in her that had long gone untended. She became friends with Angelita, who now and again visited our home. I watched as she and my mother made cafe de olla. Angelita insisted the coffee be made with piñon coffee from New Mexico, star anise and cinnamon.

As my mother fell in love with books, I fell out of all things Mejicano. In my late teens, I joined an evangelical church. I thought I met Jesus in the faces of people who didn't look like me. They told me they knew what was right for my soul. I needed saving. My job in turn was to save others.

I wasn't allowed to sing because my voice didn't fit in. I wasn't allowed to lead because I was a woman. I wasn't allowed to run on Sundays, because what would Jesus think? The rules of my parents were compounded by the church's strict teachings of having pure thoughts, daily prayer time, saving other people and a long list of shall-nots, have-nots and do-nots. The shame I carried for so long came to a head in the evangelical church.

In a movement that was supposed to be filled with the love of Jesus, I was overwhelmed with the pain of my childhood, and lonely beyond words. I could not relate to any of these people and it seemed that none of them could or would relate to me, my large Mexican family, my father's massive stroke, or my mother being a proper Mexican mother. They could not see my feelings of alienation, from myself, from my family. These feelings, combined with crippling loneliness and fear, coupled with the shame I carried, completely broke me.

The weather had been bitter cold. Everything was frozen and the snow seemed so bright and blinding. I felt utterly lost, hopeless and trapped. I saw no way out of the profound hopelessness or shame that I carried. So I decided to drive my car into the Detroit River.

It was a simple plan. Belle Isle is a beautiful island oasis in the middle of a struggling city. I knew it well. I had run it many times with my brothers and sisters. I knew where to drive my car in, easing it off the land into the frozen waters. I knew I would not survive. But I also knew I could not live this way any longer.

I put on my coat and walked through the kitchen to the back door. There was my mother, at the stove, making coffee, heating up tortillas. She must have sensed something was off. She turned to me and gently touched my elbow and said, "Just wait, Mija, things will get better. Just wait." She told me the people in the church I joined were using me, and she encouraged me to no longer listen to them. I knew in my heart she was right.

I hurried out the door and drove to Belle Isle. I sat in my car and cried for hours. My plan to end my life was undone. My sweet mama saw through my pain and threw me a lifeline. Her words "just wait Mija, things will get better," became my mantra for many years.

I didn't need saving. I needed love. I needed to realize how loved I already was, by my mamacita, by people like Angelita, and later, by *La Virgencita*.

Shapeshifter

I had a vivid dream many years ago. In the dream I was with my mother in her garden, it was full of roses and zinnias and four o'clocks. There was a wound on my arm, it was deep and open. I stared down at my arm aghast, and slowly, an insect crawled out. I was mortified and ran quickly to my mother. I frantically said to her, "Look, look." She looked carefully at the wound on my arm, and in her calm, steady way of being, she simply said, "Oh, that's just fear." And as she said it, the insect emerging from the wound turned into a bright yellow butterfly and flew away into the bluest sky. I looked down and the wound was healed.

I turned away from being evangelical and returned to my cultura, my home, overflowing with siblings and color, with its traditions of lighting candles for prayers, of loud Mexican and Tejano music, of rancheros and cumbias, of Spanish radio on Sunday mornings before mass, of making tamales and menudo, drinking too much coffee, eating pan dulce, squabbling with my siblings, reading books, and planting flowers everywhere.

I struggled with who I was until I realized there was absolutely nothing wrong with being a person who had a heart and soul shaped in Mexico, but a life born and lived in the United States. I could embrace the parts of the puzzle and make them fit into my spirit, my being, my identity.

But more so, it meant that in my heart I could be whole. I could embrace the uniqueness that came with "no soy de aqui, ni de aya." I could love all of me. Like the shapeshifter, I could change, but first there was so much I had to leave behind.

I crawled my way out of that dark, cold place. I could feel my mother's belief in me. It was absolute. I went back to college and studied Spanish and bilingual education. I went further in my education and became a licensed mental health therapist with a master's degree in counseling. Several years later, I returned for a post-master's certification in school counseling.

There were multiple Latino professors and administrators who profoundly changed my life with their kindness, encouragement and generosity. Just as my parents had been present for their community, for their gente, these professors were there for me. They were proud to call themselves Chicanos and they encouraged me to do the same. Over the years reading literature in Spanish and discovering books written by Latino/a authors, I shed the last vestiges of the shame I carried so deeply. I learned that being Chicana was, and is, a radical act of self-love and acceptance.

I struggled a great deal during those years. I often stayed in my car for days on end. I brushed my teeth and washed my face at the local donut shop that was open 24 hours a day. I stayed in the basement of my boyfriend's house at times. Other times, I made the trek home to Detroit to sleep in a regular bed and be with my family. I could not afford gas or food or rent. It took everything in me to stay focused and in school.

The factories were shutting down in Detroit at that time. One by one they were shuttered. Empty facades dotted the Detroit River. Detroit became the poster child for the rust belt. The men and women who worked the lines were offered jobs in other places, other cities, other plants. Many were laid off for what seemed to be months at a time. I knew education was my only way out.

There were times I was motivated by the generosity of my brothers. One brother, Tomas, took me shopping to buy groceries one day. Another brother, Daniel, replaced the headlights on my car that had been smashed out on campus. Yet another, Gabriel, encouraged me to not give up on my education. All of those gestures were filled with what I believed were little messages — keep going, we've got you. Don't stop. My success was their success.

Angelita visited my mama on a regular basis. I hesitated when I saw my mother and her together. There was so much truth and love they carried. Their power was overwhelming. They also held onto a deep faith in La Virgen de Guadalupe, Our Lady of Guadalupe.

One day, I opened the front porch, and my mother and Angelita were sitting there, as if they were waiting for me. I didn't know what to think when Angelita stood up and gave me a calendar filled with images of La Virgen de Guadalupe. In each picture I could feel healing and completeness. My mother had several names for La Virgen de Guadalupe. She called her La Virgencita, La Virgen Morena, or Nuestra Señora.

For as long as I can remember, she insisted that Our Lady was La Virgen Morena, The Brown Virgen, and she was brown and poor, like us. Her words and Angelita's gift pulled at me for months. There was a resignation in accepting La Virgencita as part of my story, my historia, as mi reina. There was no shame or resignation in her eyes.

I am a shapeshifter. Like the butterfly that emerged from the wound on my arm, from an insect, I made my way to owning my personhood, to being Mexican American, Chicana.

The Shoulders On Which We Stand

Recently I attended Angelita's 75th birthday party. We laughed and cried and celebrated her life. But we also talked about the eight-year-old Mexican American girl who walked over the bridge to nowhere and everywhere to get a pile of books and watch her favorite Chicana librarian. We remembered just how far we had both come.

In May 2023, my daughter Nicasia graduated from New York University. She studied Latin American and Chicano/a art. I didn't cry when she walked for her master's degree. But I did cry the first time I walked her to the building where she would be taking classes, in a former mansion on 5th Avenue and Central Park.

I cried for a year; for my mother who loved books and reading, for my abuela, who was an incredibly skilled artisan, for my tías who worked the fields. They were brave women, strong women. They endured deep poverty, and many hardships. They worked for years in fields picking cotton and other crops under an unforgiving sun.

I cried for every woman I knew who had given so much for their mijas, primas, sobrinas, hermanas and nietas. Those women didn't have the opportunity to study or draw or write or dream. Those are the shoulders we stand on.

It is the hope and belief of Mexican and Mexican American women, abuelas and tías, adelitas, hermanas, comadres and madrinas and angelitas, that carry us, like seeds in the wind. It makes us who we are, Chicana. But it is love, their love, that defines us and gives us dignity and strength, and the courage to cross bridges everywhere.

The Beat
Natalia Rivas

in 1952, at 15
i wanted to find that room
that room
where people
greet each day with sharp words and grit under their nails
and weren't afraid
to dance with abandon
to jazz and other indecent exotics
delicately explosive

i wanted to
smoke cigarettes stained red
and drink from the flask of all that is creative

oh man, can you hear the organ dragging
guitar talking of no tomorrows,
just the now, man
replied the moment… just the now
poets leaning to the left
reading from their palms
historic
in many ways twisted
catching the beat that changed the scene

hep kats
snap their fingers to
the god of grit
and melancholy

as inflammatory remarks
ignite a verbal revelation
fire and cool blues
casting primitive shadows dancing
to the drums' aggressive strokes

wearing black sunglasses amidst
a carnival of emotions

perky rhymes from well meaning
wordsmiths hanging longfellow's
laundry on a rainy day
make their point by changing the facts

i'd rather smear poems on the walls
that work at placating
mundane and stale sensible ideas

i always wanted to be in that room
ground floor melding
into the dawn

where smoky rooms
welcome
revolution daily
rugs support ideas
transported form another time, another eon
where today had its tomorrow
and the now
is intergalactic

where the cosmos
orchestrate on speed dial
the changing tide

"Proper Spanish"
Angela M. Sánchez

Author's Note: This passage was originally written regarding the ongoing controversy of the term "Latinx" and during the height of the #DignidadLiteraria movement. This work was first delivered as an oral presentation.

So, the year is 1971 and I hear there's a new word on the street. It's gotten really popular lately, mostly to refer to a specific group of people, people who in particular look like me. Like my mom and dad. Like some of the people in my neighborhood.

This popular word, it's meant to be a collective term. Really, it started out pretty low-key. In fact, before it got thrown all around the way it is now, this word had actually been around for a good 20 years now. It's just now that – man, now it's all over the place. People are putting it in flyers for community meetings, on protest signs, y todo.

Like I said this word got popular real fast.

What's weird is that some of the people in our community don't much like this word. The elders especially. They say it's insulting. That you don't want to be saddled with that made-up, butchered term. It's not even proper Spanish.

And I'm here, like, what is proper Spanish? A Castilian lisp? The proper conjugation of vosotros?

I have to hold not one but two colonizing tongues in my head at once and you're saying I have to treat them with some kind of respect? Ay pues . . .

Anyway, this new word. This new word for me and my people.

All right, you all know what word I'm talking about, right?

It's Chicano.

What? Was there another word you were expecting? Something else?

The year is 1971. We are 450 years removed from the fall of Tenochtitlan to some dude who spoke "proper Spanish." It was this guy, his cronies, and the power overseas that they represented who gave us things like smallpox, syphilis, and a caste system that said the fairer skinned you are the closer to God.

You want to know why people don't like the word "Chicano"? Chicano has its roots in the word "Mexicano." You all know who Mexicanos were? No, not "Mexicans." Or rather, not just any Mexicans. Remember the Mexica (say "meh-shi-cah") who lived in Tenochtitlan — or as someone out there might say, the Aztecs? Mexica is where Mexico comes from. Mexicanos was the Spanish way of referring to Mexica people. If someone spoke "Mexican" that meant they weren't speaking Spanish, but a Native language, like Nahuatl, Mixteco, Mam, or Zapotec. A Mexicano is a Native person. Guess who isn't fair-skinned and therefore distant from a white god? Meh-Chicanos.

But that's probably why some folks don't like the word, right? They're clinging to what they can of the Spaniard. Don't want to mess him up. Need to keep that saber clean for the next time he wants to eviscerate you, to cut out your tongue and suture his in its place.

Nowadays, April 10, 1971, we're over 20 years from when pachucos started reclaiming "Chicano" as our own. To be proud of our skin, our imperfect tongues, our demands for decency, equality, and dignity.

Dignity's a pretty significant word, too.

Dignity means getting to have an equal, unsegregated education. Most people know about *Brown v. Board*, but they don't usually know that *Mendez v. Westminster* set precedent for it almost 10 years prior thanks to our Chicanos in Orange County.

Dignity means getting to be represented as how you see yourself, not how the creators of Frito Bandito see you as some caricature standing on American dirt.

Dignity means having your voice heard. If you're good enough to be cannon fodder in Nam, then you should be good enough to hold office, to demand basic civil and human rights. Instead in many cases, our voices and our advocates are silenced with violence. It was just last summer that L.A. Times journalist, Ruben Salazar, was killed at the Silver Dollar Bar. He was on a break from reporting on the Moratorium before being shot in the head with a tear gas cannister, the kind cops use for barricades and not crowds. Who is a Chicano? And what is it the Chicanos want? Dignity's a good start.

But I also don't think Chicano is a perfect word. Let's face it, there are other Brown people at these marches who never were Mexicano either. They are from Guatemala, El Salvador, Puerto Rico, Brazil — all these other places that share a history of colonization and are just as hungry for a seat at the table.

The word "Chicano" also doesn't include Dolores Huerta. Oh, I know that when Dolores stands by herself or maybe hangs out with a group of her girlfriends, Virginia Muzquiz and Guadalupe Briseño, they can all be called "Chicanas." But the second Cesar Chavez or David Sanchez rolls up, they're all Chicanos. Voices, identities, are swallowed up and asked to conform to the dominant presence in the room. Wasn't that what we were pushing back against in the first place?

What about people like me who question the gender binary or for a few of my friends who don't even identify with the male or female. They are not Chicano or Chicana. There is no space for them because they're queer. To be marginalized within a marginalized community, it's like getting stuffed deeper and deeper into the confines of a messed up Russian doll that's more like an iron maiden. And the only thing seen on the outside is another masculine oppressor, but this time it's from our own.

Huh. Chicano.

I'd rather cross out that "o," straight up x it out, then people could fill it in with whatever they needed. Oh, but I can hear it now, too. That's not proper Spanish.

Proper Spanish is what got us here in the first place. Rude awakening here, if you're using words like "cacahuate" instead of "mani" or "nopal" instead of "cacto," you gave up on proper Spanish a while ago, too. And don't get me started on avocado.

We'll eventually find our palabra perfecta, and let's do it with the inclusion of all our Chicanxs.

Soy Chicana
Consuelo Gallegos

"When anyone asks you what you are, tell them you're a Chicana." I learned that lesson from my oldest sister and cousins, and still say it today: Soy Chicana! I first heard it one evening when I was a little girl at my grandmother's house, as the girls prepared for a night out dancing. While I watched my sister and cousins put on their black eyeliner in the mirror, looking cool in their all-black attire and bell-bottom pants, I listened. Did I know what a Chicana was at that age? Not really, but I wanted to look, sound and be like my beautiful sister and cousins who said we were Chicanas.

Although I didn't quite understand what they taught me at that time, as I got older I learned more about being Chicana, and the history being this label I adopted as my identity. I found out Chicana/Chicano had different roots. One of the earliest findings of the term "Chicano" was for a town in Baja California, found on a map from 1562. Chicano is also considered to originate in the Nahuatl language as "Xicano," with the "X" pronounced as "ch," leading to today's spelling of "Chicano." Later in the early 19th century, "Chicano" was used in newspapers as a racist term, deriding those of Mexican descent with little means. In the 1950s and 1960s, activists of the Chicano Movement united Mexican descendants into a group.

During the rise of the Chicano Movement, civil rights activists in the Southwest States, led by Dolores Huerta and César Chávez in California, José Angel Gutiérrez in Texas, and Corky Gonzales in Colorado, firmly established the term "Chicano." Some attribute an early acceptance of the term to Reies Tijerina López or King Tiger, another civil rights activist in New Mexico. As a young Texas-born man who worked as a migrant farmworker with his family, Reies Tijerina experienced discrimination and abuse against him and his Chicano family, including the near lynching of his grandfather. This greatly impacted him, leading him into activism and fighting for the rights of people along the Texas and Arizona border. After some trouble with the law in Arizona, he and his family fled to Northern New Mexico. There, he became well known for being involved in a battle for the Spanish and Mexican land grants, that had once been promised to Mexican and Pueblo families and their descendants in the 18th century, but taken by the US government. Tijerina formed La Alianza de La Mercedes and worked for years, not only for the land grants issue based in discrimination and racism, but for social justice including the right for Chicanos to preserve their culture and Spanish language. For his work, Tijerina was dubbed "The Malcolm X of the Chicano Movement."

Since elementary school, my father had taught us that we were Mexican, Raza, Chicanos. Living in the States meant we learned to call ourselves Hispanic because that was more acceptable, what we filled out on paperwork and were politely called by some white people. Otherwise, we were impolitely referred to as "beaners," "wetbacks" and "Meskins." When my father wasn't working in the fields, or on some farm or ranch, he spent his time taking us to libraries and burying himself in books, magazines and newspapers. He loved reading, learning, and teaching us our ancestry and how being Chicanos, being Raza, meant we were a mix of mexicanos, indígenos, Moors, and Spaniards. We lived where our ancient native and foreign families had fought, persevered and existed for hundreds of years. The same place our Indigenous ancestors had been for millennia was still our home. "We didn't cross the border, the border crossed us," was something my dad loved saying, and it was true.

As a young child, the small town where I lived was divided, cut in half by the railroad track, where the gringos lived on the "good side" of the tracks, and non-whites lived on the "wrong side" of the tracks in what was referred to as "Taco Town." Our teachers were white, and my classmates were a mix of the white townies, farmers' kids and the Raza kids from "Taco Town."

School was one of my first introductions to inequality and racism. Our English-only-speaking teachers immediately gave everyone with a Spanish name, an anglicized name. Juans became Johns, and Marias turned into Marys. If you were a brown child, you knew you'd be the first to get in trouble, even when your white classmates were to blame. Some white kids made fun of the poorly fitting, second-hand clothing given to us by our older cousins. They mocked our accent, our color, our hair. You would hear, "Your hair is ugly. Don't you wish you had blonde hair like us?" Hearing that hair comment made me laugh. I wanted to look like my sister and cousins; Chicanas with their black eyeliner and their dark hair, not like some kid with light hair that reminded me of an old, white-haired grandma or a pale ghost.

Towards the end of elementary school, we moved closer to our extended family where everyone was Chicano, and we could just exist without being targeted for our differentness. Most of the people we looked up to were Raza. In our new neighborhood, being Chicano was a matter of pride. Our teachers, coaches and people in our church had lived through the rise of the Chicano Movement. We were encouraged to speak Spanish and even elementary students took Spanish classes. Living around mostly Raza meant no longer being constantly exposed to a racist majority of people who saw us as some minority to belittle. Seeing Chicanos who had gone to college and were successful meant we could, too. Having strong Chicana women surrounding me, instilled a sense of how being Chicana is a strength.

In our adobe and stone houses is where we shared our language, food, culture, and religion. There, with my Raza — who both loved us and playfully mocked all our distinct features — we learned resiliency, that buffered us for anything the world might throw at us. Their digs were as spicy as the chile hanging from the ristras on our portales. Hearing people jokingly referred to as "chaparra," "cara de tortilla," "flaka," or "gorda" may have stung, but we were reminded the teasing would toughen us up, whether we liked it or not. My mother, sisters and tías joked that if anyone teased us outside of the home it would have little effect, as the teasing we received at home was probably worse. Besides giving us moments to laugh and compare our unique features, it also gave us a dark sense of humor that can only be appreciated by those in our Chicano culture.

Once I left my majority Raza community, and went out into a majority white world, my Chicana upbringing was what buoyed me. When you're the minority in your school, your field of work, your workplace, the first thing you do is look around to see if there any other people of color in the room. Even when exposed to microaggressions, subtle and overt racist behavior, you aren't deterred. You know your worth. My Chicana mother, aunts, and siblings made sure I did. When faced with bad behavior, I did what my strong role models would do, and stood up against indignities, so people would think twice before doing it again. I also encourage others to do the same.

Something that I noticed coming from a culture that is steeped in tradition and strong family value — like many Chicano households — is that many Anglos don't have that cohesiveness. They lack that closeness and commitment many Chicanos feel towards their families. We live together, or stay in close contact. Many of our elders are cared for in our homes. There is a sense of community in Chicano cultures that is very un-American. Hearing white people mock multigenerational households never made sense to me. Why would you kick out your children the minute they finish high school or put your elderly parents in a nursing home? It seemed cruel and uncaring, and made me appreciate my own culture that much more.

Chicanismo has seen some changes in my lifetime. Throughout the United States, the number of Raza has reached new highs. New Mexico, California and Texas are now majority-minority states with Raza outnumbering whites. Chicano culture is more widely embraced now, and there is still some, but less pressure to assimilate. The number of Raza-serving institutions listed by the Hispanic Association of Colleges and Universities has reached 352. In past years, more schools of higher education have implemented Chicano Studies programs. Chicano Park in San Diego was designated as a National Historic Landmark. There have been an increasing number of Chicano artists creating music, art and literature. Despite all these advances, we still face many of the same challenges as our forebears of the Chicano Movement.

Chicano activism today has a new focus on Dreamers and DACA. What has not changed is racism and discrimination — steady since the inception of this country. We still fight for social justice for our farmworkers, street vendors, and in our workplaces. The non-profit group Justice for Migrants fights for Raza migrant workers who are markedly underpaid and earn only 54% of what white, non-hispanic men are paid. Another organization, Lean In, advocates for all women and teaches Raza women how to stand up against bias in the workplace.

In my case, being a Chicana today means speaking English at work, while speaking Spanglish at home. For those of us who have continued to speak Spanish, it means battling to prevent your children from becoming No Sabo kids, yet realizing any dominant language they learn is a language of colonization. When you're in your schools and workplace, being a Chicana means putting on your daily armor in preparation for potential microaggressions and macroaggressions. Your presence in any organization will sometimes be attributed to Affirmative Action, and not because your skills and abilities made you the right person for the space you are occupying. It might mean hearing, "You talk like a white girl" or "Your English is so good. Where did you learn it?" It's also being told, "This is America, speak English." Chicanos are not homogenous. With our beautiful differences and appearances, you can expect to be asked, "What are you?" Or "Where are you from? You know, what country?", or the exceptionally rude, "What kind of Indian are you?"

Living and functioning in the U.S. is complicated. Being thick-skinned and unyielding are important tools for any Chicana. In spite of the challenges of existing in my Chicana skin, I would never trade it for anything. My culture, language and skin may be the result of conflicts and a difficult history, but I appreciate its evolution and how we continue to grow, adapt and create our unique, beautiful communities. As I go out in the world and am asked, "What are you?" I remember and appreciate those words of instruction from my sister and cousins and proudly say, "Soy Chicana!"

Hijas de Coyolxuaqui

Diana Pando

Protectors of our cultura
back bone of our gente
con sangre, huesos, y estrellas
ancient incantation
giving off Virgen de Guadalupe and Malinche vibcs
ancestral moans of pleasure and pain
expanding
contracting
birthing new versions of our gente
Coyolxuaqui's prayer is Chicanas Chingonas
rising from the dust of 500 years
our semillas recordando
roots roaring
Nepantla no more
somos de aquí y somos de allá

Xicanas Are Xingonas
Victoria Bañales

> *Sí, soy hija de la Chingada.* I've always been her daughter. *No 'tés chingando.*
> — Gloria Anzaldúa,
> *Borderlands/La frontera*[14]

Xicanas are a diverse group of people. We are teachers, students, cholas, drag queens, scientists, pole dancers, politicians, revolutionaries, and more. We are mestizas of Indigenous, Black, white, and (other) mixed-race ancestry. Xicanas are transgender or cisgender, or gender nonconforming, or pansexual, asexual, or heterosexual. Some Xicanas are monolingual, bilingual, or multilingual. Some Xicanas live in Los Angeles or the Bay Area; others live in Detroit or Kansas City. Some Xicanas live in small rural towns with names like Weedpatch or Pájaro. Some Xicanas are U.S.-born; others are immigrants. Some have papeles; others do not. Some love Banda music; others listen to Hip Hop, or both. Some drink tequila or mescal; others prefer sparkling water or chamomile tea. Most of us love atole or champurrado. Eyeliner and hoop earrings are essential — or not. Some Xicanas wear sneakers; others wear stiletto heels, some wear both. Personally, I prefer comfy boots and flip-flops. In short, Xicanas are as diverse as the list of paleta and ice-cream flavors in a Michoacana nevería.

But one thing is certain: Being Xicana requires having a strong political consciousness. To be Xicana is to strive for racial equity, to embrace feminism — our way, the Xicana way. We are vigilant and fight for social justice and liberation. We are strong, intelligent, intuitive, creative, resourceful, and resilient. We are loud and unapologetic. We denounce systemic racism, classism, sexism, homophobia, xenophobia, and a whole slew of -isms and phobias. We stand in solidarity with Native

---

14 Anzaldúa, Gloria. *Borderlands/La frontera: The New Mestiza.* 2nd ed. Aunt Lute Books, 1999.

peoples and other minoritized communities under siege. We recognize that the prison industrial complex is real, that Black lives matter, that borders and walls divide, and that women's rights are human rights. We celebrate sexual and gender diversity. We attend marches, sign petitions, and speak out. We organize, write, protest, clap, sing, paint, meditate, lead, and chant. We hustle. Somos luchadorxs.

Regardless of our political leanings, Xicanas do not sell out. We do not make exceptions for pendejos like Trump. We do not call ourselves Xicanas and attend MAGA rallies, for example. If you claim to be Xicana and wear that nefarious red hat and watch Fox News, I will say you are not Xicana. You are a Hispanic in disguise. And maybe not even that. I will say you are the Chupacabra, and with my candles and sage, I will invoke the curandera in me to wish you away, cast you off to Florida.

Do we have fun? Heck, yeah! Most of us dance, attend concerts, throw pachangas. Others of us enjoy the great outdoors and go hiking, biking, or camping. Sometimes, we dance *and* hike. Or maybe we do neither. Many of us are spiritual and believe in the supernatural. Xicanas are gifted storytellers, healers, artists, warriors, and inventors. Moctezuma, Yanga, Sor Juana, Emiliano Zapata, Benito Juárez, Frida Kahlo, Rodolfo "Corky" Gonzales, César Chávez, Dolores Huerta, Chavela Vargas, Patssi Valdez, Yolanda López. Xicanas take great pride in our culture and history and honor those who came before us and paved the way.

At the same time, Xicanas "take inventory," as Gloria Anzaldúa says, and pluck out those nasty parts of our identity that we inherited from the colonizers. It's a lifelong task that requires intentional decolonial reprogramming; it means continuously having to check ourselves. Repulsed by white supremacy and colorism, we roll our eyes and snap at relatives when they praise whiteness. We are sick and tired of anti-Blackness. We are sick and tired of anti-Indigeneity. We are sick and tired of the Nury Martinezes of the world (and there are many). With the exception of *La Reina del Sur*, Xicanas have difficulty watching telenovelas. The sea of whiteness hurts our eyes. On the other hand, being Xicana means embracing complexities and contradictions, like when we watch and actually *enjoy* those whitewashed Latin American telenovelas.

Finally, being Xicana means caring for each other and the planet in which we live. It means being a good comadre and supporting our hermanxs, but it also means setting healthy boundaries. It means practicing self-care and valuing our mental health and spiritual well-being. Xicanas embrace neurodivergence and recognize that many of us — whether we know it or not — are on the spectrum. Xicanas honor our elders and ancestors. We respect Madre Tierra and treat her with reverence, kindness, and love. We care about climate justice and weep for the Gray Wolf, the North Atlantic Right Whale, and other animal relatives that are under attack and threatened with extinction. (And if we don't care, it's time we do.)

Xicanas are this and much more. Xicanas are xingonas.

Both shores at once
Angelina Sáenz

I am the Chicana
with the *Living Buddhism* magazine
and the book of Charles Bukowski letters
at my bedside

I am the Chicana
who wakes up at dawn
to light candles and burn incense
beads in hand
chanting Nam Myoho Renge Kyo
reciting chapters 2 and 16 of the *Lotus Sutra*

I am the Chicana
who grit my teeth
and overcame all of the guilt and shame
of leaving a 22-year marriage

I am the Chicana
with a smile as wide as the Gulf of Mexico
and a heart as golden as Moctezuma's breastplate

I am the Chicana
who loves myself
my strength, my courage, my compassion and passion
my laughter and solidarity with others
and who challenges myself everyday not to seek love and validation
outside myself

I am the Chicana
who travels alone with my children to my homeland
turquoise waters and island breeze soothes our soul

I'm the Chicana
sitting alone at the corner table
at La Abeja restaurant
reading Anzaldúa's *Borderlands*
scooping up huevos a la mexicana con chile
and frijoles de la olla
into my warm corn tortilla

¿Y qué?

Xicana
Martha Alicia Rivas Maravilla

Inhale.

Listen,
I was born en Zamora, Michoacán, México
en aquel febrero del mil novecientos setenta y nueve
pero a los tres años me trajeron como la Priscilla-no-se-quien,
aya por un carro
cruzando la línea
aya por Tijuana.

I often tell folks that
that was the only time I ever went to T.J.,
that
or
that one time
se acuerdan, we went to Rosarito for spring break noventa-y-ocho.
pero sssshhhhhhh, ya después les cuento.

Pero soy Chicana

see, imma have to redefine all these definitions, and labels, and
requirements and todo
they've formalized to institutionalize and impose on us:
this process to call ourselves this one label or another, still colonial
but this process of naming simply coincides with the fluidity of language
pero
mendigos wanna keep us distracted con tarugadas —
pero se llaman historical amnesia and cultural schizophrenia
Google it, luego les escribo de todo eso.

all this informs my Chicananess.
y yes, we create and use terminology que nos da la gana.

I was raised in these lands, acá los que les llaman estadunidenses

(trust I had to Google and spell check that, porque my Spanish is what
they call pocha, still)
Sombra nos dice Norteñas
pero I just say: Mexicana y peleonera, acá en el Norte.
Raíz bien centrada.
Corazón
rosa mexicano, brillante, ardiente así como el rosa que nos regaló
Ramón Valdiosera, presente!

But what I meant to say is:
Soy Chicana
because I carry the responsibility to keep fighting, straight up.
We remind ourselves, again, to learn our history but also the historicity
of our gente.
Historicity, is for us to see
and learn,
and sense,
and feel again,
and learn again,
and all that again,
about how our gente has been here for hundreds of thousands of years,
you see?
We have a responsibility to know how our gente experienced history:
what we saw,
what we felt,
what we loved,
what we endured,
but mostly,
how resilient and brilliant and strong our gente will always be.

Y por eso mismo soy Xicana, always inspired by Malcolm X

because

we, all
still
hold a responsibility to remind ourselves of our collective fight.
the political, historical, social, y todo aquello —
shit that still keeps hurting us, intentionally,
for profit.

It is our turn to speak.

Chicana was birthed out of resilience, not just resistance.
For the reclamation of our indigeneity.
For the fight to express our identity.
For the right to be seen.

Chicana raíz, como el maíz, runs deep.

So I'm that type of Chicana, de Califas — la quien no se olvida:
we stand on land
that once was Mexico
and indigenous
prior and always.

Exhale.

Trenzas y herencias
Carolina Martínez

The first time I heard the word "Chicano" I was six years old. Sitting on the living room floor, I played while my parents talked about my "lazy" family members, "Esos Chicanos no sirven pa' nada." It felt like a bad word but I asked anyway.

"What's a Chicano?"

"They're the criminal sons of Mexicans," they said.

I believed them but I still had my doubts. I saw how my cousins called themselves Chicanos and marked it with pride on their skin. That controversy lived in my mind all the way through middle school.

In the halls of my middle school, I walked a path of self-denial. It was a constant comparison between myself and the others. Their straight, light hair against mine — long, brown, and curly. Their blue eyes and my brown eyes. Transitioning from a place where almost everyone looked like me, in school I felt foreign, like a star without a galaxy.

I was received with judgmental looks. It made me feel wrong, while everything about them felt accepted. I yearned to be embraced as one of their own, took my hair out of braids and hushed the rancheras that once played loud and proud inside of me down to a whisper. Finally, I synched into their orbit: felt like one with their crowd.

However, fate has a way of reclaiming its own. In the depths of my being, my indigenous roots called out to me, singing our ancient songs. In them, I heard the river flowing through the llano, and the whispers of my grandmother's wisdom rustling in the golden cornfield. I yearned for the wholesome feeling I once possessed.

Then, in high school, the word Chicano made a timely reappearance. It lurked in the shadows so long like a monster hiding under the bed, demanding to be acknowledged. I Googled Chicano expecting to find the monster my parents had described and instead, found a treasure.

Reading about the Chicano Movement felt like a drug, I was addicted to the truth. Each line of "I am Joaquin" by Corky Gonzales resonated with me and helped me discover a side of me I didn't know. I had found power in a word that once carried a negative connotation: the power that my identity was not defined by external acceptance, but by the internal love for my authentic self.

I was too American for my Mexican community and too Mexican for my American community. As Juan Bruce- Novoa said, "A Chicano lives in the space between the hyphen in Mexican-American" and I was fine existing in the in-between. I embraced the notion of "ni de aqui ni de alla" — neither from here nor there — recognizing that my true essence lies in the fluidity between cultures, like the intertwining of diverse threads in a braid.

These teachings — together with the profound wisdom in Nature — became my guides in understanding that my identity is a woven tapestry, encompassing both my Mexican and American heritage. With my newfound identity came a wave of celebration, education and freedom. In embracing my identity, the braid — once constricting — became a symbol of empowerment, a dance of intertwined cultures reclaiming their rightful place. Wearing my long, dark trenzas, I honor my ancestors and their traditions, no longer wishing to fit into a light-haired crowd, but celebrating the richness of my own heritage. After all, Soy Xicana! Claiming this identity has filled the hollows of my heart and given me a purpose.

Xicana Purpose
Erica Castro

I too, can poet
Although Xicana
I throw punches
With verse.

I protest
With ancestral
Blood that runs
Through me.

I teach
Future generations
The history
Of El Movimiento:

The sacrifices of the men
Who came before us —
Fathers and grandfathers
Who suffered injustices,

Beat up by sailors who
Stripped zoot suits
Off their skin,
Jailing the victims.

The Chicano Moratorium,
Protesting Vietnam,
Our brothers and
Their countless deaths.

Speaking out killed
Ruben Salazar who lay
Dead at the Silver Dollar bar,
no longer able to speak for the Xicano.

I teach the "I am Joaquin" poem
Corky Gonzalez poured out
Claiming *this is our home,*
It has always been our home.

I teach how Oscar Zeta Acosta
Lawyered our leaders,
The East L.A. 13,
And defended our activists.

We, that know,
We, that have this
Precious knowledge
Need to speak out:
Teach our youth
The power of
Xicanismo!

Our history cannot die
So, we tell the stories,
And we tell the stories
To help the legacy live on:

My true purpose as a
Xicana.

Sangre Llama Sangre
On Defending the Treaty of Guadalupe Hidalgo
Guadalupe T. Luna

My Chicana DNA is defiantly infused with family cuentos of lost lands. Including the one about a much-loved abuela — as a youth of Indigenous ancestry — hiding in a pot belly stove as Texas solders invaded her family's land. These were stories of vast discrimination and farmworker hardships planting and harvesting crops throughout the Midwest.

As a Chicana, this causes me to resist against odious state laws that are presently erasing gente de color and LBGTQ+ communities from school curriculums. I defiantly resist yielding to their erasure with two major trajectories emerging: The first shows the consistent removal of our *cuentos* and shared disparate realities throughout this nation's history, erasing — and also objectifying — Chicanas through a realm of capriciousness. The second path explores the daring Mexicanas who owned and operated ranchos in Mexico's northernmost territories prior to the war between the two nations. These Mexicanas reached out to me, and I refuse to let go of their cause.[15]

I chased the litigation battles of the Mexicanas seeking a more concise legal history as to why so many lost their property following the war, notwithstanding the constitutional supremacy promises of a federal peace agreement. Many of the women believed that the peace agreement — the Treaty of Guadalupe Hidalgo negotiated and signed by both nations — would protect their property ownership. The assertions of politicians that all the "blessings of American law," would also protect ownership status further enforced their understanding that no harm would result.

---

15 I use Mexicana as they were identified under Mexican governance. This extends to female ownership from the Spanish governance of Mexico, residing throughout Indigenous territories. Census figures of the earliest entry into California also identify Black settlers and the promises of the Spanish friars to turn over mission lands to the Indigenous remains a challenge as to which individuals actually garnered lands.

Yet within a few short years in violation of the Treaty of Guadalupe Hidalgo, the mujeres of the past lost their properties and reached out to this Chicana, seeking not only a more precise legal history, but also accountability. Accordingly, the litigation ultimately revealed a group of profound women, who, by their actions diminished the patriarchy celebrated under United States law.

Women of the past were unfairly tethered to the patriarchy of the times that denied them property rights, according to the common law — the judge-made law — of the United Sates. In contrast, Mexico's code based — civil law — recognized the legal identity of women without binding them to the bonds of male patriarchy. As such, exercising their legal autonomy, Mexicanas, petitioned for lands and operated agricultural operations throughout Mexico's northernmost territories presently comprised of the southwestern tier of the United States.

This group of female property holdings of differing sizes included, for example, María Antonieta de Castro who held 30,593.95 acres, Martina Castro owned 32,702.41 acres and Vicenta Sepúveda who possessed 17,774.19 acres. Outside of directly petitioning for land, women also witnessed recognition of their survival rights following the deaths of spouses. This legal autonomy facilitated Doña María de la Luz Chaves retaining ownership of her home, which encompassed seventeen rooms, a chapel, a store, and other tracts throughout the region following the death of her spouse.

Not only did Mexicanas hold properties, they also named them. For example, Catalina Manzaneli de Munras's Rancho Vincente, located in Monterrey County, California. María Concepción Valencia de Rodriguez, owned Rancho San Francisquito and Isabel Yorba, Rancho Guadalosa. María de Los Angeles Castro and Candida Castro shared Canada de Raimunda in San Mateo County, California. Under their agricultural stewardship, they established orchards and engaged in the production of varied food products, with yet another possessing a cattle ranch in Arizona. The Mexicanas that remain, belonged to acequia societies that protected and conserved water sources, further showing their awareness of scarce environmental resources throughout New Mexico.

The valuable investigations of Chicana and Chicano historians, illuminate Mexicana importance in the settlement of Mexico's northernmost provinces. Principally omitted from legal studies, falsehoods, however, surfaced, which privileged those seeking to erase our presence from the nation's history. This tactic parallels states in the present adopting anti-knowledge laws, denying how we identify and seeking our removal from core curriculums.

This privileges those intentionally misrepresenting our histories, sustains falsehoods and objectifies the mujeres of the past by blaming them for the loss of their property. It also protected those that asserted Mexicanas were treated "fairly" under the common law, while others declared the legal systems of the two nations conflicted and accelerated their defeat in common law determinations. Yet sangre llame sangre, and my encounters with the mujeres of the past reveal confrontations. Contrasting with falsehoods, Mexicanas fought to protect their ownership of their ranchos!

After the war, The United States betrayed the Mexicanas remaining on their property by obligating them to demonstrate proof of ownership. This newly imposed condition debased the supremacy clause of the federal constitution treaty cases, interpreting and recognizing the supremacy clause, and policies against — not only Mexicanas — but the Indigenous throughout the southwest. Consequently, they quickly lost their properties to United States land policies. This further opened the door to challenges from squatters, claim jumpers and a realm of contradictory legal rulings that stymied the defense of women holding property. The process entailing special courts to defend their interests, also defied earlier land grant law in Florida, changed to the unfair advantage of property holders. In sum, violating the Treaty of Guadalupe Hidalgo at the expense of our antepasados.

Not even the wealth and standing protected their property from interlopers and squatters such as the case of Dominga Dominguez and her Rancho Las Virgenes in 1889. Her legal history reveals she succeeded in proving ownership in the lower courts against the claims of non-Mexican land claimants. Ultimately, however the United States Supreme Court ruled against her ownership status where she lost the disputed tract of her property to squatters and claim jumpers.

A similar case was that of Teodora Peralta, for whom they made it impossible to protect her ownership claims. Teodora Peralta's daughter

María de Valencia's defense failed at the Supreme Court level because the *expediente* (title papers) that she presented were not in the official deed records. The court in *Peralta* disregarded earlier litigation where John Fremont who claimed Mariposa as his property without *expedientes* and succeeded. Even more incredulously, Fremont's actions in losing the deeds and other title papers of the Mexican property holders during the conquest of California was also disregarded. Fremont's claim as the first case to reach the Supreme Court should have guided the court in Peralta's but as in so many subsequent cases the contradictory reasoning in his case did not apply to those of Mexican, Spanish or Indigenous descent trying to defend their property interests.

The scope of external battles neither resulted from the failure to defend their interests, nor did their adverse consequences flow from the differences between the common law or civil law.

In contrast, the termination of the property interests directly resulted from violence, the failing of federal courts to preempt state law and changing procedures in the rules of evidence from earlier land grant litigation throughout Florida that should have guided the Supreme Court.

Gratuitous claims from third parties of fraud against the property owners also succeeded in depleting the resources of the Mexican owners. For a while, the United States' failure to protect, permitted a bond could be purchased to join challenges against Mexicanas to further expedite losses. In sum, eliminating Mexicanas from the properties, and in the private and public spheres.

As a Chicana, I refuse to forget their litigation battles. The voices of the Mexicanas demand accountability and obligate our continuing resistance against anti-knowledge "laws." At this divisive moment, their forced erasure continues with unmitigated restraint through states disappearing our histories from the education of youth. Our continued histories of advocacy must thereby remain vigilant against those objectifying our Chicana and Indigenous sisters and brothers into the present.

There are many ways to do this, and expand the pleas of those who confronted the violations of the Treaty of Guadalupe Hidalgo. For example, we can support the American Indian Movement-West reaching out to the United Nations. Specifically, the plea here is to the Office of the High Commissioner, the Expert Mechanism on the Rights of Indigenous Peoples (EMRIP). Seeking out international human rights law to redress the injustices confronting our Indigenous sisters and brothers would facilitate a reexamination of the Treaty of Guadalupe Hidalgo outside of the failings of domestic law. It could also bring a halt to the states that betray the federal constitution by disappearing the histories of our *antepasados* from school curriculums.

Chicanas have long joined forces with other mujeres — formed unions and coalitions across into Mexico to advocate against discrimination from manufacturing plants, relocating from tax-free havens in the United States. They have joined forces to fight the environmental racism plaguing our communities. Through their advocacy, Chicanas have brought much needed changes and medical care to colonia residents lacking safe water and other health and safety measures. Their efforts establishing La Raza Unida as a political-third-party impresses even in the present.

Xicana Fire: Fight & Liberation
Vanessa Marie Bustamante

When will you see, we were made differently?
Indigenous blood flows through me,
Igniting thoughts, visions, and ceremonial healing.
Consistently left bewildered by the colonizer's mistreatment,
Still, my Indigenous blood pumps throughout my body creating an
uproar for change in society.
Committed to creating liberation and self-determination for the people
I continue to rise, continue to fight!
Xicana: a whole political ideology.
Shared struggle and leading the fight because it's our right!
Heart full of fire and grounded in her love for her people,
She is leader, advocate, and organizer.
She is Xicana! La mera mera. La jefa!

Composed by the First Female Leader of the Raza Unida Party

Jaguar Warrior
Gaby Moreno (7 Octoberz)

La Mexicana que nació para grandeza
Si te acuerdas
Me llamo Gabriela la poeta
La mensajera con su trompeta
Llena de fuerza
La reina de la selva
Mi mente en otra frecuencia
Abierta mi conciencia
No soy de este planeta
Sabiduría de una Tolteca
Sangre de Guerrera
Jaguar en mis venas
Soy Maya, Indigena y Azteca
Adelitas son mis antepasadas
Emiliano Zapata
Una revolucionaria
Dualidad es mi naturaleza
Soy buena y mala
Geminiana
Gemela y cuata
Soy la verdad, nunca falsa
Me traicionas y habrá venganza
La fantasma con sus barras
¡Yo hago lo que se me dé la gana!
Destined for greatness since the day I was born
I'm prepared for war
I know the score
Keep you comin' back for more
The girl who's obsessed with gore
I'm nothing to mess with you've been warned!
I'm a jaguar
Got my battle scars
Get my power from the stars

I am a God!
Ushe protejo la madre tierra
La verde frontera
La que nos deja existir sin guerra
Estos poderes son de mis ancestras
Nuestra historia está en las estrellas
El universo inspira mis poemas
Mi corazón y alma en cada letra
Carácter de soldadera
Esta canción se la dedico a mi abuela
Siempre vivirás en mi, Rafaela
Me he convertido en una de tus leyendas
La Diosa de las Tinieblas
Orgullosa de mi cultura
Como yo no habrá ninguna
Yo soy única
La reina que adoran en su tumba
Agarro mi energía de la lluvia
A mi nada me asusta
Tus rezos me alumbran
Nací para la lucha
Cada pelea gano sin duda
Vengo de un linaje de salvajes
Jaguar corre en mi sangre
Nunca he sido una cobarde
I do this from the heart
You can hear pain in every bar!!!

Radical Truth-Telling: My Master Narrative
(Originally presented as a spoken word poem)
Candi Cipactli Corral

Working-class at home
Xicana outside,
Mexican American on paper.
Beaner, viejita, ruca, flaca, guerita at home.
Xicana, xingona in public: out there.
Mexican American on paper.

Soon, I knew the private and public spaces were part of the problem.
My creation-story, mis historias, of growing pains of consciousness
Split between mundos:
Nepantla — more like the different arms to my saguaro.

On the monte, the only 'R' words we had were
Rez
Reservoir
River
And
Run!

Racism without using that 'R' word:
When my abuela had a black dog and named it the 'N' word, but
abuela was ashamed when we
told her it was bad, and she said that's how life was en el campo. She
was sorry and never did it
again.

Racism without the 'R' word:
When we went down the monte on our horse and the whites in the car
asked if me and my
Primas were gonna take a bath because we were dirty mojadas,
But we just took a bath and my Hermanos just laughed, I never got the
joke.

Racism with no 'R' word:
When my own guerita mother, with red and blue Irish and Spaniard
eyes yelled, *Get the rifle!*
When I was eight years old because she saw a darker man from another
tribe
Bleeding from his head all over our front stucco fence.
I hear her yelling at my abuela, 'did you see an ol' whitty around? I bet
you that's who got em.'

Racism, sexism, ableism and more, were apparently only words for
them — mysterious folks.
All the ignorance turned the other cheek,
laughing at harmful, hateful jokes,
turn reality in the streets.

I was raised second by Westside, that move was deep.

My abuelita stayed on the monte, and I was raped in the hood I called
home.
So much violence! But time went too fast there to pay any attention.

Racism with a new 'R' word:
Radicalize young eyes.
Revolutionize the Westside!
Gangsta rap saved us all.
Had words we never heard of before. But we knew exactly what they
meant.
No need for Google or Wikipedia in time we need to be strapped.
We were still called Beaners, wetbacks, mojadas with thighs and hips
rounder than tortilla dough.

New word learned real-quick:
Savage.
Teachers called us savages. The principal called us savages.
Some of us accepted it, and wore our Aztec tats.

Anti-racism was an action before a word.

Decolonizing just happened.
One day, when we all found out the incense in church was the copal our 'savage' ancestors
Used in sacred ceremonia, during heart wrenching extraction of cora, flesh, land, …colonized.
Church tells lies.
We were pissed!
And reclaiming more: Aztec calendarios, Quetzalcoatl tats and oh ya, the Virgen *de who??*
Oh, you mean Tonantzin?
That shit f***ed us up more than drugs!

Anti-colonial was an action before it became a word.

Intersections of this capitalism, imperialism, patriarchal world was part of my creation historia,
The fight now is to make it heard:

So, I'm a beaner, guera, sexy, mami, from the hood
Mexican American on paper.

I'm an action first, before I become a word.

Editor's note: This poem emerged after participation in Albuquerque's Poet Laureate Manuel' "Low-Writing at El Chante" events, and after several nights of raising fire in protest at racist/sexist institutions.

Adelita
Natalia Rivas

the sun recedes
welcomes night
soft shadows arise

drunken
young men slide
into doowop harmonies
base notes straddle
fat moon rising

lazy cats
big eyes startled
ears twitching

voluminous shadows split open
curtains to another story

her scent arrives first
rose water and hope
dangling on a string

consciousness is stirred
awakened
flung open

robes expose
pistoleros slung low
sauntering stroll
a dancer's sway

slithering and reaching for that pomegranate
wisdom cracked opened rubies of knowledge
glistening with juice

red, green, yellow: her mighty crown

jutting branches
rustle

opaque dirt
and day long sweat
hold back the sun

it's our lady of revolution

eyes forward
shoulders back as
days move quickly

not to be held back
images of subjugation
ripped
shredded
burned

comandante
soldera
revolutionary

gun toting and ready
to drink from the bottle of wisdom
her muscles flex quietly
her belly is a quake of pleasure
her pout celebrated with a full metal
sensuality

she is
the flow of the sea
alchemist in the finest sense
old woman wisdom
and youthful vigor
your sister
your mother
your ancestors
your future arriving

she is adelita
one and many

Rasquache Liberation Love Letters

Rosanna Alvarez

Si vieras, yo como te recuerdo, past a moment or a song,
it's about how we belong,
a legacy of *cultura* where art is our song,
where *rasquache* has value and it's not just
the supposed taste[less] style of the underdog;
more like the wisdom and the fierce sensibility
of a Quetzalcoatl legacy
where knowledge lives on inside of me
in spite of all the wisdom stripped from a body of we
– *la gente decente*
as *herederas of círculos*
where the hummingbird flies,
creators and artists, whose spirit never dies,
con safos, Red-handed danzantes,
we rise.

Rasquache, a Proposal

Carmen Baca

Rasquachismo — the word rolls off the tongue like the delightful end of a carnival ride: the Ferris wheel coming to a stop, the bar opening, and gleeful passengers stepping off. The word prances out in the cadence of a Spanish polka, enticing a kicking up of chanclas to the musica filling the air. It's a noisy word, reviving scenes of las ferias, colorful paños hanging over los bailadores, the Xicana girls twirling like tops in their colorful fiesta dresses. "Ahuas" y "ópales," gritados con ganas, más altas after the frasco de mula makes the rounds a las escondidas from mano to mano. It summons the scents of chile colorado con tortillas. Vendors making enough for the year from hungry turistas seeking authentic Spanish foods.

Rasquache — the expression fulfills an itch to create, to innovate, to present, to put on display. El arte de la gente, a kaleidoscope of mediums from adobe to lana, leña, híchete, alambre; whatever appeals aesthetically, al modo de los pobres. Las ferias y fiestas feature them all, generations of each familia's talents. Los santeros, tin work artists, wood carvers, y los de más, Xicana artisans of every craft fulfilling our desire to keep traditions alive in our plebe. Esto es rasquachismo, appealing, enticing, marveling, and mesmerizing to admire and to acquire. Booths filled with visual delights: cruzes, santos, navajas hechos de cuerno, todos únicos, drawing the curious, the casual looky-loo, collectors and connoisseurs of bona fide Chicano art.

Rasquache — la palabra perfecta to describe our casitas and our yardas in vivid detail, too. An aesthetic our antepasados devised decades before one of us Xicanos gave it a name. Priceless and cherished, our unique decorations, timeless and time-worn, a part of our herencia that came with la tierra and rooted us through querencia por vida y toda l'alma. Las madres proudly display altares covered with linen cloths edged in intricate crochet, santos y velas between retratos de familia long gone beside those still living close or far. Una candela always burns for their health or their protection in good times and in bad. Eso es rasquache del espíritu, del corazon, y de la gente, young, old, and in between.

Rasquache — the name for our décor, functional or nomás por show, inside and out. A shelf en la cocina holds abuela's mixing bowls, every use bringing her to mind. Abuelo's books of alabados bring back los Hermanos' blended, robust voices as we read. Afuera, hay más. Tío's hacha and his talache still work good as new, el rastrillo, también. Pero el arado pintado rojo está parado entre flores por quebrado. That's rasquache ¿qué no? Attracting the eye in a pobre kind of way, la gente stop for photos todo el tiempo. Their ojos, always drawn to the oval nichos out in front, inside of which La Virgen or some other santo stands, surrounded by Rosas de Castilla o las varas de San José.

Rasquache — el sonido reminds me of how los pachucos back in the day used to talk when they'd pass us in the parque with a lift of the chin and a pointing of the trompa, a side eye glance and a casual "quiúbole" in greeting, mingling with the rhythmic tap, tap, tap of their zapatos on the sidewalk. A cigarro tucked behind an ear, tattooed muscles on display beneath cuffed t-shirt sleeves. Los calzones pleated shiny sharp and la cadena hanging from belt loop to pocket drew attention. El filero tucked inside, listo for any confrontation, a ready defense against disrespect or lack of deference. The rasquache attitude lingering with the scent of the pomade-slicked Elvis ducktail.

Rasquachismo — rosillo, calavera, pajarito, maravilla, dulce sonido de palabras en español. The rhythm of archaic nombres, Seferina, Carmelita, Jesusita, Secundino, Telesfor, they flow off the tongue with the undulating consonants no less fun to utter than las palabras malas shouted, say, after a hammered thumb. Cabron, jodido, a la vey, no need to spell it out, if you're Xicano, you know the vulgar variations very well. Rasquache, a funny-sounding word, satisfying the itch to board the audible amusement ride that is communication. The rolling of that R circling the mouth like the Tilt-A-Whirl, the rising of the roller coaster in the QUA before it plunges with that EEEE we say por todo.

Rasquache — I propose, should be the new moniker, the name we give our Norteño dialect. A mix of old Spain, Mexico, Nahuatl, Indigenous, Rio Grande con poquito pachuquismo along for the viaje. In the decades of our modern times, we added Spanglish to the feria. Twisting, turning, circling, rising then falling, an English word interspersed, interrupting the momentum, delighting and amusing, confirming and defining who we are with every utterance. It's the cadence, the lilt, the accent, and the stress contributing to the peculiar pronunciation, in the midway ride inside the mouth as the tongue hits the teeth or the paladar and emerges loud or soft with complete satisfaction in the intonation, in the timbre, un sonido más chingón.

Las OGs
Claudia Meléndez Salinas

They wear their canas like diamond tiaras
don their huipiles like Dolce Gabanna

Chicanas, they may have been called cholas
at one time but now ya son Xicanxs

Cihuameh, cihuapipiltin,

They are college professors, activistas, organizers,
maestras, artistas, poetas, madrinas, curanderas

They heal desde una cortadita
hasta five hundred years of gaslighting

eye rolling, jaladas de trenzas,
chanclazos, the burn of demotions

promotion passovers, denied tenures,
micro aggressions and macro chingaderas

Did you make this salsa? I spent a summer in Guatemala.
Where are you *really* from? I love your tan.

At the gallery opening honoring their own
they walk among slogans, posters,

a history etched on their skin
a bittersweet reel of protests, sit-ins

pozole for sale pa' recaudar fondos
for la lucha que no puede cansarse nunca

their linaje embroidered on their tunics
sketched pyramids imagined by the fire

by cihuameh, cihuapipiltin,
mujeres antiguas que se hacen presente

en sus arrugas, en sus miradas
in that way of walking that says

these threads, mantos de tela y de agua
are made for highlighting

an ancestral past embodied
on canas like diamond tiaras.

Fashion "Advice" to Women Over 40
Carmen Tafolla

My foolish, stylish "Expert," this advice you published
on what women over 40 should wear and how they should
amend their look to "compensate" — it lacks Panache.

You see, ma petite, I've been wearing these big hoop earrings since
way before you were born — born squiggly. And all wet, I'd add.
Bawling, bright angry red. And. Wearing. Nothing.

And I'll be wearing these earrings still, I'm sure, when you are
thick-middled and grayed, considered way too passé for this job
and hopelessly   Out. Of. Style.

My mode d'emploi, de resister, c'est ça, chérie: I'll offer you some
wise advice for free. You see it's not about just matching current runways
or looking like a perfect, fresh-bloomed, gleaming 22.

It's that the beauty comes with Chispa, flows Free with joy of spirit,
being who you'd Love to Be.   It's letting my Apache bones, Gitana hips,
dance to the rhythms in their soul, move with the beat that makes
them bold
It's   if I'm   ME,   not if I'm Young or Old
or Thin, or Pale as snow   or Dark as coffee beans   or coal

These flashing silver hoops are made of histories
and of hope flashing in the eyes of someone's dream
These fiesta fireworks I wear in turquoise skies and chile red
the happy jangle of these shell-songs, samba-ing around my wrist
this swirl of campesina skirts with room for birthing solid life
and love and earth and justice, as did the soldaderas' lives,
this stride, like all the sky is mine,
they make me Smile, and show you Style
is more than clothes

So I will dress in Echoes of the Breeze and Rippling River Laughter
accessorized by Thunder Trumpets with a Mariachi Flare
I'll absorb the Passion in handwoven Huipil labyrinths of Pinks and
Purples
Royals, Greens made by her Earth-Brown fingers, each woven tight as
loins of
Love, sure as Promise in her steady eyes. I'll shine with Dazzling Daylight
and shiver with the prayers of Shaman Trees, and blaze with Fire strings of
Heart-Red Seeds that swing like Ebony curves on mujeres africanas
ululating Joy
and waves of Motion, celebrating layer on layer
of Villages and Family, an Ancient Harmony

This Woman-Grounded Style's so strong it survives centuries,
Drums through my continents with stubborn-passioned feet
Hums in Aztec and Ojibwe, Arabic, Rumanian, Bantu, Chinese
Births babies, hunts, scribes elders   Like Tarahumara, runs free
Sounds castanets in lamp-lit cuevas, Viking horns and Maori chants

So I will wear my big hoop earrings in my dance
with huipil, rebozo, feather, sari,   beads and seeds,   chanclas, jeans.
In Style, I'll sing the Yanaguana Indians of my home   but especially I will
Sing
Me

Stereotype Me Sometime
Elizabeth Jiménez Montelongo

Sometimes,
I'm a Chicana in a chongo
With bright blue nails,
Darkened eyebrows,
Big earrings, chanclas.

Somedays,
I'm a hardworking Mexicana
Looking all sweaty and tired,
With my worn-out jeans,
Mis tenis, my daughter.

Suddenly,
I'm that spicy Latina you dream about —
Though you'll never admit it —
Red lipsticked smile and a dress.

Sunny days,
I'm a sweet, smart, Mexican girl:
Gentle, graceful, minding those manners
Even when you call me Hispanic.

Sporadically,
I'm a prissy oh-so-educated Latina
Being aggressive and combative.
So disagreeable, so defiant.

I'll snap at you, seduce you, scold you, soothe you, school you!
So sweaty, so sassy! So sexy, so sweet — so subversive!
Scandalous!

Hoops
Cecilia Sanchez

There's something about putting on my hoops . . .
I'm not sure if it's their gold, shiny appearance
But they return me to my ancestral DNA:
Golden.
Radiant.
Shining so much the conqistadoras want some
So, they pull back their blond hair,
Mask their privilege with bronzer,
Gloss and line their lips,
And, lastly,
Put on our hoops:
Out to conquer what we built
Again.

Soy Mujer Grande del Movimiento
Irene I. Blea

I was surprised thirty years ago, when a young man addressed me as señora. I guess I wasn't expecting to grow old in the eyes of younger people, but after seventy-seven years on this earth, I embrace it. It's not easy to acknowledge your abilities, challenges, and the abandonment of your own body, the side looks of your grandchildren, and the unease of your children when you can't open the ketchup packet or reach the top shelf for the flour, pee when you cough, or drop a bit of food on the floor. Nevertheless, I still identify as a Chicana: someone who understands my history, the intersection of race, class and gender, and intends to do something about it.

We, elders, still have much to offer because we have lived through much and we have resisted being consumed into mainstream America without respect. I have written much, but not much about growing older, because I have been busy and have not had time to think about it, until I hear younger women using words to describe themselves that were considered bad words of the lowest class when I was younger, or read about the new Xicana identity. Yet, I admire how they embrace their Indigenousness, use their energy to take action when it is needed, and I especially enjoy how they can use updated technology.

Since I came of age during the height of the Chicano/Chicana Movimiento my Xicana identity is rooted in el movimiento. It characterizes most of my life, what I watch on television, buy groceries, work in my yard, and even who I married. At the height of my weekend is an art exhibit, a low rider fundraiser, or a lecture by a Chicana or Chicano author.

Movement values, ideologies, political stances, education perspectives, and anti-colonialism resistance are at the heart of this brown female who writes poetry and novels of empowerment that encompass spirituality based in ancestral knowledge that gets acted out as a mother, a grandmother, a vecina as a role model for generations. Like the tomatoes, chili and calabacita that flower and produce sustenance, I am also rooted in Indigenous activism when I render a conference keynote address at La Raza Unida Party Congreso and National Chola conference.

There are some things I cannot do, like protest in the bitter cold of an early morning Women's March. I have arthritis and fibromyalgia, but I will and do speak out on the rights of women, immigrants, and more recently about senior citizens. I still switch from English to Spanish, and Spanish to English in the middle of my sentences, and I live in the barrio because I like to see children play in the streets, the smell of tortillas baking in my neighbor's house.

I now wear comfortable shoes when I dress up and tennis shoes when I work in the yard where I grow cactus and hierbas to heal my aching muscles. On a few occasions, I burn copal and talk to my Brown Beret compadre on a cell phone about what we did with Corky, when we read poetry with Lalo and marched to support César during the grape boycott.

My senior compadres y comadres and I, are well aware that our age now places us in advisory capacity to the young cultural warriors that follow us, but we are underutilized. We are well aware that our time on this earth is short and that we have not saved the world for brown people, but we have made a grand difference. This is why we are highly disturbed, insulted, even saddened, when we are cut off and flipped off in traffic by our own younger people. They don't know us, they don't know what we did. Racism has intensified, and they are stressed out over many things. All we ask for is a little respect. We would walk faster, drive faster, eat faster if we could, but we can't; we got old, but we have a wealth of experience and we are willing to share it if you ask or stop to listen when we talk.

In summary, my identity is wrapped up in Chicanismo. I am a Xicana/Chicana, a señora. I smile when I say, "Soy mujer grande." By this I mean that I am a Chicana Elder, a warrior with experience, eager to share what I've gained from it.

Atrevida

for Gloria Anzaldúa
Angelina Sáenz

Self-declared, conjurer of words
Owner, of la palabra
You take a pilgrimage to the mundane
to find our sacred

Plumed serpent
Cortez
Mestiza

You capture our continental narrative
like a feather in your palm
and then
you breathe it back to us

and it falls into our hair
tucked, behind our ear

In the new millennium
quién se acuerda del
US-Mexican War and its colonial legacy

You say

You must know your history, of exile and termination
Anglo terrorism, mass lynchings of Chicanos and their families
for daring to resist annexation

Land stolen
not by the US government
but by predatory gabachos
looking for any excuse
to take the Tejanos' land
rob them of their livelihood

And they DID!

Disguised today as corporations
Maquiladoras — new thieves

Stay south and die or go north and live (half-dead)

¿Y la mujer?

¿Dónde está la mujer en todo esto?
Violada, capturada, abusada, abandonada
silenciada, traficada, deportada

This is her home, this thin edge of barbed wire

Intelectual de la tierra
in possession of the analysis
on colonialism and its legacy

Santa de los atravesados –
the troublesome

You take
what we take
for granted

And you give it back to us

        wrapped, in our own silver and gold

And we realize
that all along
we've carried our treasure
within

Gracias, Gloria

II
SOMOS
STEMS & LEAVES

"It took me years of writing and self-reflection to get to the place where I could see my immigrant journey, including my immigrant trauma, as my greatest source of strength."

Reyna Grande

Create Birds
—After Remedios Varo's "Creation of the Birds"
Erika Ayón

Is it really that simple,
to create birds,
to stitch together hummingbirds
from a violin in your heart.

Use the moon's light
to breathe flight into them.

I have spent days when music
doesn't resonate from my center,
and crows circle. I am familiar
with a vulture's cry.

Instead of painting wings
in earth colors,
I'll fold paper into lilies.
Close to the ground
afraid to fly.

What and That, Part III
Angela Trudell Vasquez

Who hears cries douses fears   finds the lost pacifier?
The honor student with her thin old bones
who walked thousands of miles
with three brothers, two sisters, one aunt.

What did their tiny faces see perched in baby seats —
packed two by two front to back leaving the detention camps?

The building smalls

        their parents' holes
        echo in their hearts
        this is no yellow school bus
        taking them to teachers
        who care, who speak
        their language
        where hot dish for lunch
        is a foreigner, this is where no —

        parents go   a void.

        You can't write absence.

Forward
Aideed Medina

Who are we running to meet? Family? Coyotes? Or heavily armed men?
Tomorrow — behind barbed wire, in front of barbed wire?
When people are prey
when catch and release
when gasping.
Smiling sportsmen. Fish is too small to keep.
Woman. Tired eyes, tired body, tired mind, gasping, swims
through mountains, deserts, falls
into ravines, leaving child in thorny patch of cacti.
Life judged too small
for crevices, to catch.
Men, we forget are men,
turn themselves in,
      turn wives in,
           turn daughters in,
                turn sons and fathers in,
    to one group of soldiers, over another.

Running from guns,   to guns.
Running through lands   and kin
that know us, that know them, that know you.

We are one body, to catch and release

Point weapons at shadows.
Running.
Forward, to be returned.

The Flow of Blood

Katarina Xóchitl Vargas

We harvest volcanic rock
this side of El Xitle
for Mami's garden:
carry ashen, porous clumps
through Tlalpan's woods.
Whose bones do they hold?
How long have they soaked
in the hot sun?

In the nopal field, once
we found a shriveled
umbilical cord, hint
of an infant, womb, life
bursting forth at its own pace.

I smelled rain in the distance,
heard Dad's guitar in the wind.
Mi manito giggled as he slid
down a dry river bed, his joy a hawk
carving circles in the sky.

We followed the trail out of the navel,
thunder drumming around wet
lava-rocks turning black as hair
in our hands, adornments
for cilantro beds, manzanilla,
homesickness.

These are the things we take with us
when we hemorrhage north.

Our cords snap,
as we wander wet
into life after the womb. . .
El Xitle doesn't object,
though I wish he had.

From *The Half That Runs*, Huizache Magazine 11 Fall 2024, one of two runners-up for the 2024 Andres Montoya Poetry Prize, selected by Juan Felipe Herrera

Mezquite

N.G. López

Lagrimas o sangre me
escurren por el tronco
(no me acuerdo cuál,
me brotan las dos
con frecuencia habitual)
quemado por el sol y
azotado por el polvo,
sin señas de cambiar
de estación ni en esta vida
o la otra — nací mezquite
y mezquite moriré, muy
apenas protegiendo, muy
apenas alimentando,
pero aquí me tienes,
tu único alivio.

Antonio nombre de santo puesto de cabeza
Diana Pando

You were darker than coffee grinds
studied to be an accountant
pero te venistes de mojado
got a meat packing job
on the south side of the city
met woman with brown
topaz eyes
forgot your fiancée
in the pueblo
new job making 17k a year
a million midnights on Maxwell Street
third shift for 30 years
Jim's Red Hots now turned Jamba Juice
El hot dokero de mi padre
his story written in the stench of mustard and onions
every now and then
we'd have
to drag you out of
the cantina on Morgan
other days required you to hold my 6-year-old hand tightly
when the white man next door would yell at us to go back to Mexico
Our lives an endless blur of homework
olla de frijoles
trips to McKinley Park
Nosotros en los columpios
Nyquil, nariz
days spent sleeping
some sábados
Museum of Science & Industry
your summer spent
Watching the Cubs
y de vez en cuando
Riverside mall

domingos de Pine Sol
Cantinflas movies at the Ramova Cinema
mornings at la lavendería
you'd drag me to the mechanics,
the hardware store and Lee Lumber,
Daze spent with lottery tickets,
You tell me, "Ya no tengo diabetes"
run down station wagon
back to the pueblo, hospital, downtown
Dreaming
Telling stories
kitchen counter pile-up
your dusty letters from el pueblo   unopened
You came to this place never catching a break
You spent your days
dreaming of leaving
Chicago
going back
to the place you were born
You'd tell me stories
of brujas y bolas de lumbre en la sierra
How things,
were always   better
in el pueblo.

Ode to my Father's Hands
Reyna Muñoz

My father's hands used to shine
the shoes of grown men
who lived in Juarez
but worked in El Paso.
They would sell limones
on the puente libre
in the scorching sun
all the while wondering
what was in el otro lado.
His hands would play
canicas en la calle Cholula
outside of my abuelitas house
the only one a cotton
candy pink and,
if they were lucky,
had enough spare change
to watch a gringo movie
(doblada, of course)
or buy a milkshake
and play "Love Me Do"
on the jukebox
on weekends.

Later
my father's hands would pick
grapes in Delano then they'd bus
tables in Long Beach, his hands
placed dollars on the counter
after ordering a cheeseburger and coke
every night after work:
his favorite gringo food.
In the winter
my father's hands worked
in East Los Angeles

night after night
making crowns
molding dentures
the man behind the dentist
hunched over
a motor's buzz and whirr
a small lamp illuminating his hands
that look as though they are a part
of the machinery
in the dark, cold room
on Beverly Boulevard.

My mamá says
one of the first things
that made her fall in love with my dad
were his hands.
Las tenía bien lisitas
bien finas.
A mí me daba vergüenza que me tocara
mis manos, she tells me,
her own hands hardened
from a different kind of work.

And now
those weathered hands
that sacrificed for over 65 years
for my mamá and us six
kids, those hands
are busy planting
a tree in El Paso in March,
both are facing south
toward the border.
He looks up as the gusty winds
make it sway from side to side
almost as if unsure of where to go.
He isn't worried,
he tells me,
he made sure the roots were firmly planted.

El peso de las letras y los cargos
Sendy Tapia
Hija de Javier Tapia y Laura Ayala

First generation graduate, grassroots activist, hija de inmigrantes, and storyteller for life. I was raised in a small country town, deep within the 45th parallel of Eastern Oregon's Blue Mountains. For 16 years, I only knew of my heritage from what my parents passed down to me through their life lessons, work ethics, and the far and in between glimpses of Mexico living. Outside my home, I was one of 2-3 students out of 100 students in my high school who spoke Spanish, getting pulled from classes to test my ESL skills, and overlooked when it came to signing up for Spanish class, porque yo ya hablaba español así que ¿cómo se justifica un sobresaliente fácil? Code-switching, imposter syndrome, discrimination, chicanismo, and cultural assimilation were terms and intersections too abstract for me to understand how they directly impacted my childhood and identity.

"That doesn't happen to me, I've known her since kindergarten."

"I don't get bullied, I just have different interests."

"I don't know why I have to take these tests and not my classmates."

Every summer like clockwork, los campos se abrían for the cherry orchards coating the agriculturally rich valleys: once the unceded territories of the Nimíipuu (Nez Perce), Imatalamłáma (Umatilla), Walawalałáma (Walla Walla), and Liksiyu (Cayuse) tribes. Forty years of agricultural labor shared between mis padres de Michoacán, and I, a product of their sacrifices, became absorbed into the meaning of trabajando en el campo; helping translate, assisting in managing buckets picked and to whom to credit, cleaning the temporary housing shacks for the migrant workers y más. The days were long, hot, occasionally humid. While my peers went on vacations and visited family, the day started en las madrugadas beside my parents for long hours and cherishing the few family members that would migrate with the crowd. Those summers were spent speaking Spanish from sunrise to sunset with my limited campo vocabulary until school began and I would naturally code-switch into my Anglo-passing personality, again.

The physical labor of workers; elders and young adults, stretched across 169 acres of cherry orchards. The origin of blood, sweat, and skills because the faster you worked, the more money you plucked out of the cherry trees. Every summer day, I was lectured about the value of education. Every summer day, I witnessed the results of lack of knowledge, resources, and exposure. By the time I was 14, I had walked every row of the orchard and grew to recognize when the trees were ripe or still needed heat to turn the sugar sweet. Although the fresh morning air would only remind me of how much I hated waking up early and carrying a three-legged aluminum ladder that dug uncomfortably into my shoulder when finding my assigned tree; it was the motivation la gente needed to work as hard as they could before the sun peaked above the mountains and brought forth its scorching summer heat. I distinctly remember plugging in my headphones and dissociating into the endless depth of my imagination until I felt the deep rumblings of tractors that passed in between rows with swampers swinging buckets of cherries and dumping them into plastic bins: weighed, and shipped to no-so-local markets. Others were not so fortunate to have technology like la gringa que era pero no se sabía; many sang from their soul under the trees or along battery operated radios that hung off the trees, told jokes, hooted and hollered to make their cherry-picking neighbors and my parents laugh.

At that time, I read almost every day and all those stories filled me with inspiration to begin writing my own stories. As I rode the wave of middle school and high school, storytelling was there with me — shaping my thoughts and giving me a voice when a ball of nerves and anxiety would build in my throat with the need to articulate in both languages. What I never learned in school about being una hija de inmigrantes, I learned through the stories of the migrant workers that passed through my small cherry town. How they crossed the border in the middle of the desert heat, what motivated them to continue their efforts after leaving their home behind, how long it had been since they last saw their relatives or their own parents. El peso de mi raza sobre mis hombros porque nací en este lado de la frontera. El privilegio ganado por los sacrificios de mis padres.

I remember a man, aged by the harshness of the sun beaming down on his face, and although his name is vague to me, his story of leaving his widowed mother behind in his teenage years to work hard in the United States, stayed with me. He would later have enough saved up to return to Mexico in the similar conditions he went through to cross in the first place — a través del calor del desierto — only to find out his mother had passed away months after his initial departure. It was in those raw moments of sharing that I never fully grasped the entire reasoning of why my own parents would be so driven to risk getting caught crossing the border illegally, or risk their own life in the desert with limited water and food to fill their bellies. Seeing the migrant workers pile their families into a van with as much clothing and dishware as they could fit, it was a lifestyle that I could never picture for myself, but one that occurred out of necessity: a need for survival, for the betterment of life, el sueño americano. Pero aquí estoy, con la pluma en la mano, y el cargo sobre mis hombros.

The country life stayed rooted in the soul as I transitioned from a tiny town to a moderate town where the majority of peers looked and talked like me. These were the moments when I came to grips with the meaning of code-switching, imposter syndrome, discrimination, and cultural assimilation. Little did I realize how underserved the rural agricultural communities of California's Central Valley truly were. The lack of resources, the lack of bus stops and routes, limited bilingual translators, little to no option for work unless it was under the searing weather. My first understanding of what "the other side of the tracks" was, and what it meant to be from the "Eastside." What they didn't teach me about César Chávez in school, I saw day in and day out in the rural towns of California. To this day, my parents and the majority of my extended family continue to live in these areas. It is one of many pockets of immigrant-heavy, Spanish-speaking, campo-like communities in the state. One of the few thoughts in the back of my head that has me pondering is whether I'd ever return to share the wealth of knowledge that I have cultivated in progressive cities, or if I'd burn out from how set the mentality is in the area. As my parents slowly lost their bilingual skills after spending 20 years in an Anglo community, I fought to strengthen my own native tongue in hopes to better communicate my feelings and my lessons.

The blessing I received from agreeing to move in the middle of high school was the first taste of what "echándole ganas" could reap.

Becoming the Anime club president placed me in big shoes when first stepping into the role, but I quickly realized how leaders influenced more than a crowd of anime-loving individuals, and how working beside mis padres y la raza had shaped the leader growing inside of me. From organizing the group to fundraise money to attend their first ever anime convention in Fresno, California, to reaching out and inviting all the misfits and outcasts in the school to join a community of like-minded individuals where they, too, were judged for not fitting in the norm, it was the acceptance I sought in my tiny agricultural town before.

Growth didn't stop once I moved; I left for college feeling like the biggest fish in the pond, I didn't know what to expect going to university in the shark tank of San José, California. All I knew at the time was how challenging life could be when surrounded by farm labor and family that followed los caminos del campo porque eran los caminos más atravesados. As my college years developed, the intricate, almost soul-searching style of storytelling and the perspective to dream the undreamable as a boundary to push, I struggled with coming to terms with the privilege I was sitting on from all of my parents' sacrifices.

Combating imposter syndrome because I fail to recognize my worth as a first-generation, catching myself from code-switching when in unfamiliar neighborhoods or groups of people shades lighter than me. Taking Mexican-American classes to slowly unravel and heal what it means to be Chicanx and coping with the realities of ni de aqui y ni de allá? Having to justify my actions of staying in a bigger and costly city when my parents didn't see the lucrative results of an education equal to a nicer car, a corporate job, or returning home to live with them because that's what the girls did in my family. How do I explain my hunger for diversity? My thirst to see the world for what it is, afuera de la seguridad que me dio los campos donde crecí? As they question my next moves — whether or not I'd return for a graduate degree, how I'm able to pay rent and utilities but not be able to save enough money for a new car or pay off my student loans, I watch the world push and pull into itself with claws that rip into the fabric of democracy. While many stare in silence as the alluring concept of the American Dream dissipates between the cracks of the working class and the younger generations — my generation. How does Sendy fit into all of this?

Today, I stand for the folks who look like me but cannot articulate like me. The ones who couldn't fathom the opportunities to leave the country life, and the ones who left and started at the bottom of the tank, just like me. I stand for the freedom to earn a livable wage regardless of an immigration status, to have premium healthcare regardless of your health status, to live fully without having to depend on 2-3 jobs just to keep food on the table and a roof over your head. Workable conditions for the migrant workers that continue to be the backbone of this country porque mi amá y mi apá are right there on the front lines. If my voice can create an echo chamber of affirmations and behaviors that pave the upcoming wave of social and community leaders, then every story I heard as a child, de inmigrantes, adults, child, elder, and parent; these stories can continue to live a life of their own como recuerdos de los sacrificios de mi raza. Through the power of letras, I carry every title at the beginning of this article con orgullo, in hopes of adding, redefining, and passing on the lessons of my heritage, upbringings, y el amor de mi gente to everyone I can touch.

Nopalera
Marissa Cueva

Pink light shines
through the red umbrella
protecting her from the scorching sun.
A blushing haze
surrounds mi Tita,
highlighting the excitement in her eyes,
the wide smile on her face.

Allí sentada
entre sus plantas,
pelando nopales.

Los nopales amargositos
saben a la cocina de mi Tita.
Saben a afternoons doing my homework
while she cooked.
Saben a las canciones de Antonio Aguilar
y el amor de mis abuelitos.

Nopal llevo en la frente,
nopal llevo en el corazón.
Llevo el corazón espinado.
Adolorido y ardiendo.
Sangrando rojo y verde.

Como las espinas que le quito a mi Tita,
cuando me dice:
Ven Mari,
Tu con tus ojos buenos,
Tu con tus ojos jóvenes,
Tu con tus ojos que ven.
Quítame las espinas.
Quítame el dolor.

Hojas verdes y vibrantes
grow out of the brown and aged trunk.
Nopal creciendo sobre nopal.
Building on what was established before,
what was once just as bright and green.

Buenos días niña

Kelsey Milian Lopez

17 stops:
Palmetto Station to Douglas Road.
30 minutes of music that sends me
hasta las nubes with summer plans.

The city is hot and humid.
Today, more than ever before.

I sit down next to large handbags,
cheap flats, petite women.

They remind me of alternate universes:
my life
and my mother's life.

Standing here as early as 6:15 AM.
Conversation after conversation.
Bus after bus taking them to Hialeah.
Taking them home.

A new brown-skinned woman approaches
the bench every 15 minutes.
Besos, names, and preguntas about their families
exchanged, as usual.

I sit there, listening to their conversations
about forgetting the laundry upon reaching Hialeah,
about working in a new house in Coral Gables.
Then, it hits me:

They were maids.
Las que take care of your children.
Las que spend hours cleaning
homes they wish to own one day.
Now, I taste salty tears.

Long before I appeared
my mother had also been one.
A life we would have continued,
but my destiny was different.

I sat on that bus stop to catch
the next route to a future mis papas
dreamed for me:
Lo que soñaron para mi.

The women from the bus stop
reminding me of a culture and people
I refuse to forget.
Respecting what they do,
their sacrifice and ganas
are noticed.

I hope someone notices
mis sueños too.

Empire
Irene Sanchez

Life in the Empire is made up of / Concrete Dreams / Smog Horizons and Dirt / This is not the U.S. they sing of / Oh say can you see / Pastures of Plenty / I remember when it was green / But I saw how Dairy Farms and Citrus Groves / Became warehouses in Free Trade Zones / Creating pollution / And the most colorful sunsets / That are among the most beautiful I've ever seen to this day

Living in the Empire will confuse you / Like when you moved there / And white boys in big white trucks and confederate flags drive down your street / As you watch them from the bigger house your parents you never see because they work so much moved you to / Bigger doesn't always mean better / But you try to convince yourself it is / Like they told you to / Don't be ungrateful

Living in the Empire will / Consume you / I remember how my friends were pushed out of school / Never to be seen or heard from until years later and how the air wasn't the only thing polluting us / Holding these secrets and self-medicating them / Was killing us / Even as we did our best to travel straight lines and still are called less than / We begin to believe it / As we leak out of pipelines that were cracked to begin with / And the only pipelines that weren't cracked led directly from School to Prison / Or told us we could be successful / Just sign names on dotted lines so we could / Be all we can be / I remember my friend who wanted to go to college / Signed his name and years later aside a dusty road we ate tacos in Texas / One of my first loves Brown and beautiful he told me he had a family and wanted out / He only joined to go to college / Two years later he was killed / Why is it then we allow them to continue to tell our youth be all you can be / But how can you be all you can be if you're dead? / From Vietnam to the wars of today / Chicanos die on front lines abroad and at home / And we are still marching like our ancestors did Chicano Moratoriums and dodging tear gas cans fighting for our brilliance / Brilliance we already had before they told us they would make something out of us as if we were nothing and no one without any history to begin with

Living in the empire will confuse you / Until you remember where you came from / I remember when I walked out for Prop 187 / We demanded our rights / Because they hated us-Mexicans / These rights we've been trying to get since Mexican Schools / We've been trying to get since Walkouts / We've been trying to get since they took our land / And made us foreigners on it / And called our grandparents wetbacks / I remember my parents / Growing up in East L.A. / And the pain they didn't want to talk about / And how they believed the American Dream meant / They wanted to give us better than where we were from / As if where we were from wasn't good enough / But I learned it was good enough we just couldn't afford to live there / And my parents thought bigger was better / Because it cost less / But it really costs everything / When you cover up generational trauma with things / In the Empire/ they say / You don't have a choice / This is the way it is and always will be / Just accept it / But you can't because / Living in the Empire teaches you / That the Empire / The Empire is everywhere and it must be changed before we lose another child to the lies the school system tells us / our communities have had learning loss not just in a pandemic, but for generations / and it's our time now to rise up and change for our children, and all those who will come next...

Missing the Monarch Butterflies
Marissa Cueva

There are no monarch butterflies here.
There are no Mexican flags waving.
There are no taqueros on the street,
or mercaditos on the corner.
I miss L.A.

I miss the monarch butterflies.
The migrant butterfly.
The one that reminds me of my sweet Tito.
Le decían "Popeye" por Bracero
And Bracero he was.
Strong, brave, hardworking.

I stand on this land in
complexity and duality.
On my two brown feet,
los pies de tamalito como
dice mi mami.
On my two brown legs
that are shaped differently than theirs.
My body is not elegantly slim,
I am shaped like the mamis
and the abuelitas that shaped me.
A bit plumper, a bit rounder.
Softer hugs and harder hands.

I have no history on this land,
yet their little espressos
and their little cappuccinos
would not exist without conquering mine.
The tomato on their bruschetta,
the avocado on their toast,
the nopalitos sitting
on their window sills,
and so much more,
would simply not exist here.

I suppose one thing they couldn't steal
were the monarch butterflies.
Without the monarch butterflies,
how am I to know
that I'm going the right way?
I miss the monarch butterflies.

Nashon...ality
Gloria Delgado

1946: I'm alone on the sidewalk outside my house, fussing with a too long, too twisty jump rope. Actually, I'm on the only large level area on our block, a spacious common driveway and parking area two houses down from our building. The parking area is conveniently vacant this sunny Saturday morning, the perfect time and place to practice the art of jump rope. All of my cousins, even the boys, can pepper and double Dutch with the best of them. But, that's only because most of them have flat wide sidewalks to practice on, I complain. Everyone knows it's much harder to learn in a neighborhood with steep streets, like Ashbury Street, where I live.

A sudden distracting noise makes me trip over the tangled, uncooperative jump rope. With arms and legs pumping like an engine, a young girl about my age strides up Ashbury Street shouting out something I don't quite catch. I glance around. No, there's no one else close by, so it must be me she's yelling at. But why does she look like she wants to fight? I don't know her, but imagine she belongs to the new family that just moved in, somewhere down Waller Street.

Uncomfortable with the newcomer's aggressive attitude, nevertheless I've been raised to never show fear. Faking some courage I hold my ground, keep a wary eye on her as she approaches. The stranger stops directly in front of me, places small brown fists on skinny hips, juts a narrow chin right up into my face. Still shouting, she repeats her question: "What nationality are you?"

I'm fascinated. Close up, the girl reminds me of a sizzling firecracker about to explode. Now I understand. Her aggressive attitude is not a challenge, just the reflection of intense feelings roiling inside her. I understand her intensity (the feelings, not the word), because, except for her eyes, something about the girl reminds me of a favorite aunt, petite, volatile Tía Elvira, my father's older sister.

Never have I met anyone quite like this girl. Maybe she's Chinese? I stare right back at her, struck by our similarities, by our differences. She's probably about my age, five or six years old, but smaller, shorter, browner. Where my long straight hair is carefully and lovingly woven into two neat braids every morning by either Mami or Abuelita, her hair, the same brown-black shade as mine, has been carelessly chopped into shoulder-length clumps that move, wild and free, blown about by today's warm late morning breeze. And, as revealed by her white shorts and sleeveless top, the girl's arms and legs are covered by a generous sprinkle of dark hair, also just like mine. Strong black eyebrows form one line over her deep-set dark almond-shaped eyes that burn with an intense, forceful gaze, nothing like my vague, slightly dreamy near-sighted gaze. She can't be Chinese, I decide. None of the Chinese kids I've seen around the neighborhood are dark skinned or fuzzy like we two are.

"What's *na..shon..*?" I manage to blurt out, never having heard the word before.

"You dummy, everybody has a nationality, you're born with it. It's the place, the country where you were born, where your father and mother and your grandparents came from. It's the language you talk, and what you like to eat!"

"What's yours, then, your *na..shon…*?" I counter, stalling for time. This is a completely new notion, that something I've never heard of, something called *na..shon…* is part of me. The stranger's sophistication is suddenly intimidating.

"I'm Filipina. I thought you might be too. You've got lots of hair on your arms and legs, even a mustache! But close up I can see you're not one of us. So, what are you? Or are you too dumb to know?"

Now that hurts, and makes me mad! Not the 'dumb' part; having dozens of boy cousins means I'm practically immune to teasing and insults. No, it's the mustache comment that hurts. Having fuzzy arms and legs I can tolerate, but I absolutely hate that sprinkle of dark hair on my upper lip, and especially hate being teased about it. Mami always smiles and says not to worry; it will all disappear someday when I'm older.

Nevertheless, I deliberately ignore the girl's rudeness, avoiding the too simple, too obvious retort of "so do you" by changing the subject.

"Is Fila...a language or a country?"

"Both!"

"But how can you be Fila…if you speak English?"

"I learned English like you probably did, dummy. In school!"

There's a brief pause before her next question. "So where were your parents born?"

"Papi was born in Mexico and Mami was born in Hawaii."

"So, you're Hawaiian, then!"

"No, I'm not. Papi always says he's puro tapatío and Mami is borinqui…I mean Puerto Rican!"

"She can't be Puerto Rican if she's born in Hawaii! That's impossible!" Another pause. Then, more calmly: "So, what language do you speak at home? Hawaiian?"

"Not Hawaiian! Well…yes, but only a few words of pidgin. Spanish, mostly, especially with my abuelita, my grandma, since she lives with us, but English too since I've started first grade at St. Agnes School. And Puerto Ricans speak Spanish, like Mexicans do. They sound very different, though."

"Then you're Spanish!"

"No! Not Spanish!" I emphatically reply, recalling one of my father's favorite derogatory phrases, malditos gachupines. "I'm Mexican! And Puerto Rican!"

"You can't be both, dummy. It's impossible! I already told you, you can be only one thing; you can have only one nationality!"

I pause, very confused. This is getting way too difficult. The girl seems to know what she's talking about, so, if we can only have one *nashon*, well then, how do I choose just one? And which one? That's impossible too, choosing between two loving parents.

Maybe there's a way out of this problem. Remembering another new phrase we recently learned in school, I *grasp at straws*. Yes, I know what I am! … maybe … .

Hesitating, I pick up the twisted jump rope, wind it casually into loops, think things over a bit before answering. "Maybe I'm — English? Yeah, I'm English since that's what I speak now, mostly. English."

She explodes. "No, you big dummy! You're American, like me! English people have pale white skin and blue eyes, and they live in England, way across the ocean! When you live in the United States that makes you American!"

I give up. "Maybe I don't have one, maybe I don't have a *nashon*!" I shout back at her, completely frustrated. "Besides, you just said we can't be two things, so I can't be 'merican! And I don't live in the United States, I live in California!"

Then, after a pause, more meekly, I ask: "What's 'merican?"

The little girl snorts, shakes her head in disgust at my appalling ignorance; and with a fierce, scornful parting glare, stalks off back down Ashbury Street, turning right at the corner onto Waller. We never talk again.

Later at school I catch occasional glimpses of the girl, learn that she's in third grade, two grades beyond me, and so about two years older. Well, that explains why she knows so much. When our classes pass in the hallway or on our way to the playground she first gives me that same fierce stare of hers, then grudgingly returns the briefest of waves. Unfortunately, like so many others in this highly transitory neighborhood, her family soon moves away, and I'm left without the benefit of her wisdom and experience.

Becoming Chicana

1947: About one year later, I have an eerily similar encounter with another girl, again a stranger I've seen only a few times previously in school. She's deliberately waiting for me this afternoon, grim faced, half-hidden behind the main exit door. This meeting is a complete surprise, as the strange girl is obviously several years older than me, and I don't even know her name; we've never before spoken or even acknowledged each other.

In a brief, whispered conversation she quickly says: "There's a secret word I just learned that you and everyone like us should know and use from now on. Don't share it with anyone else, though, not even your friends, just with people like us, people you trust. Promise?"

Reluctantly I nod yes, not liking to make promises I can't keep, curious as to what the mystery was all about.

Before responding, the girl checks to see if anyone else is around to eavesdrop. "The secret word, the one I want to share with you, is 'Chicano' or 'Chicana' and it means people like us, but not like our fathers or mothers, or any other relatives. The word belongs to us, because we were born here, in the USA, and they were not, so they don't understand that we're different from them, and we will always be different. Do you understand?"

Yes, yes, yes! I nod again, wholeheartedly, enthusiastically. "You mean it's our own private word for nationality!" She smiles in agreement, a wide, generous approving smile. As she turns to leave, I ask if it's ok to talk to my father about the word. "Yes," she agrees. As with the other girl, we never talk again. But she's been the first one, the only one, to answer my enduring question. Finally! I feel satisfied, happy, content.

That evening, I sit on the edge of the armchair waiting for my father to look up from his newspaper. I'm eager to ask him about this new unexplored, unexplained word I've only heard once or twice before, and only in passing. To my surprise he explodes with anger.

"Chicano, chicana!! Never! Not pocho or pocha or wetback either! Don't use those words, they're insulting! We're Mexicans, you and I, and we're never ashamed to say so out loud, unlike those vendidos who call themselves chicanos!!"

"But..." I interrupt, "What about Mami? She's not Mexican!" He abruptly cuts me off. "Never mind that. Don't ever forget, you are Mexican, like me!"

Papi is wrong, of course, I know he's wrong, he doesn't understand what I'm trying to say, or maybe I haven't explained myself well enough. I've never forgotten what he taught me, I only know that I am more than what he thinks — not better, just different. It's late, so I get ready for bed, deeply disappointed at Papi's reaction. This topic is immensely important to me, but obviously, we two can't and won't be able to discuss it. It hurts.

You know what also hurts? The reactions of other adults, family, Mexican and otherwise, who also refuse to accept or even consider the term Chicano. Mocking, sarcastic, ignorant, they make fun of the younger generations for our lack of proficiency in Spanish, our use of Spanglish, call us agringadas, accuse us of "forgetting what we are and who we are." I don't know how to answer.

No Spanish Spoken Here

1948: St. Agnes Grammar School, San Francisco - Third Grade Recess Playground Supervisor to small group of us:

"Now, girls, remember that there's no Spanish allowed in school during recess or lunchtime, even out here on the playgrounds. You wouldn't want to be reported to The Office or have your parents called in, would you?"

Mean, bossy, crab-faced Mrs. Baxter walks away, leaving us feeling embarrassed, ashamed of being called out, our averted eyes staring down at the lines and cracks in the asphalt covered playground. But we've done nothing wrong. We *were* speaking English. Mrs. Baxter hadn't even been listening. She just assumed, because we were playing together, that we were speaking Spanish. The thought of deliberately breaking a school rule had not even crossed our minds!

Until now, until today...

When Mrs. Baxter turns away, we look up, silently exchange furtive glances. With that glance comes a gleam, a defining moment in which we instantly, instinctively become aware of shared emotions of pride, arrogance, unity, resentment, anger, and fellowship. Although we are of different nationalities (as I'm beginning to understand the concept), we share similar histories and the same imposed or inherited language, Spanish. We have no name yet for this feeling, but it is powerful, buried deep within, enduring, as old as time. Probing, tentative, we try out the secret word among ourselves. It fits, it feels right. It is right! We just know it!

Without any preliminary discussion or decision, from today on we deliberately, subversively, speak Spanish with each other every chance we get, everywhere we can. Even as young third-graders we know the school and teachers are wrong to forbid it. Another of my father's familiar refrains (¡Ay Jalisco, no te rajes!) rings in my memory. Like those from Jalisco, my Mexican father's birthplace, we will not be commanded, we will not give in, we will not be beaten or submit meekly to injustice.

This solidarity, our new camaraderie, our defiant use of Spanish, our use of the word Chicana, endures for several years until one by one the others change schools or move out of the neighborhood, and I am left behind, alone again.

Well, not really alone, as I've had a best friend since early first grade. She has beautiful long auburn braids and is Italian, Scots-Irish and Cherokee. Over the following months and years Milly and I grow as close as sisters. We never quarrel, never chatter, and even in silence, feel comfortable and compatible to the point of often hearing each other's unspoken thoughts. Nevertheless, the togetherness and understanding we share is not enough to fill that empty place I sometimes feel inside now that the others, *my* others, are gone.

Still Invisible

1957: Presentation High School, San Francisco, my junior year. A group of Spanish-speaking classmates on a Muni bus, riding home to their Mission Street neighborhood. Leader of group to me just before we all exit the bus:

"Oh, hi there, what are *you* doing on this bus? I've never seen you here before." Dora smiles, stops her chatter for a moment, switches to English as she directs her question at me. Dora is a petite, vivacious girl from Central America, always smiling and laughing at school, the invariable center of a tight circle of friends who buzz at each other in various accents of rapid Spanish.

"I'm on my way to 25th and Alabama, to my uncle's house," I answer. "And I've been coming on this bus to visit since my Abuelita moved in with his family."

"Your uncle lives in the Mission? Really? 25th and Alabama... That's near St. Peter's, isn't it? Too bad you don't live here, like we do. And too bad you don't speak Spanish. We could've been hanging out together all this time!" Dora is still smiling.

"¿Y quién te dijo esa mentira?" I answer, keeping my voice light, flashing a tight, polite smile back at her to mask my growing irritation and resentment. Dora had seen me, of course. Seen and not seen. Self-absorbed, she and her group had walked right past me again. Dora's clique had always politely ignored me — in the classrooms, in the cafeteria, in the homeroom, and today, on the bus. Of course, our junior class was huge, almost 200 girls divided into six homerooms and three lunch periods. But still, all this time, until today, I've been invisible to them.

"Oh, you do speak Spanish! Well, we never suspected."

"You never asked!" I answer, still smiling, still trying for a light and non-accusatory tone. "In fact, this is the first time all past three years any of you have ever talked to me."

"What? Really?" Dora pauses, thinking it over. "You're right. I'm so sorry! We never bothered to ask if you were one of us. We never heard you speak Spanish, so just assumed you were Portuguese or Italian or something, like that red-haired Italian friend you always hang out with."

By this time everyone is off the bus. Dora gives me a graceful sideways goodbye wave. "Well, see you later!" She and her friends start down the sidewalk. I head in the other direction, towards Tío Memo's house, to meet up with my grandmother and cousins.

So, they had noticed me. As I walk, mulling over our brief conversation, my head fills with an overload of new thoughts to ponder. They're a sociable, outgoing, not particularly academic group. Did they really think I was Italian? That's hard to believe, but it may be true. Maybe I'm not one of them because I'm not from the Mission District? No, it's got to be more than that. Dora and her circle have never been exclusive or petty, like so many school cliques.

Then I'm struck by a sudden revelation! It's our language that separates us! I speak English everywhere in school, having no close Spanish-speaking friends at this time, and little opportunity for contact, while Dora's friends are always together, all the time, everywhere, during class or in the Mission neighborhood.

Dora and her circle have made high school into an extension of their neighborhood. Everywhere they go they bring with them the same feeling of camaraderie and intimacy that comes from living in the village that is the Mission District. I remember that feeling, from way back in early childhood. At best it means safety, security, protection, warmth and understanding, knowing who you are, who others are, knowing your place, not having to explain yourself. I still miss it, that warm, enveloping closeness we felt when we defied the school by speaking Spanish, by our use of the word Chicana, the term we freely and spontaneously adopted that afternoon for ourselves when subjected to yet another injustice in school.

But at its worst that same closeness, that village mentality, might grow constricting, stagnant, divisive. I miss being part of a group, but could never accept anyone else as my leader, no matter how charming her manner. I've enjoyed mixing with other nationalities, listening to the cadence of different languages and accents, exploring similarities and differences among us. What have Dora and her circle missed of life outside that circle? A village, no matter how comforting or attractive, may create invisible walls impossible to scale, walls that separate people from each other. The safe fortress may become a prison. Which way of life is best? They may have ignored me, but then again, I never reached out to them either, I never made the effort. What's right, what's wrong? Who knows? Not Mrs. Baxter, not Dora, not even my father. Somehow, somewhere along the way, I'll have to figure it out myself.

Spics and Spans — 1967
Juliana Aragón Fatula

My tenth birthday, in the backyard,
my school friends twirl around the mulberry bush.
I walk Linda home and wave goodbye from the sidewalk;
she lives three blocks away.
The next day Linda tells me,
"My mom saw you out the kitchen window
She said that you was a Mexican and I wasn't allowed to play with
Mexicans."
I don't mind; I have lots of primas
and they're all Mexican like me,
so, I never miss Linda.
I think she misses me.
She sees me at school
smiles with her lips upside down,
then bounces away to play with the other Patties.
That's what we call them, Gringos.
They call us Spics and Spans,
I guess, 'cause our moms are all maids,
'cause our eyes and hair are shiny like polished silver,
'cause our dark skin makes our teeth gleam bright.

From the author's unpublished manuscript *Chingona Corn Mother: A Spiritual Memoir*

¡Ya basta!
Diosa Xochiquetzalcóatl

When I was a little girl…
We had to take my dad's shoes off after a long day at work
even though my mom's day was much, much longer.

When I was a teenager…
I was pulled out of a restaurant by my ear for flirting with a waiter
while my cousins were encouraged to pursue without avail.

When I became an adult…
My brother and I took after my grandpa's promiscuous ways.
He has always been a "player" while I am forever stuck at "slut."

Chola Heroes and Cholo Saints
A semi-autobiographical account
Elvira Carrizal-Dukes

I've never been a fighter. I was more of a book nerd. Growing up, Cholas and Cholos were my heroes and protectors when my parents couldn't be. They were part of our community. I saw them at church, at the grocery store, at the park, and at school. I grew up in a small colonia called Chaparral in Southern New Mexico. It's an unincorporated town on the border of El Paso, Texas. As small as this town is, Chaparral is split into two counties, Doña Ana, where my family lived, and what we call the Otero Side (for Otero County). Our town doesn't have a public library, but there is a private prison on the Otero Side. It's a low-income and mostly Mexican community.

When I was coming up in the eighties and nineties, there was no middle or high school. Instead, we rode a public-school bus across the Franklin Mountains to attend schools in Anthony, New Mexico, the next biggest town close to us within New Mexico state lines. After sixth grade, we started taking the bus about sixty minutes each way to and from Gadsden Junior High and High School. There were students from other colonias near Anthony that also attended these schools, but Chaparral was the farthest. It was my first time experiencing a traditional period scheduling with various classes and teachers within the same grade.

My first gym class in junior high was especially eye-opening for me. It was the first time taking a physical education class with a locker room, where we were expected to change into gym clothes. I had never changed clothes in front of strangers before. The gym teacher was a white man with tiny shorts, a Gold's Gym muscle shirt, knee-high socks, and he wore his hair in an afro like the painter Bob Ross. It was also the only class where I didn't know anybody. I didn't especially like running around the track in the desert heat. Many times, I finished my laps last with a few other students, some who chose to walk instead of run.

A few weeks into the semester, the gym teacher, Mr. "Bob Ross," asked me to stay behind instead of running around the track. He asked me to help him grade the P.E. test. Because my parents raised me to be respectful and polite to adults, I didn't ask questions and agreed to help him grade the tests. I felt embarrassed because the other students noticed, and it wasn't fair that I didn't have to run my laps. It was also uncomfortable when Mr. Bob Ross sat right next to me on the gym floor as I graded. But I did what I was told and didn't question authority.

It wasn't until I was in the girls' locker room that three Cholas came up to me. They were the same ones who walked and usually came in last. We smiled at each other before, but in the locker room is where we had our first conversation. The Cholas were Luz, Violet, and Carmen. They dressed in traditional Chola clothing, such as Black Dickies and Charlie Brown shirts, and they wore black eyeliner and mascara, and teased their hair high, held in place with Aqua Net.

It was Carmen with the orange dyed hair who first spoke to me saying, "Hey, why do you let that gabacho make you grade papers?" And then Violet, "Yeah, he's a f**kin' creep." Finally, Luz spoke up. She seemed to be the quiet leader of the three. You could see in her eyes that even though we were seventh graders, she had been through a lot of grown-up shit. She was wise beyond her years. Luz offered, "Let us know if you want us to f**k him up."

It took me a minute to respond to realize what they were saying. I knew I felt uncomfortable around the gym teacher but didn't know how to express it. I didn't know if it was just me, and I was afraid if I said anything, I would feel foolish. But these girls understood me without me having to saying anything. I responded, "He said he'd give me extra credit."

Carmen quickly shot back, "In exchange for what?" Violet seemed to always back up Carmen, saying, "Ese cochino wants something. Watch." And then Luz, "If he touches you, break his fu**in' fingers." I responded, "Okay." Then Carmen, "From now on we're going to call you Sad Eyes."

After that conversation, every time we'd exit the locker rooms to head to the track, the girls would mad dog "el Bob Ross." One day, he tried telling the girls to run instead of walk. I could see them from a distance where I was sitting and grading papers. The girls got in his face and pointed at me. El Bob Ross looked over at me as well.

From that day on, no more grading papers. I started walking laps again. El Bob Ross left me alone, but for the next three years in junior high whenever I saw him, he would awkwardly stare at me. I forgot about him, until I revisited my junior high yearbook and saw his photo that I painted over with green marker. I suddenly remembered the sick feeling I got whenever I went to gym class and the Chola Heroes who stood up for me.

My senior year in high school, I got my first job as a bagger at our local grocery store in Chaparral. I worked after school and on weekends. I was trained by an older Cholo in his thirties, his name was Santos. He was a cashier. He would ask me about school and what I wanted to do after high school. I told him I wanted to be a writer. He encouraged me to graduate from high school, and when I finally did, he invited me to a party on the Otero Side. I learned through our conversations that Santos was a veterano and high-ranking Cholo in a gang. He was very down to earth and humble. He was also positive and encouraging. He agreed to pick me up for the party. Him and his street lieutenant Verde, picked me up, and I went to the party with them.

It was an outside party with a bonfire on someone's property. There was a trailer, and the party was in the back. I didn't recognize anyone at the party, but Santos kindly introduced me to his friends, and I hung out with some of the Cholas. We were drinking and smoking. In Chaparral, the moon and the stars in the sky light up the desert. It was a beautiful night and a great way to celebrate graduating high school.

Then suddenly, there was a lot of commotion. Members of another gang showed up. I didn't know exactly what was happening, but I could tell some violence was about to break out. The Cholas quickly left my side. And then Santos and Verde came up to me. Santos spoke first, "It's not safe here for you right now. Verde's going to take you home." I responded, "Okay." I knew not to ask questions, and time was of the essence. Verde gave me a ride, and I got home safe thanks to the Cholo Saint.

I've never been a fighter, and Santos knew that. I was more of a book nerd. The Chola Heroes from junior high and the Cholo Saints from my neighborhood knew this before I did. They protected me, and I survived and graduated high school, and soon I'd be heading to college across the country in Minneapolis, Minnesota, where I had no Cholas or Cholos looking out for me. Instead, I carried with me the memory of the moon and stars that light up the sky in the Chaparral desert at night as a reminder of where I'm from and as a sense of protection wherever I am.

Afterword

Later in life, I ended up pursuing a doctorate degree in Rhetoric and Composition. My topic centered around the Chola and Cholo culture. Because I was raised by a village that included protection from Cholas and Cholos, my mission was to study, research, and write about the history and present state of this subculture. I grew up having respect for Cholas and Cholos, and it's disappointing when they are portrayed negatively in mainstream media. My way of giving back to a community that helped raise me, is to write and use my academic experience and creative skills to pay homage to Cholas and Cholos, and the Pachucas and Pachucos before them. I'm grateful for this space to share my positive experiences.

La guerra de la independencia es de todos los días

Angelina Sáenz

Ríos de rebeldía
Desbocan en mis venas
Encimita de mi carne

Desvelos y dudas
Me siento inútil
Estúpida e impotente

Rabia cuando no consideran mis deseos
No me dejo de los hombres

    Tengo alergia al obedecer

Pero ya no solo boto

    También recojo
    Las partes de mi cultura
    Que sirven

what we don't teach them

jo reyes-boitel

we don't teach them about men   not really
we don't teach them about how men can and do
hurt women, especially young women

instead, we spend our time guarding against those
who look in passing, who slow down when
a group of girls walk through after soccer practice,
who whisper as they pass
– things we already understand

we don't tell them the world is here to destroy us,
turn us into obedient things, to be held down

we don't teach them
until they come home
with their own horror

and then the walls within us   fall away
        we say too much   we say we are scared for them
        and pissed at the circumstance   this world has put us under

        it takes everything then   to keep our voices crisp but calm

and, in the quiet after, we wonder, was it denial that held us back? do
we hope
they will be seen?   or was it my own fear? to be named a
troublemaker when,
look, the world is changing.

>   see now   how my own child will
one day be a doctor and she will also,
one early morning, miss her ride home
and stuck sitting outside a bar after closing,

while a man   sits six feet away
but calls to her   sweet
>   like she's a kitten
>   tells her she's pretty

that man,
calling from the dark,
will say this is a kind of equality –
that she can be both a doctor
and a victim.

how could I think there wouldn't be a price to pay?

First appeared in *the impracticality of silk*, Gnashing Teeth Publishing, October, 2024.

Too Drunk to Consent
Amalia Ortiz

Necrophile likes to get it on with the dead.
Drinking will go to her head,
or slip a roofie instead!

Hey! Hey!

That kinda game works for him every time.
It's your word against mine.
No witnesses to his crime —

Hey! Hey!

He thinks she looks so hot when she's sleeping.
No small talk. No speakin' —
That's when he comes a-creepin'.

Hey! Hey!

Stumbling, tumbling to the ground —   He
thinks she wants a pounding.
Pervy and rapey is how it's sounding.

She's too drunk to consent.
Your actions are no accident.
You waited all night long.
Now, she's too drunk to get it on.

She's too drunk to consent.
I smell your rotten intent.
Don't take your mother truckin' pants off!
Keep your fu**ing hands off!

She's too drunk...
She's too drunk.
She's too drunk!
She's too drunk to consent!

You think the green light is no protests, no tears.
No memory means no fears.
Tonight won't haunt her for years.

Hey! Hey!

If she was sober she'd say you're idiotic.
Black outs are not erotic.
Asshole, keep it platonic!

Hey! Hey!

You'll claim she's lying, being overdramatic.
You're beyond problematic.
You're psycho-level traumatic.

Hey! Hey!

Ya te conozco, because #metoo.
Watching your shit's deja vu,
but this time, it's gonna f**k you.

She's too drunk to consent.
Your actions are no accident.
You waited all night long.
Now, she's too drunk to get it on.

She's too drunk to consent.
I smell your rotten intent.
Don't take your mother truckin' pants off!
Keep your fu**ing hands off!

She's too drunk...
She's too drunk.
She's too drunk!
She's too drunk to consent!

Hey juan,
(and all you other rapey assholes out there)
Even though you got away with it,
I won't let the world forget
you're shit!

She's too drunk to consent.
Your actions are no accident.
You waited all night long.
Now, she's too drunk to get it on.

She's too drunk to consent.
I smell your rotten intent.
Don't take your mother truckin' pants off!
Keep your fu**ing hands off!

She's too drunk...
She's too drunk.
She's too drunk!
She's too drunk to consent!

Momentarily Blinded
Maria Miranda Maloney

My dad walks the length of my tío's five-acre ranchito. He walks between the rows of watermelon. He stops briefly here and there and begins to study a tender shoot. My dad's body is designed for the outdoors — slim and agile at seventy-eight. He grabs a handful of weeds and plucks them out. He does this for hours, rummaging through the earth, looking for disease.

"I liked your poem 'Plucked,'" my friend Raquel says. I am on the phone with her while I watch my father from afar.

"Thank you. It's real, you know. I read about the girl in the newspaper."

It is 2011, and the murder toll of women keeps piling up — 298 young girls dead. Their remains are found in graves on the outskirts of Juárez, raped and mutilated. Their breasts are cut from their bodies. My friend, Gloria, a fronteriza, who crosses the Bridge of the Americas to Juárez every day to teach English in one of the maquilas to mid-management staff, tells me she sees the dead on the streets. Senses their anguish, and she can barely breathe. Gloria communicates with the dead, and the toll of death in our sister city of Juárez is wearing her down. She sees dead women everywhere. I laud her power, but I don't envy her. Every day, the TV news from Mexico flashes a photo of a young woman who disappeared or was found ravaged by men who use their bodies to mark their territory.

"Perros," I whisper.

I think I'm lucky to live in the United States, where I don't have to wake up to another young woman dead, where I don't have to hear mothers wail and angry voices rise above the rooftops like black smoke. I think…I'm lucky.

But I weave lies. The fabric is thin and rotting. I'm blinded by too many days of false prosperity and security. I don't know the rest of this land — the rural towns of Texas, beyond this frontera, masked in tranquility, the false bravado of old men sitting outside their porches, dazed by the yellow light, spitting tobacco from their dehydrated lips, racism embedded in their soil, and young girls sold to neighbors for meth and cocaine. Girls I will come to know one day.

"Perros," I say. "Why can't Mexico's people rise against this violence?"

I blame it on the people before I understand the root of its cause. I blame its corrupt government before I trace the guns back to this land I call my country. Before I trace the hunger for drugs on our streets.

I am angry. So, I write poems to record the violence. To remind me how great my life is here in the United States. But I lie. The poems are unremarkable. They are rants, aspiring only to paint a picture, spill my anger without resolve.

"I'm glad my grandma died before she got to see her land go to shit," I tell Raquel. "I hear the streets of Juárez are empty." I'm referring to my 102-year-old abuela who died before the killings began and her beloved frontera fell into cartel and military chaos.

"They are. Businesses are closed, and there are no more tourists. Only the fronterizos cross," says Raquel.

I was once a fronteriza, too. Waterfill and Zaragoza, two small towns on the outskirts of Juárez, were my home. We visited Grandma every Sunday. Those Sundays were filled with haircuts, shopping, doctors, and church, and primos.

Al otro lado was our lifeline — a needle in our veins that pumped sounds of raucous life — vendedores at the bridge, tiny hands stretched for mana, glittering velvet paintings of Pedro Infante, la Virgen de Guadalupe, and Pancho Villa. Al otro lado was my home away from home.

Even then, at nine years old, in the ninety-degree heat, sitting in the back of our blue Falcon, sharing space with my four sisters as we waited in line to cross back to the U.S., even then, I felt lucky — to have another home, this frontera.

"Fuck Mexico," I say to Raquel, angry over the death of another young girl, a maquiladora worker on her way home, plucked from a street corner. I was angry for what I felt I had lost — the safe streets I had roamed as a child when I roamed by Grandma's neighborhood.

I sip my cold drink. I look over at my dad's bent figure. My abuelo Pablo did well to sell his lands in Mexico and immigrate to the U.S. But even then, I know I lie, just like all the white-washed books I had to read in school.

I look up at the sun — I am momentarily blinded.

And now I am crying

Jesenia Chávez

when I tell the lady at the yoga studio counter that I don't like strangers touching me, and that they are all too close, and now I am crying in the car because I don't always feel safe, and when I said it out loud I got sad, sad that I don't feel safe in this body, in this city, in this planet sometimes. Other times I do feel safe in this body: it protects me, it holds me, it remembers to be gentle even if I forget, it tells me things, but I don't always listen. I wear armor in this brown female body, I prepare for dumbass questions, I prepare with Nike Cortez and hoop earrings, and zarape hats, y con hablando en Español. I wear my brown skin and love my brown skin and big nose, sometimes. And other times I don't, and I am sorry body. I am sorry. I will love you always, I will remember what you said, what it took to be born in Martin Luther King Jr. hospital, when my Mexican Mami walked in ready for me to pop out, (and maybe I was ready too), on August 25 early in the morning. Her first baby girl born in the U.S., in a big hospital, my birthright to have papeles. And my little 4'9" Mami, held me and I was loved, and I am loved, and my tías and my grandmother love me from the heavens, and from the hell they went through. And I will not be erased. And I will not annihilate my body, even though I want to jump into the concrete river sometimes and be eaten by the crows and coyotes, I will not. I will not be devoured.

History of Complicity
María Elena Fernández

My white skin comes from the hacendado
my mother's father
the grandfather I knew my whole life
I have just learned
was his town's exploiter

How was I to guess?
On a lifetime of every other year pilgrimages
to Amealco, Hidalgo
land of my sacred rural origins
place of my mother's birth
I saw only a splinter-thin man
blind in one eye
shuffling 'round the courtyard
of a dark, dank ranch house
no running-water
a dried-up corn patch in front
the empty stables out back
were our communal outhouse

Heard my mother and aunts coo only adorations
and whisper worries that his one good eye
would betray him
and his frail body tumble down the front steps

How was I to guess?
That in his young, strong years
he seduced the women of his pueblo
leading each up the ladder to the barnyard loft
promising marriage in the morning
Their babies were born
my tías and tíos Beatriz, Chela, Fay, Erasmo and Esther
and no wedding ceremonies took place
until he married my grandmother

How was I to guess?
That my grandfather once had many peasants
harvested his acres of cornfields
their reward was to owe him money
because what they bought at his store
cost more than the wages he offered

I got the hacendado's white skin

Me, who always thought
I came from the downtrodden
loved to tell my American dream story
"My parents came to this country
with only sixth and eighth grade educations
worked hard and sent us to college."
In the university I seared into my memory
statistics on the disparity between Mexican and white
learned the history of gringo imperialism in the Southwest

On the streets of downtown L.A.
I marched down Broadway against
police brutality, racist immigration policies
held my picket sign high against our exploiters

How was I to know?
Just one generation before my mother
we were the exploiters

Hidden
Cecilia Sanchez

I hide under skin people want to see,
       like Tonantzin:
            hidden,
feeding into what society demands.

I do believe truth will set me free.
But why be truthful when I am not believed?
Slipping through crevasses
       of oppressor fingers.
By oppressor, I mean the white man,
       the brown man;
           men.

I am what they want to see:
       My body's curves fit into the fissures of their brains —
       Maybe not all men, but most.
          Or so, it seems to me.

Tonantzin hides under La Virgen.
       Not by choice
          but by the powerful will of man.

Maybe, she is not scared to be seen.
       Maybe she knows she won't be believed:
Forcibly stripped of her beauty.
       Forcibly stripped of her essence . . .
And we,
       forcibly stripped of believing in her.

Still, those who know, *know.*
    And those who believe, *believe* . . .

        even if we are hardly seen —

        Hidden, but still powerful,
            like beautiful Tonantzin.

I Will You Forward
for RJ
Amanda Rosas

Sometimes I imagine
I rush out the door and drive the three nights and
four days to rescue you from your wilderness therapy.
I've no bags packed, my hair whips rapidly in a dilapidated
highway wind. The minivan shakes as if its threadbare
tires need canes. I find you folding your sleeping bag in
a heavy woods. Lord knows how I found you. The misty
morning tree bark crawls off the glare in your glasses and
I know you are surprised because incidentally you smile
just enough to tell. Maybe we hug. Maybe we just stare
each other down like two birds on a branch understanding
our lot in the mother nature of things. Our faces gesture
like language and so we do not speak. Because it was never
about talking, no. It was about becoming present, a reuniting
in one another's silence, that messed up place, that swamp of
sugar and sand that peels our skin out of our skin and there
is nothing more naked, more scared, angrier than the fresh red
salmon of raw skin. And I made this false journey thinking
this is how we escape and when. This is us standing up to
change the world starting from within. But you are unreachable
and I am idealizing again and maybe there is no real road that
leads to a second birth or healing. Nevertheless, I'll close my
eyes, and I'll will you forward.

Casino Mamas
Carmen Jackie

Lourdes thought that the only thing better than acquiring the best parking spot in the parking garage is using a free burrito coupon before it expires, and she planned on using every free food bonus from the casino to justify why she didn't stay home to cook something from scratch. In her mind, every dime and peso she could spare is just a little bit more cash that could go on her casino playing card.

Panchita picked up Lourdes in her driveway. She didn't have to knock or even honk because she knew that Lourdes would be standing in her doorway. Lourdes didn't use GPS tracking to know when Panchita would get there; she just knew. Even though Lourdes and Panchita were just cousins, they fought like sisters. They were the only two from their families who lived on this side of the border.

"Buenas," Panchita said, as Lourdes climbed quickly into the trusty Toyota Sienna with more than 300K miles on the odometer.

"¿Qué pasa?" Lourdes asked, because Panchita didn't even look up at her. She was too busy tapping on her cellphone, which was very unusual for her because she preferred to talk on her cell. They were both in their late fifties now and reluctantly learned how to text but found true joy in their life downloading new casino game apps.

"I need to pick up Nadia." Panchita replied.

"¿Por qué?"

"I guess one of the men at the bar grabbed her arm, and so I am going to pick her up. She says she isn't bleeding, but she doesn't feel good."

Nadia, Panchita's daughter, started working at a sports bar near the college. It was supposed to be safe and full of mostly young college kids, but lewd men seemed to be drawn to Nadia like a magnet. Panchita thought that her daughter's purple hair, along with the arm tats that she got on her eighteenth birthday, made her look especially tough. She wondered if her daughter's appearance had anything to do with attracting men that treated her roughly.

Lourdes started to pray. There are some people that pray, and you just know they are talking directly to God. That is what Lourdes sounds like when she prays in Spanish, her skin around her face gets tense and almost begins to glow. Lourdes talks so fast and hardly takes a breath when she talks to God. When she finished her prayer, Lourdes noticed that Panchita squeezed her hand while she waited at a stop light. So, she started another prayer, this time, to María, then to every saint she could remember, until they got to the bar.

The *Last Campus Bar* had seen better days. Panchita drove to the side where she knew Nadia would be waiting, trying to hide her vape pen before Panchita saw her. However, Panchita knew she never gave it up, but just became more creative on how she hid it. Nadia wasn't vaping this time, and she also wasn't alone. She was standing with a woman clothed in a white dress who had bloodshot eyes, and at first, both women thought Nadia had found an angel. When the car pulled up, the woman froze and tried to blink away more tears as Nadia approached the driver's window.

"This is Luna, ma."

"¿Estás buen, mija?"

"Ma, I am fine. She just needs a ride."

Panchita and Lourdes took a deep breath as Nadia waved to Luna to get into the car. Lourdes thought that Nadia did look fine, but Luna looked cold and so very young. Lourdes just wanted to get to the casino before midnight but now that seemed rather selfish.

"¿De dónde eres, mija?"

"Guanajuato."

Not even Nadia knew where Luna was from. She was very quiet in high school, and they had different friend circles, but after high school they finally became friends, on social media platforms at least.

"¡Que linda!" commented Lourdes. Maybe it was the tone of Luna's voice or the fact that she spoke perfect Spanish, but Lourdes knew that this girl needed a compliment. Luna breathed a little easier and used the headrest while she wrapped her own arms around herself a little bit tighter.

Panchita turned up the heater and gave her a beach towel that she had in a grocery bag for her weekly water aerobics class. Panchita assured Luna that it was clean, and the faint Tide scent filled the van as Nadia helped her wrap it around her shoulders.

"Do you want us to take you home?" Nadia asked.

"I don't want to go home just yet. I feel so stupid," replied Luna.

"Hey, it wasn't your fault," said Nadia.

"¿Qué paso?" Panchita asked.

Nadia tried explaining what happened, that Luna had met someone online that was going to meet her at the bus station heading to Vegas. Both Panchita and Lourdes nodded as the white dress made more sense now.

"But then…" Nadia paused and looked at Luna, who looked even more emotional at the recounting of the events.

"He didn't steal me, but I handed him my bags with everything that I own and my savings because I thought he was going to carry them for me till we got on the bus," Luna said, starting to cry again.

All the women told her to breathe and that everything would be okay. She was lucky to be alive and that her parents would understand. She described how she had managed to explain everything to a security guard, and he wanted her to fill out a police report, but she walked away before the police arrived at the scene. San Bernardino police were spread thin, and she was still alive, so they took their time getting there.

The security guard scoured the trash bins and found her tiny pink faux leather wallet with only her ID still inside. The five hundred in cash was long gone. It was the first five hundred dollars she had ever earned, and she had managed to save, which left practically nothing on the debit card that was also missing.

The police took so much time getting there that the security guard gave her some pocket change so she could get something to eat from the vending machines. Instead, Luna climbed onto the first city bus she could find to just get away. She didn't care where it took her, and the last stop on the bus route was by the college campus, where she walked to the bar, hoping to buy more time before she had to go home.

No one had bugged her on the bus; most thought she was a runaway and didn't want to get involved. At one point, she was the only one on the bus and wondered how she was going to replace her cell. The man had taken her shoulder bag with all her savings and her best outfits. The worst part of it all was that he looked exactly like the picture on his profile, if not even better. Luna thought that if she told her parents what had happened, they would just pack up everything and go back to Mexico.

Luna couldn't go back, but she wasn't thriving in the states either. Luna was young enough to learn English when she immigrated, but old enough that she would never lose her Spanish accent.

"¿Y tu brazo?" asked Panchita.

"It's okay, ma."

Nadia even pulled off her black faux suede jacket and showed her arm was red but not quite purple. She explained that some jerk was trying to sit too close to Luna. He grabbed Luna's thigh, and that's when Nadia told him to stop, and he said it wasn't any of her business, so she "accidentally" dropped a tray of drinks on his lap. Then he grabbed Nadia's arm and wouldn't let go until the three-hundred-pound bouncer made him let go.

"It's fine. It's not the first-time, ma." Nadia said as she crossed her arms and reclined her seat.

This didn't sit well with Panchita at all. Panchita had worked her share of waitress jobs and had a small scar near her hairline when she had gotten in the way of a brawl herself. It was a long time ago, but she still held her breath just thinking about it. Lourdes knew Panchita was driving back into town a little tenser now.

Lourdes managed to get Panchita to keep driving to the casino. Maybe a little diversion was all the women needed and maybe they could all get their minds off everything for a bit. At the casino, they weren't caregivers, college students, or scam victims. They were just four ladies going out to enjoy their night with some free burritos.

Sure, they could have gone to a fast-food place that was open late with ample parking, but both Panchita and Lourdes were a bit tired of all the crying. Lourdes had taken care of her kids, who were now out on their own, and she also ran a daycare. If she was tired of anything, it was people crying. She only watched funny movies now, or animated films. Lourdes needed to find goodness and light in the world. All the casino lights are what attracted her to them in the first place.

When Panchita got in a long line of cars to get inside the parking garage, Lourdes' heart sank a bit. It would take hours to park, Lourdes was sure of it. Then Luna pointed out that another entrance was opening, and workers with light cones were waving them in.

"Good catch, Luna." Nadia said.

Nadia hadn't noticed the new entrance because she was too busy looking at how high the new cinderblock fences were now around the surrounding streets. The tiny postmodern houses that were built in the 1950s looked like doll houses next to them: doll houses with security bars on the windows, but still wooden doll houses set in the desert. Multiple cars parked at each house. There were so many commuter cars, it did seem like everyone commuted from the Inland Empire to other surrounding counties where they could easily charge double for the same haircut or whatever they did for work. Nadia tried to figure out how old she had to be till she could afford a little doll house of her own.

After changing her majors so many times, Nadia was now just taking one class a quarter and working as much as she could, so she never had to take out a loan. Her still living at home had made the Cal Grant stretch a little further. She would rather be driven around by her mom until she could afford a car on her own. Nadia was sure that a loan would just tie her down, and she wasn't sure that she was going to stay in the area much longer. Nadia might go somewhere tropical like Miami or fun like New York, but later when she could afford to. Miami and New York were bound to be filled with people with all kinds of fun-colored hair, and she was sure to blend in. At least that is what she told herself. Nadia had stopped getting tattoos and only bought clothes at the thrift shop so that hopefully she could make that big city dream happen one day.

Luna had been out to a casino in the desert before so she thought it would be filled with smoke and shady characters, but it wasn't. Everyone inside looked friendly. The casino even scanned everyone's face before they entered. For the first time in a long time, Luna felt safe. The deafening sounds of people playing loud slot machines made all the women feel at ease. It was chaotic, but they didn't have to control any of it, and there was a calmness in that.

Lourdes weaved in and out of the crowds to see if her favorite machines were being used. Luna stopped for a free bottle of water that had the casino name on the label. Luna was expecting to see women in cocktail dresses and men dressed in tuxedos like in the movies, but other than a few men wearing their blue-collar uniforms, everyone was dressed super casual.

Luna caught up with the women and drank all her water. Luna then found a seat and wrapped the towel around herself as best she could to cover the white dress. It was more of a slip-style dress than a wedding dress, but she didn't want anyone to stare at her. No one was really staring at anyone. *This is great*, she thought to herself. She just needed to go to the restroom because she hadn't gone since she had left home in the afternoon.

"Nadia, where is the restroom?"

"I'll take you. I need to go too. Plus, this machine isn't paying out," Nadia said as she tapped the side of the buffalo machine before pulling out her casino card.

Nadia led the way and walked like she owned the casino. Nadia's wide shoulders and long arm swings made Luna look even smaller as she waddled behind her, struggling to keep up. The small kitten heels she wore didn't make her look older tonight, while she wore a beach towel and appeared like a child looking for the locker room.

Luna knew very little about Nadia but wanted to know more about her. She didn't know Nadia's favorite color or animal, but just knew that Nadia had strong confidence in herself. Nadia would never have been scammed like she had been tonight. *I could learn from her*, Luna thought to herself, studying Nadia's every movement.

When Luna was washing up after using the restroom, she could hardly recognize herself. Something about her had changed. A new frown line had appeared, and her eyes were swollen from all the hot tears that rolled down her face at the bus stop. Luna felt like she might start crying again, but she was distracted by a woman digging in the side of the trash bin next to the door, who put something in her pocket and left the bathroom. She hadn't meant to stare, but she had watched the woman through the reflection of the mirror and couldn't remember ever seeing anyone dig like that through a bathroom bin. As Luna walked back to Nadia, and told her what happened, Nadia explained to her that the lady was probably looking for drugs. Luna thought that Nadia was probably right, since there weren't cameras in the bathrooms.

"Hey, just go have some fun tonight," Nadia said, as she put a twenty-dollar bill in Luna's hand.

Luna just wanted to put the cash in her tiny wallet that she stuffed in her bra but was a little too excited to try a slot machine for the first time. She walked around many machines and rows of chairs just to find one that was unoccupied. She found four machines clustered together with no one around. She began to insert the bill and press a button since the pull lever was just for show.

The machine went through the motion and she immediately lost five dollars. She looked around and the rest of the women were all busy with their own machines. Luna pushed the button again. Another five bucks were gone. She wondered if she could just have the machine return the ten dollars that remained. Ten dollars could at least get her a bus ride home. She pressed the button again and lost another five. Luna paused, exhibiting the kind of internal pause that makes one feel like a mannequin with nothing left inside. There was nothing left to do but to press the button again.

The machine twirled and hissed like never before, so loudly that other women stopped playing on their machines all together. All of a sudden, Luna had hit the jackpot! She just won ten thousand dollars. The women stood next to her, and Luna just kept covering her mouth like a beauty queen that had just won first place. One of the managers helped her cash out. Lourdes, Panchita, and Nadia stood around her talking about what they wanted to order from George Lopez's Chingon Kitchen to redeem the free food bonus.

Luna sat like a child while the others waited in line for the food. She drank her Coca-Cola in peace while the rest gathered the food and utensils. All of them ate quickly and in silence. Luna looked less pale now that she had eaten. Nadia cleaned her teeth with a toothpick as Lourdes and Panchita played slots on their phone. Luna handed each of them an envelope.

"¿Y, esto?" Lourdes asked, trying to count all the hundreds and twenties crammed into the envelope.

"Gracias para todo." Luna replied.

The women hadn't noticed that Luna had the pot winnings divided evenly into four envelopes. Each of the women got up and took turns hugging Luna. The tightest and warmest hug was from Lourdes, who whispered, "Gracias, mi amor."

Her Favorite Little Word
Diosa Xochiquetzalcóatl

She don't want the good guy!
She wants the one with a past.
The one people see and say, "Dang girl!"
Tatted-*hasta-el-tuétano* son-of-a-gun!
She don't care too much for bangers,
But, *uy Cucuy, ¡esos pelones!*
The baggy pants and *q-vo* attitude.
White-tank-wearing, *mota*-smoking-*vato*.
Yet her inner-*chola* never seems to want to learn
That playing with that fire always gets her burned.
But you tell her over and over, like she ain't ever heard
And all she does is snap back with her favorite little word:
¡Chales!

The OG
Sandy Shakes

For years—too long to keep track of—you dedicated melodies in the style of lowrider oldies. I'd hear a ding, and there you were, tunes in hand and a "good morning beautiful."

That soft beat. That love song. Just like your demeanor mixed with a gentle ruthlessness. Like my favorite John Coltrane track: "In a Sentimental Mood." That Pisces kinda mood where we can be romantic as hell or plot how to disappear you … YOU. It was always you. 15 years later it became, US.

You reminded me of Brooklyn Ave. NOT CHAVEZ.

This was BEFORE Instagram's time, before we were gentrified. When Cortez still belonged to OGs. When outsiders had no idea where "La Brooklyn was." It was the equivalent of a Spanish Harlem, a complete cultural hemisphere of speakers going off, vendors scrubbing yesterday's dirty intentions off the concrete, and food that made you feel like home. You were reckless in the streets but contained the softest eyes for this short Mexican chic.

You were original, like wearing gray dickies to Hollenbeck. Like the original idea someone had of putting us in uniforms to solve gang issues. Except Ben Davis carried standard gray and 8th graders still wore size 42, trying to get sent home or to the homie's home.

You were cool, like removing "caution tape," and tying the ends back together so they didn't know we crossed over another hood barrier. But we did, both of us, unintentionally.

You were original, like LAUSD's coffee bread. That small piece of nourishment before our ADHD kicked in.

I'll remind those hipsters that HOODNESS existed before the vegan joints served overpriced (gluten free) bread. This bread was never free of anything but guilty of taking over another tiendita because Boyle Heights rent went up 300 percent %!!!

How is it that our tenants get lighter and lighter?? And the prices get higher and higher??

These were small immigrant homes. These were where a mouse named "Fievel" could go west and rest … if he was Mexican, or Japanese, or of Jewish descent.

Boyle Heights was our Ellis Island and now they have stolen all our housing, and left us with artificial stress causing non-organic illness. We were kings, these viruses were gifted to us in Trojan horses. They then ditched the horses and used our backs to carry their fortune for them.

But again, I digress…

After all of it came and went, and I left and returned again, I found him slightly battered and bruised, and renovated him, cleaned his vision, and loved one of Boyle Heights original gentlemen.

It was a feeling of simplicity, an urgent hydration when the pavement melts your skin, / we were water, and I TAUGHT him how to let the ocean kiss him…

I found an OG and he was willing to share me with my bag of pens, scribbled napkins and open mics. on concrete—now healed from our past mistakes.

I thought I would finish my story with him…but Boyle Heights called him back to the streets … and our love became someone else's CHISME.

I still pass by the pavement with the crack we promised to heal. I will come back once I spiritually can…and plant a rose just to watch love bloom … again … despite all of them. Despite whoever loves my broken petals otra vez.

The Ghost of Trees
Erika Ayón

Our love lives inside a valley
that once grew orchards of peaches,
pears, and almonds, but since
has devoured two avocado trees,
a fig tree, and a plum tree,
our effort to make the backyard greener.

After each dry branch, fallen leaf,
I wonder how much water does one need?
We need so much to survive.

This valley gave rise to our romance.
A romance because unlike a love story
it was never supposed to be. I came
from the ocean. You were raised
between mountains. I looked into
your blue eyes in search of a sea.

I played with words, you used letters
to make things work. I came from
a big family, you were an only child.
We had to learn to talk to each other.
Not let the past corrode our present.

When our son was born,
we almost didn't make it
out of the dust storm.

Every day this valley reminds me
how close the sun is to our bodies.
Here the moon sometimes feels
like a heat lamp. In the night, I feel you
drift away to escape the warmth.

Before our love, a tarot card reader
told me a former lover had taken
a lock of my hair and buried it
in a box under a willow tree. I needed
to reverse the spell, sacrifice a white dove,
dance in circles.

I did my own cleanse.
Filled my pockets with rocks.
Placed feathers in my hair.
Covered my walls with hummingbirds.

Now to ward off evil,
I pray to the ghost of trees in our yard.

In the vastness of this bed
Jen Yáñez-Alaniz

The laughter of children down the hall is gone.
                                       I am left desperate
to wake from a dream,
                  such distance. I am twenty-one and in love,

but the mirrors are shattered.
                  I have not seen my reflection in thirty years.
A dog-eared book lies tattered, bulked in my hands.
                            Every page swells

wide with wedding gowns, cake, and bible scriptures sacred and
condemning against divorce.
               My breasts are tender and heavy with warmth. I am wet

between the legs, but my groom is old.
                       He sits at the edge of our bed,
and I need only to wake him, to call to him, my love.
                            The man I knew

when I was twenty-one.
               But he sleeps within the shaking shoulder blades
of this man who shares my bed.
                    He is lost to the furrowed brow,

to the shriveled bird in the fist.

From the unwinding music of an empty bassinet,
I hear the sorrowed song of a lullaby reaching to comfort my infants.

A pillow is pressed against my chest.
                         And it smothers me, yet my
tongue continues to sing of the moon for my children.

                         My book of marriage is gone.

the impracticality of silk

jo reyes-boitel

I have dreams of full-length gowns, red or orange
or pink organza and silk, beaded bodice,
sweetheart or strapless,
jupon or bustle or asymmetrical hem

anything that lets me push a leg through from behind
hooped panniers and lace in a serpentine line,

       though sometimes I
imagine I have little more than silk,
spaghetti straps falling from my shoulders
some expectation of being wanted.

     The executive director tells me I am lucky I have beautiful tits,
that they are the only thing that saves him from writing me up.
     Even better that I was a lesbian because *these other bitches
will get pregnant and leave their jobs in an instant
to play Mommy.*

And don't forget the makeup.
How I cannot have enough red lipstick,
from blue red to rust to near fluorescent
to maroon for a casually bruised lip.

Bruising along the jawline too,
covered by primer then contoured.
And jewel-toned glasses to distract,
hone in on my eyes, lightening
as the years move along,
from cocoa brown to oiled hazel.

And she holds me at a distance in everything we do.
We play house where I am the pet, dozing on the couch,
taking liberties until she decides
whether I will be loved or denied
on a whim.

My lover holds my chin, her fingers lining my cheek bones.
Until, again, I'm on my knees, waiting for permission
to be wanted.

More and more I cannot deny myself the mermaid
bottom, how it hugs the hips and flares out after the knee.
Seemingly, I float across a space
until the entirety of my body
is water,
and my skin viscous membrane
plated in turquoise and green glass sequins

the back tied tight, the near breathlessness.

The assistant manager at a music store
calls me over to his office. I don't report to him
but he finds it important to ask if that was my mother
who came in moments before
to drop off my lunch.

I have three calls on hold.

She's pretty, he says. Then,
She has solid hips, like for having babies.

I look at his face.

Like you, he continues.

I was never a showy girl, never
fell for the allure of jewelry and abundance,
          but something about
diamond bracelets sliding over silk gloves

leads me to polished metal chains around a delicate neck
and my ears with their own temptations.

                    The father of my best friend took me out into the river
                              when I said I couldn't swim.
                         He held me, his arm across my waist then
                              his hand across my bottom then
                    his fingers finding their way into my yellow swimsuit
                         – a new outfit my mom bought me for summer –
                              while he whispered
                              in my newly-pierced ears
                                        There.

                                   Isn't that nice?

I never thought myself pretty enough
but in dreams I'm soothed by velvet and tulle,
by dresses long and billowy, by silk across my shoulders.

                    Why are their hands always cold? This boy
               Who asked me out on a date, who said I was interesting
                         Now waits by the door after *good night*

                    Still, he doesn't leave. In no hurry either,
               his shoulder leaning against the door frame as he says
                              but I like you
                    And I think that means I have to fuck him
                              because no one has told me
                                   I get to say no.
                         Besides, he won't leave otherwise.

I never thought I deserved the finery.
At best I could try for a temporary beauty
or special event beauty, like graduation pictures
or weddings when everyone has the chance to be special.

As a girl I bought plastic mules made for third graders,
pink soles and shimmery, stretchy fabric crossing my toes.

Older and away from my parents, I bought kitten heels and knee socks
On sale. Lounging in them and bodysuits when the days were rainy.

And always hair in pigtails or curls.
My small moment thinking I'm cute, worthwhile.

These things were just for me.

No one ever bought me a thing.
I was never taught to expect flowers.
I was considered easy going,
someone who didn't need the extra attention.
I was the *sweet kid* or *easy lay*.
                    And the older brother of my best friend watches me
one late night I'm at their house. We were listening to records in her room,
                    surrounded by blankets and pillows.
            I stepped to the kitchen for Kool-Aid when he corners me.
                                            He tells me
                            I have a pretty mouth.

                    Then tells me he'll show me how to use it.

Soft fabrics and tenderness are wasted on me.
Faux fur and coral cheeks, costume jewelry
and the joy of pretend, all without a place
to root. In this life joy is not a guarantee.

I soil the tender flesh of fabric every time.

When I am not in dreams, I choose a practical outfit.
Perhaps it's me hiding the gorgeous slumbering cat
within, that enjoys the mess of naps,
and who insists I have made my own
trouble when I've wanted.

If anything I was never allowed to be
innocent. This is what happens to girls like me.
We are born already owned, without
the chance for freedom.

I slept with a man twenty or more years ago now
and who I chance bumped into at a small gallery:

How he looked at me as though no time had passed,
as though what he had once put his hands on
still belonged to him.

I never belonged to him.

But he did not see me, not the delicate within
me. He saw the shape of me, the way I could
help him because men must have their way.

Reaching over,
I thought he was trying for a hug. He
grabbed my breasts
with both his hands, shaking
them as he smiled.

I did not speak.
I could not move.

I stepped back.
And back again.
Until his hands couldn't reach me.

I couldn't say a word
though the inside of me was screaming.

He followed me with his smile, never doubtful he is clever,
then walked over to the jazz collective
to take his seat at the drums,
his mouth against the microphone
reading some old poem.

And people saw him.
People saw him
and said nothing.

There is no elegance in sackcloth or canvas
but it has its purpose:
the way it fumbles both to hide what sleeps beneath it
and to shout out against those who would attempt its touch.

No delight.
No wonder.

But canvas has its protections.

Thought ugly or queer, with mottled skin
and unforgiving heft, I have made it through
the stories that don't show up on printed pages
yet still, alter me
in terrible ways.

I have survived. I have found joy.
This poem may not have a happy ending.

But I, the poet, still walk around this land. Build my voice. Write some
poems.
I've found I am persistent. I know now I hold a kind of beauty
no one can take away from me.

And that is the finest kind of love, velvety and rich.
Heavy and sweet syrup dripping through my fingers.
It churns within me. Milky and shimmering.
Flawless cut like a gemstone. This cannot be denied.
Look at me. For as long as I will breathe. I am beautiful.

First appeared in *the impracticality of silk*, Gnashing Teeth Publishing, October, 2024.

Time
Jen Yáñez-Alaniz

it exists
in a sky above my home

on one
October night

when I didn't step outside
to look

yo sé
que en esas horas
las nubes iluminadas
exhalaban

Imagino mi hogar
como una madre
dormida

como una iglesia
agotada

cansada del matrimonio

unraveling herself
from sterling light

unraveling herself

from the moon

First appeared in *there is so much I want to tell you: a Corazón Collective anthology*, Mouthfeel Press, March 2024.

Mycelium
Amber Ortega

It was in the dirty snow that I dug deep for the roots covered in wet compacted soil. I dug through the invisible, hidden in Meijer's parking lots at 9 a.m. on Sundays, covertly stepping in '90's college dance clubs, sifting through drunken bodies. After trying all the beds and sweating in multiple lovers' sheets, I touched a root. I felt the mycelium of ages pulling and calling to me. My heart. The root was dispossessed but it would do. I could replant it, feed it, show it where the sun shone best so that it helped me bear the fruit of the motherland. I sliced my belly open trying to find the vein of a thread. Like a cyborg I connected. Uploaded. Processed. Centuries of RAM, pain and joy.

Pain so vivid and deep. Protracted through centuries. Making infinite promises of rest, endings, destination points, fruition. These are ghosts. Boring holes through my body. Probing. Searching. Attaching. Burrowing. Nesting. Electric online. Telematically engaging. Sending vapor for wisps of names, dates, profiles, backs of hands, fingerprints, old velvet shoes. Raspy hips aged through flexion and extension. Deep wrinkled sides of necks, whites of eyes turned red and pink from winds blown miles and miles of ages. Loose thighs, tight brown calves, elbows that no longer bend. Bellies wrapped in loose cotton, warm, cradling birthing places, sweet blue onyx stars, night ghosts.

Each year, I take my corporeal inventory. Where is the attachment, the umbligal connection to the place I long for? Que me echo de menos, aguantando mi cuerpo in new places, twisting my spine, leaving spiral pathways through my femurs and tibias, lacing down the middle of my arches, sewing them to the earth. What dirt, what zacate, what charco, what cenote, ¿cuál pedazo de aire? ¡Ay que me caigo! ¡Ay que no me caigo!

Tie the feathers to my burial sack. Send me back. Send me in. Send me out. I brush my fingers across the algorithm printed on my skin. It sets a surge throughout my limbs, irradiating vibrations to my fingertips and toes. My knees rattle. My thighs shake. My belly laughs, full of pain and joy, full of breath and sighs, full of hunger. Este niño llora con razón. Es que ha tenido hambre desde que nació.

Each feather is asked for, quietly, con humildad. You must have no expectations. You must be satisfied with nothing in return. They will know what to leave and how many. Each feather is a symbol and a function. Each feather carries a code, a key to trigger a communication. Electric earth bound and housed in dirt. Verdant. Moist. Saturated. Mycelium LAN, networking my knowing beyond body and into each gram, channeling through the mycorrhizal.

I now inhabit the other side of the threshold. My resting place. Warming the motherboards of dark ethereal floors. Waiting for you to step across. I'll reach my hand to touch your shoulder or the rib closest to your scapula. I'll feel your heart suspended. I'll hold your breath and linger in your lungs as you weep. I'll be the old woman nestled in your chest. My calaca bones will enwrap you, protection from unwelcome keyloggers tapping your clavicle and hip bones for residual data. I'll guard your logged memories, entered in neat rows and partitioned by columnal moans of proximal ancestors.

Mi Tia
Natalia Rivas

so let's face it… the statement flounders
questions spring forward
and baffle me in abundance
scatter

a rustle of butterfly wings harmonize
reminding me that my journey isn't over
rainbow silk rebozo wraps me in memories

hot steam rises powerful scent of corn
fresh tortillas warm and bubbling
scent of wet dirt after a rainy day
it as about 1955
i was 4 or 5
a warm roseville day
my grandmother stood behind me
her faded floral apron flapped in the summer breeze
as the car approached
it was turquoise and white
round headlights and a curvy lines
delivering her majesty

a red chinese silk dress caressed her body
buttons from her neck to her knee on the side
the thinnest piece of leather buckled on contour of her ankle
she wore her aztec brow proudly
and adored her body with mystical airs
her hair in a pompadour
my tia sat perched on the white leather

magical incantations followed her through her day filling the air
scenting the rooms with that glorious smell of secrets exploding
sandalwood scented chinese fans fluttering at important moments
my tia was the best of many worlds. poet, organizer, astrologer, mystic
endangered species.
magical creatures bore the breath of her wisdom
i'd like to say, she lived a charmed life,
casting spells of freedom with herbs and good intentions
she proudly marched for the rights of others
carrying her signs and reading her poems

carrying her grief and sadness
a badge of a broken heart
her pain became her grief and marched for freedom
she bore the pain
until her legs were eaten by disease

there were days of darkness that draped the wind

secrets
well-kept in a jar next to haunting fear and rage
rattled and secrets spilled

the walls dripped blood on the floor
imprints of her hands on the rim of the tub
ajax and tears cleaned the tub, the bloody walls and bitter truth
our souls tortured provided smiles
walls dripping blood
feet sliding on the blood-soaked floor
my child eyes didn't understand
and as much as we scrubbed
we were imprinted with pain
of grownups and cruel monsters with smooth voices

my grandmother praying and baffled at her daughter's sorrow
and failed death
prayed her "ay dios mio's" throwing her arms in the air
as if, god would know the answer

Nina
Maria Miranda Maloney

It smelled of home when Nina roasted serranos, split tomatoes open on top of the comal, palmed flour and corn to make perfectly round tortillas, while all the pots of pinto beans boiled in unison. Outside Nina's kitchen door, whirlpools of dust teased her. She could smell incoming rain just by the scent of dust on her doorstep. She could also smell trouble.

"That daughter of yours is going to make you pay for your sins," was her favorite reminder to my dad. She was referring to me when I would squirm out of her embrace. She said I was already too independent for my own good, and I would be trouble.

When she died, Dad drank his paycheck every other Friday; he'd punch walls in our home but never made a hole. The walls were made of adobe and bruised his knuckles. I watched him cry over the table. He said he missed his Nina. His rage would come in waves — a mourning man; then, he'd go after my mother. She'd run to the bathroom and lock the door, and I'd stand between the locked door and my father, who threatened to break it down if she didn't come out. I'd beg him to leave her alone, and I softened his rage when I reminded him of how much I loved him. I was six. He'd back away and return to the table, where he sobbed loudly.

My sisters watched him, wide-eyed, afraid he'd go after them.

I guarded the doors to the rooms — a cat ready to pounce when the rage returned.

Who said men don't cry?

When Nina lay dying, she was home in her Juárez house. My parents lived in a two-room house across the street from her. They owned a small corner grocery store. Their best-selling item was oranges. I was two. Mom would peel oranges and pluck the seeds out, and I ate the fleshy segments because there was nothing else to do.

Across the store, Nina was dying of diabetes, but it was her heart that killed her. Back then, Dad spent his days and nights at her house while I spent my days eating oranges as my mom worked the counter and stocked the shelves. I was a busy toddler, running wild among the customers, and often dashed out onto the street when the screen door opened. Mom chased after me. In time, she was too exhausted to run the store and run after me, and she begged Dad to help her at the store or help care for me, but he wouldn't have it. His mother was dying. Mom once told me Dad was Nina's favorite son, and she was her least favorite daughter-in-law.

When Nina died, the family buried her at Jardines Eternos, an upscale cemetery with acres of green grass, trimmed ledges, and tree-lined cobble-stone pathways. Headstones and mausoleums rose from the green earth in intricate patterns and marble. This was not a cemetery for the poor. The poor buried their poor in La Chaveña, in the dusty cemetery smack in the middle of the city. I remember returning to the cemetery every November 2nd — Día de los Muertos — with my abuelito Pablo to clean his mother's grave, sprinkle water over the dirt rise, and adorn it with cempasúchitl. Outside the cemetery's entrance, flower vendors sold marigolds in buckets of water, and men with shovels waited to be hired to clean graves and sprinkle water from the buckets they filled from a water spicket outside the cemetery's doors. On that day, every grave became a garden, a celebration of life and death, of exit and return.

But Nina deserved a headstone and a stone grave, in a lush garden. Jardines Eternos lined its closely guarded entrance with stalls of lavish flower arrangements and heavy prices.

Years after Nina died, my parents, sisters, and I visited her graveside and bought our flowers from vendors in the small town. We sank our knees deep in the grass and waited for something to happen. Perhaps she would give us a sign to tell us she was happy. Maybe she would miraculously resurrect, and we'd watch her spirit float to the heavens. Perhaps I'd hear her whisper from deep within the core to remind my dad that I loved him when her death anniversary drew near and my dad would become sad, angry, and violent.

We all would wait quietly, kneeling in the soft grass, next to her grave — my father lost in thought. I always hoped she'd wake up and make him happy again.

From the author's unpublished manuscript *The Moon in Her Eyes*

Coins
Petra Salazar

grief reciprocates
it gives and it takes
like a curandera
offering a candle and sage
and accepting payment

it spreads its arms
and i open to it

embracing

ready to receive the pain
i let my tears fall
like coins from a purse

¡Abuelita Josefina presente!
Jesenia Chávez

I wish I knew my abuelita more. I realized I didn't know much about her when she died, and this felt like a huge tragedy. I only have stories that have been told to me, stories I have made up, a few pictures, and I have a whole lot of feelings. One story is that I am alive thanks to her care. I was a fussy baby and grandma fed me a little at a time. I did not like anything. I would not eat, but grandma fed me de a poquito so I would not starve.

There is a picture we all have; we treasure this photo because it tells us something about who she was. It is a black and white photo of her in a dress and she has guns across her chest, like the women of the Mexican Revolution. We asked her about it countless times,

¿Por qué tenía pistolas, abuelita?

Para defender la tierra mija.

¿Pero por qué? ¿Por qué?

No answer. We would move on, drink our café quietly. That was all we got; she didn't talk about herself much, ever. She only listened, she only prayed, she only cooked and cleaned and worked. She let us hug her and hold her hand, she cooed at babies. She never complained. She suffered in silence, I think. She was lonely, I think. She sewed our pants and braided our hair. Her love language was acts of service, ¿verdad que sí abuelita? What a frivolous thought, love language.

Primo Rigo called us. "Grandma is not well. She is in the hospital. You need to come now if you want to see her." Rigo, the eldest grandchild, had always reminded us to visit, had kept us updated on grandma. He had told us before it might be her last days, but this time we knew he meant it. My two sisters, Erika and Lucero, my mom, and my cousin Carmen texted each other and made plans. We would go as soon as we could. I was at work, and when I read the text I began to cry. Luckily it was after school, and no one saw me. I drove home. I let my school know I would need coverage. The next morning, we met up early to make the 5-hour drive, all packed into one car. Cozy, like the many times we had driven up to Modesto to our Tía Chayo's, to visit and sit around and eat. This time it was different. Grandma, always so considerate, had chosen to die on a weekend.

We drove straight to the hospital.

We knew she would leave, but we didn't know how much it would hurt. We knew she would die someday; she would move into the spirit world like all her brothers and sisters already had. She had defied so many expectations already. She had married older than most girls from her pueblo, she had ridden horses and shot guns to protect her land, she had come to el Norte to help her daughters. She had stayed with all of us. Abuelita had lived in that first house with us in South Central and walked up and down and had been held at gunpoint once, the story goes. She had walked us to school in Maywood and gotten lost and found her way without knowing English.

One time I went home early from school. I had a fever, and she was home, so she came to pick me up. I felt so special, to be doted on by my grandmother without my siblings or cousins around. She put a pañuelo, soaked with rubbing alcohol, on my head, and comforted me as she tended to me. She made me teas to drink from herbs plucked from the yard, hierbabuena y hojas de limón. When I was a first grader, grandma would wrap roses from the garden in aluminum foil for me to take to Ms. Dawson, my generous teacher, who would let me hang out in her classroom before class started. Grandma knew about kind gestures.

Sometimes it was five kids with her in a cramped apartment in Maywood, as she cleaned and cooked and managed our conflicts. She watched us ask for rubber bands from the mail carrier or beg for coins for the paletero. It must have been so strange for her to see us in this country, speaking a language she didn't understand, making demands for things she never had. Being ashamed of her, like that time she had walked us home from middle school, even though it was only three blocks away from our house, in her umbrella hat, and we walked across the street to avoid walking with her, embarrassed at our grandmother in a long skirt with medias on and a short white sleeve shirt.

She had nurtured, loved us, and been devoted to us kids despite our English and rude ways. She had survived, but now it was her time to go. She was tired. She lost weight. She didn't talk much, and she already had never been much of a talker to begin with. To our never-ending questions she had always just responded with a, "Yo no sé." She didn't know what answer would satisfy us, her American-born Mexican grandkids. "No sé, mija," pero sí supo cuidarnos y cocinar y salir para adelante. She was tired, and it was time to let her go.

When we walked into the ICU in Modesto, California, grandma was lying there, her teeth and dentures all messed up and moved around in her jaw, a fucked-up jenga. Her eyes closed, I hated the tubes in her mouth. It looked painful to have your mouth open like that for so long. Death smells all around, people's fluids everywhere, the stench of human decay, of moss and dirt and bodies transitioning. It smelled like soiled pants, and not being able to shower for many days. It smelled of oily hair and rotting meat. I was not prepared for the stench, and I worked hard at hiding how unpleasant it was by smiling and holding my breath. Even though grandma was not aware, she would not have liked it, she was a neat and tidy lady.

The doctors and nurses told us there was not much more they could do for her. The noisy life preserving machines, beeping, and whirring. I wanted to sing a sad song like Björk in *Dancer in the Dark*, with all the sounds. There were other families standing around their sick loved ones. Young and old folks in the worst part of the hospital with many vulnerable patients who probably wouldn't make it, or maybe they would. Now Rigo, and Tía Chayo, her oldest daughter greeted us, and explained what happened,

"No quería comer, estaba inconsciente y llamamos a la ambulancia."

We started to cry.

"Solo pueden entrar tres o cuatro a la vez a su cuarto." Don't they know we're Mexican and there's a lot of us?! I wondered.

My mom would go in first, "Entre usted, amá."

She would go in first to see her mom. I braced myself for the grief. The grief my mami would feel, the grief my sisters and cousins would feel. The most important woman in our lives, the one to whom we all owed our lives was leaving us.

We were there a couple days, crowding her little room. Only a few of us at a time could go in. We held her hand and sang her songs:

Ay, ay, ay, ¿qué voy hacer con este amor que se perdió? Lo que me duele más es no saber por cual razón me abandonó.[16]

We sang and laughed at how loud we were; we were probably annoying to the hospital staff.

"¿Cuál canción le cantamos abuelita?" said my oldest sister Erika. She was at ease next to grandma, holding her hand and talking to her. I admired my older sister so much for her care with our dying abuelita. I wished I could too, but fear stopped me. Fear of the finality of it, fear of hurting her, fear of not being heard.

"Cantámos 'Dos gotas de agua,'"[17] Tía Chayo said, "Okay, pues, ¿quién se sabe la canción?" I said.

"Ya se me olvidan las cosas, mija," said Tía Chayo.

"A mí también," said my mami.

"Pues busquen en los teléfonos, hombre," said Primo Rigo; he always had a joke ready for us.

Carmen laughed and playfully scolded us, "Cantamos bien desentonadas."

"Pero canten, hombre," said Lucero my youngest sister, that is her song, "Dos gotas de agua."

Tía Chayo sang beautifully. She always did, she sounded like Las Jilguerillas when she sang with Tía Panchita. The rest of us sang pretty well, too; we can sing in my family. We sing together, we pray together, we grieve and celebrate together.

We shuffled in and out, three or four at a time. In the tiny waiting area, we sat and traded snacks and stories.

"¿Cómo le decía a las hijas de Rigo?"

"Pajarita for Raven," we laughed. She couldn't pronounce the English names some of the family members had given their kids. "Yake for Jake," and she would change all our names, but we didn't care; we were used to it.

"Remember when she called Robert 'Saralailo' because he wouldn't stay still?"

16 "Llorando a Mares," Mario Saucedo, *Hay un Mar*, 1971.
17 "Dos gotas de agua," Luis M. Dueñas Singer (Chelo), *Chelo*, 1976.

"Remember when she sang at the party in Santa Paula?" She hardly ever sang.

"Remember when she got mad at you for not wearing medias under your dress to church?"

"¿Te acuerdas cuando fuimos a Dolores?"

"Sí fuimos muchas veces," but it was never enough time.

Remember, remember, remember her alive, not laying there in that tiny room in the ICU.

I chased my cousin Vero's kids in the hallways of the hospital. I liked chasing the kids, they were three and seven years old; it was a nice break. When it was my turn to sit with my grandma, I would walk in through those doors that require a badge, the kind you have to use a phone to call the nurse's desk to open them. Sometimes, the door would already be opening, although it was because a body was being wheeled in or out and I had to move out of the way.

I got close to her, I touched her forehead lightly and her tres pelitos grises. Le hablé un poquito, "La quiero mucho, abuelita." I didn't know what to say. I wish I knew her more. I wish I knew what she wanted, what she dreamed of. "La quiero mucho, abuelita, si se quiere ir, yo entiendo, ha sufrido mucho." I told her it was okay to go.

We all waited our turn in the waiting room, no changes in grandma, todo conectada con tubos, the machine helping her breathe. No other signs of living, except a warm body surrounded by her loved ones. Then the social worker and hospice nurse came to talk to us.

"It is time to talk about options for your grandmother."

"Okay, what are they?"

"We can move her to hospice care, where she will be more comfortable. She won't be in pain, she will be medicated, but medically there is nothing more we can do."

Mi mami said, "No, tienen que hacer algo, la pueden salvar, la pueden ayudar." My mom did not want her disconnected, she held out hope for her, her mother. My mom had already lost so much. She wanted this, so we let her talk, and then we decided it was time for grandma to rest. We got the pamphlet and read about death. We had read about it before when Tía Panchita was dying and we were going to take her home and take turns taking care of her, but Tía died in that hospital in Long Beach before we could do any of it.

We knew some things about death, but as we listened to the social worker explain the process, it didn't make it easier. All of us were exhausted from waiting and watching our beloved grandmother in pain.

She was transported to hospice, and we followed along. What a terrible feeling to leave your grandmother alone in some medical van with strangers that don't speak Spanish. She arrived, and we arrived. We parked our cars and walked into a home, a cozy home with plush couches. A place that seemed to have been decorated by an old white lady from the 1980's with a little bit of money. It was a quiet and somber place, a welcome change from the noisy ICU. It smelled pleasant, like potpourri. No death smells here. It felt like we were the only ones in the building. It felt like a decent place to die. A tall nurse walked in to greet us and led us to her room. She showed us where to get coffee or water. She told us that grandma could be there a day, or a week, or a month, no one knew how long she would last in there. It is a mystery when people choose to go. We nodded okay, okay, we had heard this already at the hospital.

Grandma would not be in pain or have tubes stuck in her. She would not be in a tiny ICU room where only a few of us could enter at a time. She would be here ready to die in a cheesy but comfy hospice care home. I noticed some other elderly residents all alone in their rooms. I wondered how long they had been there, dying. I wanted to comfort them, too, because it seemed tragic to die without anyone around to hold you. A Christmas tree sat at the center because it was late November, and there were couches all around.

Grandma had her own large room. This was nothing like the rancho where she grew up in Dolores, Chihuahua.

The rancho would have had many relatives all around, eating and talking. It would have been outdoors. It would have been much different, but there was nothing we could do. She would leave this earth in the United States surrounded by her daughters and grandkids. It was such a foreign place for her; her life had been devoted to us. We walked into her room, and we talked in English, in Spanish. I could not bring myself to touch her, and I deeply regret this now. I was so scared.

We lay down to sleep. It was late at night. It was the longest night; it was the shortest night. My sister Erika squeezed into the bed with our grandmother, and my sister Lucero took the couch. I lay down on the cold tile floor. (Later my lower back would hurt for many months, so much that I went to a chiropractor. The pain was part of my grieving.) My aunt got in the lounge chair. My cousins Rigo and Carmen found another couch. My mom curled into a chair in the room.

Ya era la madrugada, Friday at 1:00 a.m., we had finally settled into a couple hours of sleep. "Ya vamos a descansar un poco," said Tía Chayo. We couldn't get much rest, but we tried. A few moments of quiet, no sounds, only my mami, my sisters, my cousins trying to be still.

"Ponte en el la cama, Jesenia, o algún sillón, mija," said my Tía. I was in front of her on the floor, I could see her orthopedic shoes. They sparked a tenderness in my heart, she was old, too, she was sick, too.

"No, está bien, aquí estoy bien, tía, solo denme una almohada."

They threw a pillow at me, we laughed a little.

"Regáñelas, abuelita, me tiraron la almohada," I said; I got jokes too.

"Ya apláquense pues," my mom said playfully.

Finally, we were all quiet, laying down.

After what seemed like only a couple of minutes, my sister Erika said, "I think she stopped breathing."

"What?" We all said softly.

My mom and aunt got close to their mom. They held her and kissed her. We all approached after, we hugged her and kissed her and said goodbye, rest, abuelita.

She had taken a last gasp and was no longer in her body. She was gone.

"Ay, mamá," cried Tía Chayo, who had taken care of her these last few years.

"Ya descansa, mamacita," said my mami. "Ya no sufras, mami."

We cried and prayed, and the nurse came in to clean her up. Someone had gone to tell her, I'm not sure who, or if maybe she just knew, if some alarm went off in a patient's room. We had to leave the room while she did this. We walked out hugging each other.

"Ya estaba cansada," we murmured. My mom folded into herself, holding her hands the way she does when she is sad. We hugged each other and held hands while we waited in silence.

When we walked back in, abuelita looked so peaceful, she had been cleaned up, her mouth was closed. With gentleness and mercy, the nurse had put so much care into making my grandmother comfortable on the bed. She had even put some flowers in her hand. A sad little bouquet of white flowers, weeds almost, but they were beautiful in grandma's hands because she was at last resting. Abuelita dormidita with the covers up to her chest, her hands holding a bouquet. I felt a giant swell of tears burst out of me, I wanted to shout, but I stayed quiet. It felt wrong to be loud in this place, in the presence of sacred death. We took turns hugging grandma, trying to be close to her. She had waited to arrive to hospice to take her last breath. We had only been there a few hours. She knew we needed that. She knew. She held on to her dignity, she was able to die in a quiet place. She did not have a lot of control over her life, her life was one of service, but at least she held on long enough to die in hospice with us asleep by her side.

My Tía Chayo began a prayer. We prayed a rosary together. It was comforting to say those *Padre Nuestros* and *Ave Marias*. We sang some church songs, and consoled each other.

Then it was time for the business of dying — the paperwork. We stood outside her room speaking in quiet voices; who would arrange everything? We needed her to be transported to Los Angeles. She would not be buried in Modesto even though Tía Chayo had paid for plots there. We wanted her in Los Angeles, and my mom also had paid for some plots with my dad in the Catholic cemetery, Calvary Cemetery and Mortuary in East Los Angeles. A cemetery we were familiar with because my Tía Panchita is there in a crypt in the wall. We talked and looked at each others' exhausted and sad faces.

We huddled in a circle next to the large couches, and we looked at each other.

"Okay, we will have to get her home to LA." Carmen spoke. She had buried her mom only four years ago; this must be so hard on her, I thought.

"We will get her to L.A., and let everyone know," said Erika, always the one ready to handle difficult situations.

"Yo también tengo un lugar aquí en Modesto," said Tía Chayo.

"Pero, la vamos a llevar allá, tía," we said gently.

Rigo spoke. "Sí está bien, we can get the paperwork started."

We looked at each other, who would take care of it. We all had busy lives.

The three oldest grand kids who take care of everything, my sister Erika, Rigo, Carmen. Then me and my younger sister Lucero. My Tía Chayo and my mom off to the side, no longer the ones that made decisions. The adult children did it now, for them. We had to decide. I took a deep breath, and I said, "Okay, I'll do it." I knew I could take days off to help figure things out with my mom, to get the paperwork arranged. The rest of them had taken care of medications, paperwork for Medi-Cal, visited and consulted and planned so much all the time, and I thought it was my turn to help. I immediately regretted that I volunteered, because I wasn't sure I would be strong enough to do it, but I also knew how much everyone had already done, and they had their kids and jobs and spouses, and I only had me to worry about. Then they came with the body bags; another elderly gentleman had died that same night, I found some comfort knowing that some viejito would be with my grandmother. I wondered if he spoke Spanish, so he and abuelita could talk and be dead friends. They took his body out in a black body bag like you see on TV. I think they took abuelita out, too I don't remember, it was too much to bear.

Once we returned to Los Angeles, the planning began, the mortuary, the cemetery visit. The arranging of transport, the coroner report, all of this took so long, and everyone kept asking and asking me when we would have the services. I felt frustrated; I had no control over how long this process would take and the thought of our grandmother sitting in some basement awaiting transport was difficult for everyone. I felt upset and worried, and angry with the way we treat bodies and death. It is tragic and dehumanizing. I spent hours worrying and wondering, my back aching, my heart breaking. I had to keep it together at work, while out with my mom making the funeral arrangements, but my body hurt. My head hurt. I wondered why my grandmother had to suffer in the ICU instead of being allowed to die at home, comfortable. I would be teaching, and suddenly my phone would be going off, and I knew it was some member of my family asking when the services would be held. I wished we were Jewish or had some religious reason to get the body moved faster, but we just had to wait. I had to call and see what the issue was. She would be transported in a cold van, not in the car with us anymore. She would not stop with us to get food and use the bathroom. She would not hear us arguing or laughing or singing in the car down the Freeway 5, past the Grapevine, past Magic Mountain, back to Los Angeles. She would come back all alone.

Finally, they got her to the mortuary in East Los Angeles we had found, and I sat in the tidy office that smelled like Fabuloso with a man who set it all up for us. We brought grandma's outfit, some jewelry for her to wear. Later they called us because we forgot the calzones. *I mean, does she need underwear*, I thought. *Yes, I do, mija*, said abuelita's voice in my head. She was a classy lady.

It was winter in L.A., and the sky was a gray mass. Not one ray of sunshine for us on that day, the soft rain pelted my car windows, and the sound of the windshield wipers soothed me. Here we were alive, driving around while grandma lay awaiting her burial. I drove around with my mom, and we smoked cigarettes, cried, sniffled, and talked. We planned everything as a family, the flowers, the pictures, the rosaries, the food — including the pan dulce, the eulogy slide show, the program, the little cards with her picture and a prayer. Everyone pitched in. Together through it all to send off our abuelita in a dignified and Catholic way she would have wanted. We could not bury her in the Campo Santo 1,245 miles away, but we would try our best to send her off in a rancho-style way.

At the cemetery I sat with my mom in another office. My parents had bought their plots long ago after church one Sunday. We flipped through a catalog and picked out a light blue coffin that we thought grandma would like. A black one would be too basic and masculine for a badass lady like my abuelita. They took us in a golf cart to see where she would be buried. Grandma "quiere estar en la tierra," in the ground. Those were her wishes my mom told me. We decided on the inscription on the tombstone, it would have a picture of the Virgen de Guadalupe etched on it. I consulted my sisters and primas every step of the way, thank goodness for group texts! Every decision was made collectively.

The funeral day came, we piled into the cemetery. We wore blue, to honor abuelita. The priest came and said some words I don't remember. Then it was over. We stayed until she was in the ground. Until they made us get out of the way of the tractor piling and moving dirt around. This is the hardest part, the finality of being in the ground. This is when women wail and try to throw themselves in with the dead, in real life and on TV. We wailed, we cried, we held each other close. After, we drove to Bloomington to drink tequila and grieve together. All the grandkids, all the siblings, little kids and big kids all together. We had food, and my grandmother's only son, my Tío Tino, paid for a banda norteña, a banda like the ones our family frequently hired for quinceañeras and bautismos because they played well and knew all the old songs. Then it was my turn to sing the song I always sing for grandma with the banda, one of the only banda songs I know, "Mi Ranchito."[18]

> *Alla tras de la montaña,*
> *Donde temprano se oculta el sol*
> *Deje mi ranchito triste,*
> *Y abandonada a mi labor*
> *Allí me paso los años,*
> *Allí encontré mi primer amor*
> *Y fueron los desengaños,*
> *Los que mataron ya mi ilusión*
> *Ay corazón que te vas*
> *Para nunca volver, no me digas adiós*
> *No te despidas jamás, si no quieres saber*
> *De la ausencia el dolor*

I sang and cried-sang, and I sang loudly and proudly for my Abuelita Josefina Vizcarra de Meraz, 7/31/1921-12/1/2018, que en paz descanse. I sang about leaving a small town, the heartbreak it causes because you might never return. You might not have money or papers

---

18 "Mi Ranchito," Chicho y Margarita, *Chicho y Margarita,*1937.

to go back. You leave the mountains, the trees, the rancho life behind, you come to a new country, you help raise all the babies. You don't understand all the English, you walk around everywhere and cook and clean. You buy tortillas instead of making them, you buy meat at the market instead of the fresh slaughter of farm animals. You make a new life with your three daughters in California. You take turns helping them in this country where everyone has to work all the time. Once in a while you can go back home to the rancho, but then you get diabetes, and your daughters bring you back because they don't want you to get sick. There is no regular health care you can get over there. You come back, sad because you know you will not get to die with your sister in your home in Mexico. You are resigned to this life back in California, in Maywood, in Huntington Park, in Modesto. You know the kids need you. We needed you, abuelita. Gracias.

I sang and sang, and we all drank and danced, and we even sang one big group song with the banda. One more hour, let them play one more hour, extending our collective grief together. Let us sing together to remember our grandmother, our dear abuelita, the matriarch of our familia. The strongest and quietest one. The one that never complained. The one that helped raise all of us. She had left us now, and we were heartbroken. Gracias, Abuelita Josefina, lo siento que sufrió al final en el ICU. No sabíamos como dejarla ir, pero usted nos enseñó. She showed us how to let her go. She showed us how to take care of each other. Sometimes I dream about her, and she tells me she is okay. She tells me to let her rest. She tells me not to worry so much. She is watching over us.

> *Ay corazon que te vas*
> *Para nunca volver, no me digas adíos*
> *Vuelve a dejar el amor, al ranchito que fue*
> *De mi vida ilusión*[19]

Never say goodbye, mejor dices, hasta pronto, nos vemos. See you soon, Abuelita. Cuando Dios quiera. Maybe I did know you, Abuelita; your actions were enough. Your actions were enough to guide me.

19 "Mi Ranchito," Chicho y Margarita, *Chicho y Margarita,*1937.

Desideria
Inez González Perezchica

Desideria,
no one in our family spoke your name.
Generations later
you demanded attention
you did not want to disappear without a trace.

Great maternal grandmother
who my family never talked about,
you were forgotten
until, at a family constellation,
I felt the presence of an ancestor:
a strong woman.

Maria Desideria Rodriguez Perez
I inherited your strength,
flowing through the generations.

Trying to understand you
Desideria,
I think about the Mexican women of your time,
born in El Saucillo, Aguascalientes in 1861:
there wasn't much happiness for Mexican women then.
Especially, poor women.

Your husband, Juan Ruiz Chavez,
a widower, was unfaithful and abusive.
The only joy in your life was
Maria Guadalupe: the daughter you birthed.

You became a widowed, single mother
living in poverty.
So, when Manuel proposed to your daughter,
planning to move to the United States with his new bride,
your one condition was
that he take both of you to el norte with him.

Through the years and with each of the twelve pregnancies,
Guadalupe's health deteriorated,
and she was buried alongside Dolores,
her second stillborn baby.
She was forty-one.

Dolores — pain in Spanish —
named for the pain that came with her
and stayed with you.

Diabetic and blind
you could still point to the moon at night.
But, when you ended up in a nursing home,
did anyone come and visit you?

Great maternal grandmother,
I can only imagine what your life was like.
But I know that your suffering made you strong.
I wonder if you ever smiled.

Life is much easier for us, your descendants.
We inherited your strength.
for that, we should at least know your name:
Desideria Rodriguez Perez.
Born February 11, 1861
Died January, 1945.

Cempasúchil

Rosalilia M. Mendoza

Flor de muerto,
Marigold,

This is how I know you:
yellow to brighten our sorrow,
strong scent to ward off the decaying.

I didn't know your petals were edible
until I saw a reel on IG, with a recipe:
atole de Cempasúchil.
How the cocinero molia tus pétalos
en un molcajete, with maiz.

How long have you been around,
Cempa?
And your name is still indigenous:
Xochitl.

I wonder how you feel, in between the
living and the dead.

Somehow your offering is sacrificial.
Sacred, returning.

Well, we all know our inevitable truth:
what is birthed on Mother Earth will
be swallowed by her one day.

The least I can offer is my bones
for all that she has given me:
clothes, food, shelter, water.

I wonder what you think
about rent, bills, discrimination, consumption.

Pretty flower,
have we forgotten our higher purpose?

Cempa,
will you help us remember?

Dreaming with Aurora

Sonia Gutiérrez

"Ay que bonito es volar
A las dos de la mañana
A las dos de la mañana
Ay que bonito es volar
Ay mamá".
     — "La Bruja"[20]

It was November — in the time of memories and dreams. She wore her long black hair down over her shoulders and her favorite white gown touched her calves. Her bare feet were dry like the desert dust, craving for a drop of water. Under the cherimoya tree, she sat on a concrete bench while she took in her surroundings that looked like her home and then continued on her journey. She saw the rabbit on the moon peer through the tall almond tree heavy with flowers; its leaves glistened and danced feverishly as she passed by. Even though the smell of eucalyptus trees permeated the backyard, she couldn't smell them as much as she tried. Something else called her — a smell more powerful — the smell of bright orange cempazúchitl flowers.

As she got closer to the backside of the house, she recognized the geranium clay pots lining alongside the house. The estafiate and ruda plants were well taken care of — for a second, she thought they were hers. But as she approached a bedroom window, she saw her face reflected. She didn't know if she was la Llorona or a bruja or the two of them in one. Through her eyes, she didn't look terrifying — not to herself. Looking at her face did startle her a bit, but what startled her most were her feet. They weren't touching the ground. Her body moved slowly, heavy with time on her shoulders, to her altar, where she found her picture in a wooden frame, the only picture of her, the one with her hair tight in a long braid. The candle's flame flickered, and the red, bright pink, royal blue, green, and

20 La Bruja is a popular traditional jarocho song from Veracruz, Mexico. The
   author is unknown.

yellow ribbon hanging from the window's frame swayed as she moved to a corner in the living room next to la Virgen de Guadalupe. Her favorite dish — mole rojo, frijoles, and arroz — was still warm with her daughter and granddaughters' hands. Next to the mole, her family had placed a glass of water to quench her thirst. She remembered who she was — she was Aurora. And her granddaughters, Paloma and Sofía, had guided her to the place of the living.

After reuniting with family members placed next to her on the family altar, Aurora then visited Helena, sleeping next to her husband. She found her in the same position she slept as a child. Staring at her daughter's grown woman's face, Aurora leaned over and kissed her daughter on the forehead. Helena woke up, stayed still and asked, "¿Mamá, eres tú?" With no answer and heavy with sleep, she went back to dreaming.

In the morning, I woke up confident my grandmother had visited the altar both Paloma and I had set up for her the night before. I sat on my bed recollecting my dream then rose to my feet and stared out the window. I had dreamt I was walking. No, I was floating like la Llorona but wasn't sure if the woman in my dream was my grandmother — Aurora, a bruja, or la Llorona.

It was November — in the time of . . . *Ay de mí, Llorona Llorona, Llorona, llévame al río. Tápame con tu rebozo, Llorona, porque me muero de frío.*[21]

---

21 La Lorona is a traditional Mexican folk song of obscure origins believed to have its genesis in Isthmus of Tehuantepec, about the legend of La Llorona.

First appeared in *Dreaming with Mariposas*, Sonia Gutierrez, FlowerSong Press, 2020, and in *The Dreaming Machine*, April 2021

El Nido

Anel I. Flores

It was almost time for Lita's most independent gallina, Sofia, to hatch her eggs. Lita Eva went outside to check on gallina Sofia's status. When she got close enough to the gallinero to see the silhouettes of the birds, gallina Sofia's spot on the roost was empty and her nido, made from a wood apple box, was only filled with grass; no gallina Sofia. Solitaria's Lita was aggravated and grunted curses into the wind. Virginia watched her vecina Eva from her back porch and chewed into a strip of dried venison from the winter elk hunt.

"Pinche Sofia! Gallina desgraciada! Anda en la calle otra vez!" A stranger would have judged Lita Eva for talking to spirits, but Virg watched on in admiration.

After Lita Eva's last child was still-born, her viejo cried until he dried up and didn't wake again. Lita Eva cut her losses, out of habit, and accepted the peacefulness of life with gregarious gallina Sofia's flock and La Vecina Virg to coffee with on the porch. Lita Eva expected the melodic interruption of clucks from las gallinas and depended on la Sofia's longing look from the gallinero's wire window each morning. "Tan obediente, mi triste Sofia, sad girl gallina, I love you." Lita Eva gently kissed la gallina Sofia on her soft pillowy head. La gallina scooted and stood over her coop, just enough for Lita to slip her hands into the nest and gather a few eggs.

"Always ask the gallinas permission to take their babies, and tell them it's for food. They understand you."

Sol remembered her Lita teaching her how to reach in for the eggs when she was little.

"And, always thank them for their gifts."

Huevos were all Lita ate. If it wasn't nopales with huevos, it was puerco con huevos, calabazita con huevo, huevos con frijoles, papas and eggs revueltos, eggs with wieners, huevos estrellados, crudos con jugo, with tomate, and her favorite huevos a la copa, or boiled eggs with sal, pimienta and cilantro from her field.

On Lita Eva's last morning living, in panic at Sofia's absence, she went barefoot searching for the gallina, first in the vecino's coop, then under and within each tree in the thick monte behind her orange grove, and finally under the house. The mint green painted house at one time or another creó over sixty stinky and sweaty mocosos, if you include Lita's own kids, their kids, their kids' kids, the vecino's kids, and even the kids who showed up after papá grande died, claiming to belong there. Tilted, but firmly balanced on stilts, the space between the ground and the floor of the casita always had a steady breeze and stayed cool against the humidity of the dirt. Sometimes Sofia would go under the house to protect her eggs, safe from any hungry creature wanting to take the babies. When Lita got to the edge of the house to check on Sofia, too confident in her psychic mind and eighty-three-year-old body, she bent over at the waist, possibly too quick, and blacked out. Virg lost view of Lita Eva, dropped her venison in the dirt and ran over to see where she disappeared to. By the time she arrived, Lita Eva's eyes were open, she was on all fours. Lita Eva pushed herself abruptly off the ground, leaving comadre Virg behind her, ran over to the coop, opened the little door, crouched down to fit all the way in and stopped again, almost dead in her tracks, at the peering eyes of a snake.

From her belt holster, Lita grabbed her viejo's abalone-shell handled navaja, switched it open, and with a quick whip of her hand out in front, sliced the snake's head off. The snake body fell limp along the edges of Sofia's nido, his head dropped to the floor and rolled to a dark corner. Blood dripped through the fruit box, onto Lita's feet. Without question or hesitation, she grabbed the open end of the snake with her left hand, letting blood seep through her fingers like a leaking manguera, and with her right hand used the tip of the blade, slowly and carefully to slice the black snake all the way down the middle. Lita Eva felt guilty for cursing at her última hija, gallina Sofia, and gulped back tears as she pulled each of Sofia's children from the snake's long belly, placing them each carefully into the nido while she finished her rescue.

With cupfuls of warm water she rinsed off each egg individually, wiping them down with a small wet toalla and then drying them off with her ruffled delantal, to reveal their pastel green shell. Lita replaced the blood-soaked apple box with a freshly prepared nido made from a Ruby

Red grapefruit box. The sun shone into the nido at the bottom. Lita wiped her forehead with the back of her hand in relief and slowly backed away from the gallinero. Sliding her chanclas backwards through the thin dirt, Lita walked to the empty rocking chair on the porch and sat down. "Gracias a dios," Lita whimpered. "Si, comadre. Gracias a dios." Las comadres sat on the porch.

"We waited and waited, Sol, for la pinche Sofia to come back."

Finally, as the lowest tip of the South Texas sun hit the horizon of woods surrounding the rancho, Lita's most fierce gallina came swooping in to warm her liberated eggs. Lita exhaled slowly and let the tightness of her muscles drop like a noodle under her bata. Simultaneously, Lita Eva pulled out her green pañuelo, a pinch of tobacco and a disobedient little rolling paper. Slowly, while studying each of Sofia's movements she placed the pinch of leaves into the papelito, pinched the edges, twisted her fingers together in front of her mouth, lifted the cigarette to her bottom lip, extended her tongue and slid it across the paper. Lita did this without breathing and without looking down at her cigarette. With a final twist and one strike of a match against the windowsill behind her, she took a deep, long drag of her cigarette, and fell to her knees from the chair onto the dusty, cracked porch.

"¡Y nunca se levantó!"

Sol was in a daze, looking out the window. Virg, tapped Sol's knee.

"Fue como una telenovela, Sol."

"Wow, comadre Virginia, are you okay?"

"Pues sí, she was better off away from all the heat. I brought her into the shade and wrapped up her cigarro with intentions of making an offering."

"What happened to the offering."

"Pues, tú sabes, your familia didn't want to do a ceremony. They wanted a traditional Catholic mass con priest y todo."

Sol looked out the window at the flat horizon and counted the random corn fields and orange orchards that popped up. Virg exhaled loudly out her half-open window.

"Wow. That's a lot of information to digest. Do you mind if I take a little nap while you drive."

"Yeah, mija. You can sleep while I drive. Get it? The song? Tracy Chapman."

"Yes, Virg. I get it." Paloma smiled, leaned her face onto the warm window and closed her eyes.

Virg slowed her tires down over the roll of loose gravel under them. "We're here, mija. Wake up." The dust rising from under her tires came into the truck cab but Virg's eyes didn't flinch. Sol felt a tickle in her throat. The truck finally came to a stop, slanted slightly up where Virg carelessly rolled over the wood track-tie aligning the dirt road and separating the street from the small front yards and cinder block homes.

"I'll be back en un ratito. Okay, mija?"

"Back, *here?*" Sol felt disoriented and lost, unaware of what to do from here.

"What do I do?"

"Go in. Walk around. Take your time."

"Can I text you when I'm done."

Virg squished her lips together like two pieces of bread.

"Mija, your Tia Virg don't text."

Sol felt even more lost. It was at least 100 degrees outside. Lita's house stood alone and the brilliant mint green paint Sol remembered was dusted with gray, peeling off in places revealing the original orange paint underneath it. A white burro tied onto a wooden bus stop post cried out.

"There's a bull!"

"Sí, mija, there is a lot of bull here, but that's just a burro, city girl!" Sol stepped down out of the truck. Alarmed by the loud screech from the heavy door she laughed. Then reached in, grabbed her red backpack, swung it over her shoulder, slammed the heavy baby blue metal door with both hands and leaned into the empty space where there was supposed to be a window.

"How long are you going to leave me here with this burro?"

Virg smiled even larger and swayed her head from side to side. She leaned over to the window sill and placed her brown, thick, wrinkled hand on Solitaria's fingers clinging over the door frame.

"Voy a levantar un copal blanco. Then, I'll be back."

"Okay, Tía Virg. But I won't be here that long."

"I won't be that long either. After the copal, I'm just going by the farmacia to pick up some alcohol verde. Real quick."

Through the truck cab, Solitaria saw the corner of her Lita Eva's house. A white, lace curtain blew through the busted kitchen window out into the wind. Sol didn't know what she was going to do while Virginia went to the botánica up the road, but she asked for this trip across the Chalan so now she had to face the spirit of her Lita. Virginia slid her butt across the bench seat, closer to Sol. She reached out and cupped her chin in her hand the way Solitaria remembered her mami Flora used to do.

"Vas a estar bien, mija. Nomás tienes miedo de los fantasmas."

"Are there ghosts here?"

"Solitaria, no te preocupes. Tu abuelita's ghost está contigo, no matter where you are." Sol looked behind both of her shoulders.

"You'll be right back, right?" Sol was scared but didn't want to come off as being a baby.

"Sí, mija. Go say goodbye to your Lita's house. I'll be back."

Sol grabbed the straps of her backpack hanging over her shoulders and pulled her chin from Virg's hand. Before Sol could change her mind, Virginia was gone. Only a cloud of dust was left floating in the air where the truck once was. A hairless bird that Sol couldn't decide was a gallina or a duck stood tall and skinny on top of an old dusty toilet leaning in the corner of the neighboring yard. She stared at the hairless figure, perplexed. The sweet, peppery smell of cilantro blew between the lines of hanging clothes swinging with each push of wind from the coast. The nostalgic smell jerked her back into the reality of why she came to her abuelita's house in the first place, to say hello, goodbye and sorry for not coming back to visit after so many years.

Most of the house was ransacked. The beveled mirror once hanging from a golden chain in the living room was on the floor against the wall, missing a corner shattered into tiny sparkles at her feet among dust balls. Bobby pins and several dehydrated flies that looked like they suffered a bad landing scattered on the floor in the abandoned home. Mami was too sick to be part of the family battle over which hermana would keep the house and Tia Chita insisted it should be left to her because she took care of Sol's Lita the longest. The truth was, Tía Chita moved back in with Sol's abuelita after losing her job and her roommate, but didn't take care of her at all, unless you call sleeping there some nights proper care of an old abuelita. Sol didn't think her tía deserved the house but felt worse that she didn't do anything while she was hiding away in San Antonio to help her Lita Eva.

"If you tell your grandma about you liking girls, she will drop dead, so please Sol, keep your mouth shut." Chon's words over the phone to Sol when she called home to let her parents know she was safe and not coming back to Mission. He frightened her to the marrow in her bones. She never told her Abuelita Eva, and she never saw her before her death.

A gallo clucked in the distance and Sol wondered why, way out here, en México, a ki-ki-ri-ki roared every hour, instead of just in the morning. Did they know something we didn't know? Was their call some kind of prophetic message? Or, were they just mimicking the church bells? She laughed and felt the warmth of her abuelita's presence. The memory of her voice materialized, cursing at the "pinche gallo," she used to call with her hand swatting flies out in front of her face when it was too hot, and she had enough of Abuelito's late nights out at the baile. Sol slid her feet across the smooth gray cement front porch, flipped open the swing door and stuck her old key in the knob, hoping to find it still worked. At the pressure of her key, the door opened up on its own.

The hot wind blew a tart orange peel fragrance through the back screened-in porch that soaked up the entire house. Sol could see the dust particles floating among themselves through the sun pouring in. She kicked a small brown trash bag with her foot by accident. There was a little weight in the bag that made Sol curious so she reached down and picked it up, uncurled the closed-top edge and found her favorite childhood bar soap, Rosa Venus, tattered but still protected in the box and untouched. Under wood scraps and countless yellowed issues of *El Mañana*, Sol found a couple tubes of paint and a pair of leather lace-up boots. She kicked up the periódicos hoping to find at least one picture left behind by her abuelita.

Arriving in her Lita's bedroom, out the window she witnessed the view her mami used to always talk about. A tall arched galvanized steel entrance gate, reading Los Ebanos Cemetery was close enough to throw a rock at. Her abuelita chose this room as hers for the perfect view of her mami y papi, sus abuelos y sus bisabuelos. As she approached the window, her knee ran into the halfway-pulled out drawer or her 'Lita's vanity and her eye caught the light coming in through the crack in the bottom of the drawer. Inside the drawer, she fingered a soft tela. Wrapped in a green and yellow flower-print pañuelo, Sol slowly unfolded each corner to find a cigarette, blackened at the edge, a tattered leather pouch of almost burgundy colored tobacco, and an envelope of transparent rolling papers. She knew the yellowing cigarette was wound, licked and sucked by her buried Lita Eva, right before falling to death.

She pictured her at her vanity, smoking, watching the aire blow dead spirits into the window. The wind came in at Sol's face and she forced herself to imagine spirits circling her torso. She shut her eyes halfway, trying to force her imagination to materialize her Lita's espíritu right beside her, but only light and specks of dirt circled around her.

Before the next gallo cluck, Sol ran out the front door, down the dusty, broken road to the cementerio. The sky was still overcast. The sun found its way to blare through the clouds and the tombstones were massive blocks of cement with life-size vírgenes y estátuas de San Antonio y Jesús. Almost every tumba had a white cement bench that was smooth and warm to the touch. Sol drug her fingers against each tumba as she walked through the tight maze, over dead flowers, ribbons, melted candles in pink, yellow, baby blue and white, deflated balloons and plastic roses rained with imitation glistening teardrops, as fresh as the first day they were never picked.

Solitaria decided the only way she'd be able to face her mami without her Lita would be with a flawless sky, the kind that hovered over her head in the Rio Grande Valley after the hurricane moved on, surprisingly blue and crisp. With Lita's recovered cositas at her side in the bag, a squished metal tube of paint smothered in her palm, and a daydream behind her eyes, she laid her heavy body down on a cement bench belonging to another one of the dead at the cemetery, and enjoyed the burnt stench of Lita's hand rolled cigarette already lit once before and the blue sky above her. She felt peace finally knowing her Lita Eva had Virg with her during her last days. The air filled with sweat, citrus, onions and dust must have been just like this the day Virg found her on her back.

Solitaria felt the heat permeating onto her skin from the sun, through her clothes from the sky and from the hot stone under her. She regretted not being here to defend what her Lita wanted and enjoyed the pillow of multicolored plastic flowers beside her Lita's tomb on their side. This was her last nap with her Lita Eva and their only smoke together. The singing Chalan rope whistled against the steel pulley for the ninth time today. Her Lita's spirit was there and Virg was probably near.

The old woman slapped her calloused hand on the outside of her car door. "Ya, es tiempo."

An excerpt from the novel, *Cortinas de Lluvia*, Anel I. Flores, Jaded Ibis Press, February 2024.

Ode to mi hermana, Irena — 1989

Juliana Aragón Fatula

Then you whispered in my ear,
Live the Golden Rule
You'll always be blessed.
I pushed your wheelchair up the hill.
You pretended not to be in pain
Grey pallor and sunken eyes
In your cheap chemo wig.
Your beauty like a perfect day
Your love, the sky-sigh you hear,
But can't see
Beneath this abode of gods.

From the author's unpublished manuscript *Chingona Corn Mother: A Spiritual Memoir*

Letter #3, To My Brother
Carolina Monsivais

Dear brother/mi hermano,

I try not to think of myself years ago there
collapsed on a hotel floor when my back

finally splintered. A dark pain sucked
every breath and pierced every movement.

Walking became a matter of will. My son's
cries that day, a pearled guilt that guts

my memory and chokes me still. Every pill
I counted after, like the ones you hid.

I considered keeping all of my selves from
waking because I felt an inconvenience to love

and be loved. And I loathed the face a husband
saved only for me. It was the patriarchy

that kept me alive. Can you believe that?
I would be damned if anyone else were

to raise my son. I do not like to write this
because it would be deemed too

sentimental. Neither the poet nor the historian
wants to bear that accusation.

But, my brother, when I saw my son's cocooned
heartbeat pulsing on a screen, I knew he was

my destiny and I was his. Until you find
a tether to live even broken, this can be just

enough. Maybe I should have told you this.

death runs in my blood
Petra Salazar

aunt tita sits straight up
an empty-eyed omen
in her casket full of dirt

plumped & powdered skin
tortillas mourned & charred
over seasoned iron flame

all of my ancestors
have died by death

i cannot disown it
i stink of compost
rattle of bone

something old
passed down
under white gowns
clouded iris crystal
hoarded heirlooms
a spinster's estate sale
with newspaper stacks
& euthanized cats

in my panty drawer
a collection of baby teeth
a rusty copper IUD
lengths of cut hair
my father's right eye
rolling around in a box
willed to my child

El Pozo
Amanda Rosas

No one thought to check the pozo. The well, abandoned to calamity and the elements, a squatter of strategic solitude somewhere along the property lines of the ranch. An inverse reflection of life. There it sat staring at the sky blankly, necessarily.

My mother came with her family to the ranch each summer to live with her grandfather and his sisters. I can hear her comprehensive sigh of relief to see the untamed space of savage overgrowth that could honor and embrace her energy. Her feet must have traveled wildly acre after acre, the bottoms dusted and gray with the dirt of The Border. Her small sunshiney frame bouncing in full liberty each burst of day, as she danced to the chicharras' soft percussion and the voice of cricket choir.

She was the youngest, and the one who challengingly disobeyed the elders. She never could resist the warm, fried cinnamon of buñuelos, and so she ate them out of turn, knowing a nalgada awaited. She indulged like a magical magpie, smiling through shut eyes, time and again. Her indifference to punishment earned her something deeper than a reputation for disobedience, something more scarring, like rebelión encarnada.

So when she complained that her stomach was all knots and pain and too cramped and twisted to eat, they blamed the buñuelos and the peanut butter and all the secret foods she'd devoured that were twirling like mangroves in her gut. When she vomited, the tías claimed God was avenging her for her sins and cravings. Still, no one bothered to look inside the belly of the pozo.

Then the aunts themselves began to feel the calambre, and headed conspicuously to the outhouse with bundles of cornhusks clasped desperately in their hands. Then my mother's mother and father, followed by her brothers and sister were clutching panzas, and the rancho swelled with the rotting of illness and the smells of sour foods. Everyone lay drenched in the sweat of South Texas heat, questioning the collectivity of their illness.

It was then that someone decided the pozo was suspect. My mother's grandfather, who had legendarily once been a Mexican vigilante, marched with the ranch hands to inspect the well. The wood cover was removed bearing the pozo's abundant water source…and a bloated, floating, filthy yet somehow serene corpse of an unknown man whose decay was poisoning anyone who needed long gulps of hydration in the high heat of summer.

No one tells how the pozo was purified or when they fully trusted its water again. And no one knows why a man lay sepulchered in the rancho's water well, his eyes reflecting the claroscuro of earthly living. Some say it was an attempt at an equalizing revenge from Grandpa's days as Mexican police. By summer's end, the tías were a little less round and a little more giving of their bendiciones. Especially to the little girl, who confronted mortality so unexpectedly one transient summer where life became less about mischief and more about the erosion of secrets, slowly sinking incognito in the family well.

My Myth at my Brother's Wake
Carolina Monsivais

Her spine-twisting howl broke
from my body
my hand hovered over my chest
and ridges rose

a river cut through
and gave her ground to wander
because every Chicana needs
space for her own Llorona

on one side the father hushes her howls
on the other her mother whispers unleash

she releases and breaks everyone in the room
that is her myth

she undoes every part of myself
and makes me spend every
year getting to know the person
grief made of me

Coyota Kingdom
Aimée Medina Carr

Tell me where you were raised, and I'll tell you who you are.
— Levi Romero[22]

I became a genealogy junkie after I wrote my second book, *Wisdom Keepers*. My poeta, prima / hermanita Juliana, warned me:

"Be careful, comadre. Once you start, it's addictive; you'll be on the computer, and hours will flit away," she said over the phone when I called to ask her to send me what she had compiled of our ancestors. She started the family search about six months before me.

"Give me all you got," I won't risk being labeled a pretendian. If I write about Indigenous wisdom, I need our heritage and origin stories documented to show how they shaped us." We said our goodbyes, hung up, and later that evening, she emailed a six-page document with generations of grandparents' names, dates, and places of birth. It kickstarted the search for our ancestral roots.

I did this process to use a crass phrase of my father's: *ass-backward*. I spent the year pre-pandemic writing inspirational essays celebrating our rich, Native culture. Then I read a barrage of vitriol and nasty, ruthless attacks toward those claiming to be of Indigenous heritage, writers, scholars, musicians, etc., on Twitter and other social media websites. I needed solid proof of my Indian lineage. It took over a year *and continues* as I discover new family history. I became my own archeologist; websites and books contain information not commonly known about my ancestors. The digging of data inspired the historical novel that I'm currently researching. The working title is *Coyota Kingdom.*

I got busy and lucky. I found the New Mexico Genealogical Society and participated in a weekend Zoom workshop. They provided helpful websites to find pertinent info about my grandparents and great-grandparents. Family Search software works like a charm (and is free). After typing in three or four sets of grandparents, the next set appears automatically. On some sides of the family tree, it worked up to the tenth

22 From *Querencia*, Levi Romero, University of New Mexico Press, 2020.

generation of great-grandparents!

I was elated and relieved because I had no idea what I was doing. The information given is names, places, dates of birth, baptisms, marriages, and the children's names. Some profiles listed history, photos, and memories, but not all. It was difficult to detect actual Indigeneity, which required more detective work. Later, I got better at reading clues and researching family names and birth locations.

The New Mexico Genealogical Society has a program that collaborates with Family TreeDNA. A saliva test determines the exact percentages of DNA genetics. My mitochondrial DNA is Haplogroup A2. Mitochondrial DNA is passed down from mothers to their daughters. Haplogroup A2 is common among Native Americans.

I'm a Native daughter of southern Colorado. The most surprising discovery in the ancestry search was that *all of my family's ancestors* were from New Mexico. Our family trees linked back to ten and eleven generations of **Nuevomejicanos**. I've traced my antepasados roots back to the 1600s and to the "first families" of Nuevo Mejico — the ambiguous heritage of Indigenous territoriality and European sovereignty.

While writing my debut novel, *River of Love*, my ancestors gave me a miraculous and mysterious gift. I had a visitation, a sighting of my ancestors (Indians) on a Sierra Nevada Mountain ridge while skiing on a bright, bluebird winter's day. They led me to reveal stories that *deserve* a voice. We have been dismissed in the history department. Women especially are missing from historical pages, monuments, and at every level of narrative significance.

I write stories that focus on women. The antepasados' history was a hushed secret complicated by the imperial transition of the U.S. conquest. The evil secret that haunts my ancestors is slavery — a taboo and uncomfortable subject no one wants to discuss. It is easier to erase the fact than to admit that this country was built on slavery. As citizens, we can't discuss genocide and then claim how great we are.

The systematic destruction of the Indigenous Peoples' entire way of life is one of history's most shameful and greatest tragedies. The decimation of our culture continues with truth denied in history lessons and textbooks. The government refuses to deal with the cruel past because it would shed light on longstanding racism, mistreatment, and economic neglect, which prevents the necessary healing.

A glimmer of hope in 2023, the state of California signed into law the California Indian Education Act. School districts are to work with local Native American tribes to develop history lessons for students. It's a start, but there's a long way to go to rectify the injustice and prejudice we have suffered from the lack of knowledge and respect given to our Indigenous population.

Parents are asked, "Where do we come from, and who are our people from many generations back?" And if they don't answer directly, find out for yourself before family members die and can't answer your questions. There's so much value in first-hand experience and memory. Also, photographs, letters, and even family keepsakes can tell a story about a time and its people.

When I was growing up, my dad's family told us that we were Ute and Apache Indians. They gave no tribal affiliations or proof of enrollment. And when pushed, they would say, "That's all you need to know."

My college professor uncle was the first to discover the Genízaro connection. He wrote a book about it, but when struck with dementia, it was lost. I received confirmation after a serendipitous stumble upon a cousin on my mother's side of the family — primo Bernardo Gallegos, an 18th and 19th-century New Mexican history scholar and sociology professor who spent a lifetime educating about our people's postcolonial hybridity due to slavery. Through personal stories, he tried to make sense of the identity conflicts outside the "tribal" paradigm of not belonging to a specific tribe where Native American identity tribal membership has permeated the dominant culture.

Both sides of my family's ancestral roots are entwined with the Genízaro — detribalized Plains Indians kidnapped and sold at a young age by Spaniards in colonial New Mexico. It made it impossible for the Genízaro descendants to maintain any form of ethnic identity over the centuries. A term used for mixed-blood ancestry of Indian and Spanish was Coyote(a), also Mestizo(a). These terms defined the generations of Nuevomejicanos — Indo-Hispanos of New Mexico. Genízaros and their descendants have created a new category and demographic of people in the political, social, economic, and culture of New Mexico and the United States.

I identify as a Coyota, and the stories I've discovered reflect the strong, resilient women who survived and established communities that worked together under extreme and adverse conditions in New Mexico. Ancestors give us agency — their blood coursing through our veins is our credentials.

I dislike Western civilization's cultural amnesia and blindness toward silenced and unheard voices of women and choose to focus on these courageous first settlers and pioneers of Nuevo Mejico. *Mujeres muy mujeres.*

Maria Pascuala Bernal (1583-1626) found herself at the intersection of two distinct cultures when she and her husband, Juan Griego I, came north from Mexico between 1598 and 1601 with the Juan de Oñate expedition that included several hundred soldiers.

The colonists were disappointed by the lack of silver and gold in New Mexico. They called this desolate place *the land of misery*, and many deserted. By 1608, only fifty Spanish soldiers with their families stayed among the thousands of Indians. Juan Griego was from Greece. Pascuala's family were Aztec Indians from the Valley of Mexico.

The village of Bernalillo (little Bernal) is a town near Albuquerque named after my 10th Great-Grandmother. North of Bernalillo is the Pueblo of San Juan. In January of 1599, the men were away arresting the Indians that killed 12 colonists. Pascuala Bernal, Doña Eufemia de Sosa Peñalosa, and twenty-two other armed women took to the rooftops to defend the Pueblo.

Doña Eufemia de Sosa Peñalosa embarked on the epic eight-week sea voyage from Spain to Mexico with her husband, Francisco. She was a rarity as few women came from Spain, resulting in many soldiers marrying Indian women who acculturated into the Spanish culture.

She rallied the soldiers when morale was low during the long journey on the Camino Real De Tierra Adentro with Juan de Oñate's expedition. Many women in this era demonstrated that power is not always tragic *and grows by giving, not taking.* They built communities, new myths, stories, and configurations for the betterment of future generations. Doña Eufemia isn't an ancestor but is worthy of being included in *Coyota Kingdom.*

My aforementioned primo Bernardo Gallegos and I shared a common ancestor in Doña Josefa de Hinojos, a Zuni Pueblo Coyota, and sister of Ventura, War Captain of the Zuni from the village of Holona. She is my maternal seventh Great-Grandmother.

Another descendant is Doña Inés, a Tano Indian of the Pueblo of San Cristóbal, who was captured in 1591 during the Gaspar Castaño expedition. She became the matriarch of the Martín Serrano (Martinez) family in New Mexico. She had a child with Hernán Martín Serrano, a Zacatecan, one of the soldiers who came with Juan de Oñate in 1598. She is my ninth Great-Grandmother.

The Spanish soldiers called New Mexico tierra de guerra, *the land of war.* They defended against hostile bands of nomadic Apaches, Navajos, and Comanches. Drought, famine, pestilence, and the constant lack of food and supplies produced a harsh existence. Our descendants were made of tough grit and perseverance. We build on their sacrifices and owe it to them to be radically responsible ancestors for future generations. Our antepasados work through us: *we are their wishes and dreams come true.* We are the result of the love of thousands and are all walking family trees. Love is the power beyond power.

Here are a few free resources to aid in the search for your family's genealogy. Use a simple family tree template to list the names of a couple of generations of grandparents from your mother and father's families. *The more, the better.* The New Mexico Genealogical Society is a dedicated and talented group that donates time to help make family connections of Nuevomejicanos — *we are all primas y hermanas!* Please support them by becoming a member. They have a list of resources and articles on their website. Webtrees of the Great New Mexico Pedigree Database is another invaluable resource, as is Family Search.

Facebook has numerous genealogical groups: A favorite is Gary De Leon's Descendants of the Oñate Expedition, which includes countless Indigenous groups (usually listed by tribe).

José Antonio Esquibel is a genealogical researcher, historian, and author of articles on Spanish colonial genealogy and history, particularly seventeenth-century New Mexico. Estevan Rael-Gálvez was awarded a Mellon Foundation grant to oversee *Native Bound — Unbound Archive of the Indigenous Enslaved —* a digital project centered on millions of Indigenous people whose lives have been shaped by slavery.

During this profound, fulfilling, albeit perplexing search for my origins, I was clueless that all of my ancestors were from New Mexico. I was born and raised in southern Colorado, as were my parents, grandparents, and great-grandparents. As wealthy white ranchers bought up all the land and water rights in New Mexico, our families migrated to Colorado to look for jobs.

Research shows that when children learn about family history, it keeps them healthy and happy. The world is better when it's common knowledge that we are all related, which helps reduce racism. We hunger to know our heritage, who we are, and where we come from. We want to be remembered and honored, as do our ancestors.

We are still here.

Ancestral Mathematics
To be born, you needed:

2 parents
4 grandparents
8 great-grandparents
16 second great-grandparents
32 third great-grandparents
64 fourth great-grandparents
128 fifth great-grandparents
256 sixth great-grandparents
512 seventh great-grandparents
1,024 eighth great-grandparents
2,048 ninth great-grandparents

For you to be born today from twelve previous generations,
you needed a total of 4,094 ancestors over the last 400 years.

The centuries of Love and heartbreak, pain, sorrows, triumphs, joy,
victories, failures, creation, and destruction the ancestors had
to live through to produce the *miracle of you.*
In many ways, the past remains our present *when your children
find their history in your face.* We represent what life can be.

*"Scientifically, it's been proven that humans are one people. The color of our
ancestors' skin and, ultimately, my skin and your skin is a consequence of
ultraviolet light from latitude and climate. Despite our sad conflicts here
in the U.S., there really is no such thing as race. We are one species, much
more alike than different. We all come from Africa. We are all of the same
stardust. We are all going to live and die on the same planet, a pale blue dot
in the vastness of space. We have to work together."* — Bill Nye[23]

23 Source: https://lyricalzen.com/ancestral-mathematics/

Fog
Alma Luz Villanueva

Teen breakdancing, backward
flips immense energy traffic
stop, he bows such grace
light changes, people hand him

pesos, if I were there I'd smile
BRAVO hand his spirit 200
pesos at least enough four
meals street stands sabroso

taquitos- as I eat nice place with
fountain behind me, a familia
passes me, "Provecho" enjoy eat,
each one smiles of joy "Gracias"

I say- my casita, fields, a horse
grazes, the peace of beauty,
jasmine scent, monarchs resting
their flight, young man with 5 year

old son brushes the horse gently,
talking laughing, son's eyes of wonder,
lifted to horse's back, father leads
them home home home in

Mexico- I carry enough pesos the
grandmother's hands out, they bless
me, equal exchange, I tip a waiter
50 pesos he places it to his corazøn

"Gracias" "De Nada" small gestures that
tell me I'm home home home in
Mexico- 60 Minutes Ukraine man, he
his wife, two small sons in car,

Russian tank blast his wife, two small
sons bleeding no life, his left leg hanging
by skin, crawls out, watches his familia
burn, he weeps openly this man, I

weep with him, "Why" he asks weeping
"Why"- these are moments photos of my
Time, I at home counting small gestures
"Gracias" "De nada"

*   *   *

Dawn fog the fields, trees, marvelous
hills, white cranes, eagles, monarchs,
humans gone, this time gone, I
exist in no time breath by breath,
no war, no hunger, no Russian tanks,
no husband father weeping "Why?"
I exist only in
small gestures
this gift of
fog

Manuela Monzón de Mendoza, The Poet
Isabella Santana

Chica tells me that
her mother was a poet
>>she had it all:
>>the dead husband
>>the alcohol addiction
>>the insanity
>what is my talent, then
>generational gift?
>generational curse?
>>when I was little,
>>Chica would tell me stories
>>of her mother–
>>the beatings
>>how grief grabbed her by the neck–
>>stuffed her into
>>a bottle,
and dragged her away
until she couldn't handle her
existence.
>>I am eerily similar to
>>Manuela Monzón de Mendoza.
>>the insanity,
>>the fragile balance between
>>tolerating existence and
>>tormenting myself to death
so I google search: *how do you break generational patterns*
it seems as if nobody has the answer.

>>Manuela Monzón de Mendoza
>>you are the shadow I cannot shake off
>>you are part of me, through history.
>>I will never be able to escape
>>you, but god, oh god
>>I will certainly try

When Your Grandmother was First Named

Lorna Dee Cervantes

When your grandmother was first named
mine was a slave, working for a line
in the census. "Savage Wench" they called her.
Christened after the saint in the mission
that once housed her people. She was named
for her prison, her relatives' bones
adobed in its walls. She was
all alone. A small band on the run —
all dead now, but her, the eldest
of seven sisters. Seven Sisters
like the stars they descended from.
My grandmother was a mute
survivor, never telling
who her mother was, even
to me, a descendent
to the dead, the massacred,
the slain seed. When your grandmother
was first named mine rode her horse
to escape her naming. Going deep
into the land to discover
her word.

III
SOMOS
FLOWERS & FRUITS

"To be Xicana is everything. From this breath to my last breath. It is politica, cultura, and espiritu. It is to be, to embody, to speak, and to live knowing I am Indigenous. No matter what I write or speak about, it is always rooted and nourished by being Xicana."

ire'ne lara silva, 2023 Texas Poet Laureate

Poema de Fuego
Diana Pando

Ember eyes flicker
On the fifth day she ate fire
humo negro
chokes you back into being

Candle cracked by heat

Throw papelitos into the fire
With your name on them
You wonder if i am a blessing or a curse

Cover me in copal, romero y alcohol de maguey

They whisper: *que mala bruja*
Others yell: *¡quema la bruja!*

A wildfire of palabras burning

Throw a papelito into the fire with my name on it

Soy tu poema escrito en fuego

Sometimes, we burn
and eat our own ashes

Con poesía
Xánath Caraza

Con **poesía** disipamos
los tiempos oscuros.

Palabras que sanan
los aislados corazones.

Fluye, poesía, entre
las nubes cibernéticas.

Trae pensamientos curativos,
pequeñas **dosis de alegría**.

Sé la medicina para este corazón sin luz,
para esta **sangre** que aún palpita.

Artificiales pulsaciones como
flores se tatúan en la pantalla.

Como **dulce música** que nos baña,
que nos trae dorada felicidad.

With Poetry

With **poetry** we disperse
times of darkness.

Words that heal
isolated hearts.

Flow, poetry, amidst
cybernetic clouds.

Bring healing thoughts,
small **doses of joy**.

Be the medicine for this heart devoid of light,
for this **blood** that continues to flow.

Artificial pulsations like
flowers are tattooed across the screen.

Like **sweet music** that bathes us,
that brings us golden happiness.

Preparing to Explode
Carmen Tafolla

I hear your vientre growl with hunger
your jaguar soul searching for something more
your mirada filled with all the fierceness of black night sky
and the heat of stubborn stars burning siglo after siglo
refusing to disappear
or dim their fire

These stars in your visión are our velas eternas
our esperanzas intent on seeking salud
intent on the long-denied justicia
intent on letting you be your real jaguar powerful you

I am not fooled by your silencio
though sometimes others are
Your silence is full of story
a grito that can no longer be contained
Unwilling to whisper permitted sound bites at permitted moments
within set limits   set by others   and then restrained
Your voice is ready to explode with power
Your courage aching pa' abrirse to its full red bloom

Mija   recuerda   deep in our veins queda la historia
Somos guerreras   We do not swallow injusticia
Sin miedo   Sin dudar   Con mucha paz   y mucho amar
We will arm ourselves with our dignidad
with our courage or our copal
or our vote   or our vecindad
We will throw molcajetes if we have to
or even more dangerous   we will use words
Words of power   Words of truth   Words of compassion
Palabras pa' curar

Do you hear the low growl now, Mija?
A ronca purr right below your skin
It is our history chiming in   It is our vision for justicia   al fin
It is our grito   preparing to explode
fiercer than the jungle of injustice through which we forge our soft paths
with strength of spirit and strength of truth
It is our voice, our story, our power,
our curandera's curación

Ahmo Nimahui | No tengo miedo | I Am Not Afraid
Axolotita

Sometimes, we do not remember
we are the seeds of our ancestors.
Se nos olvidó,
que florecimos mucho antes de que nuestros pulmones sintieran el
primer aire.
Ahmo nimahui

Sometimes, we do not remember
that we must build community for our roots to thrive.
Se nos olvidó,
porque nos robaron nuestra identidad, la cual fue sepultada junto a
nuestras historias en el infierno de Dante.
Ahmo nimahui

Sometimes, we do not remember
that we are the world and the world is us.
Se nos olvidó,
que el mañana se construyó con lo que hicimos el día de hoy.
Ahmo nimahui

Sometimes, we do not remember
that the promise of life is death.
Se nos olvidó,
que nuestras almas siguen viviendo a través de nuestro amor o nuestras
culpas.
Ahmo nimahui

Sometimes, we do not remember
that we are descendants of warriors.
Y se nos olvidó,
la magia de nuestra resiliencia, la cual siempre lucha en encontrar
nuestra paz.
Ahmo nimahui

she said she didn't know how to make medicine

ire'ne lara silva

but i do   i know how to make medicine what else
was i given life for i have been watching and
learning whispering and praying   breathing and
weeping   living and living and living

and breaking my skin and breaking my eyes and
breaking my heart and breaking my thoughts
grinding down the fragments in a molcajete made of
what survives when a star explodes

so many drops of my blood in this   so many drops
of my bile   so many drops of my tears this is what
no one tells you   that there is medicine you can
make of yourself no green leaves no blossoms

we are in the place where there are no recipes no
instructions   but where you must walk gently on
the earth and clear your eyes and do no harm and
break none of the laws of medicine

do you see it's taken everything everything i am
and every second of what i've lived to even begin to
learn my heart has died and my heart has died and
my heart has died and i keep breathing

medicine lives under my skin and in my eyes and in
my tongue and in my breath i know how to make
medicine i speak medicine i walk medicine i am
becoming i am making myself medicine

First published in *the eater's of flowers*, ire'ne lara silva, Saddle Road Press, 2004
(Reprinted with permission from Saddle Road Press)

Coyolxauqui
Claudia Meléndez Salinas

Even when you're fractured
You are whole

Coyolxauqui II

Guerrera
dismembered

por las batallas
contra la migra

el IRS, the Department of Corrections
el Fentanyl y el meth

Running breathlessly
spinning, eternally in motion

woman of bells and snakes
serrated limbs

swimming, drowning
on a crimson whirlpool

Guerrera entera
en encrucijada

aligned with Orion
for the winter solstice

at the crossroads
of what is possible

axis mundi
por donde circulan

las fuerzas del universo
laughing at la migra y el IRS

aún

Martha Alicia Rivas Maravilla

aún cansadísima
de todo aquello,
I birth
strength
to
dream,
love,
fight,
for
us.

On June 29, 2023, the U.S. Supreme Court issued a long-awaited decision addressing the legality of race-conscious affirmative action in college admissions programs in *Students for Fair Admissions, Inc.* This poem was composed in response to this ruling on Affirmative Action.

Los pajaritos
Christiane Williams-Vigil

One thousand miles between a classroom seat
and the place they call home.
The roar of migration and the never-ending span of merciless desert.
These are my people.
Hungry for safety.
Our children forcibly tossed into iron cages
or pinched by bear traps left by men in green uniforms.
Here, they come to my classroom
to learn the difference between *here* as in
'you can stay here'
and *hear* as in
'open your heart and hear my words.'
My classroom is sacred.
Here, no hands will take them into the night.
Here, it is alright to rest their heads on a desk.
I will drown out the shouts that say 'send them back.'
I will hold the door open so more can come to make nests.
For birds are meant to move with the changing season.

My Daughter Begins Her Flight
Elisa A. Garza

Early spring in Houston, sunny with cool breezes from the West, not yet sultry. On days that do not rain, my toddler and I walk around the block, noticing which trees are leafing that super bright green, which are no longer new, already faded. Azaleas are bursting their pinks and birds are chattering branch to branch. Rather than hold my hand, my daughter, wearing her favorite pink vestido, pushes her doll Rosa in a little pink stroller, as I once pushed her in the big green carriola. Every now and then, the tiny stroller wheels stop short on the uneven squares of concrete, and m'ija lifts her carriola up, keeps going. Then, she stops walking, her arms flapping; she believes they are her wings, that she is a bird, and that she is flying, her little legs hopping unevenly on the sidewalk, one folded up and the other straight down, flamenco-style. Doll and stroller forgotten, her mouth opens in the smile that dimples her cheeks while she chirps and caws. (She does not cuu like her namesakes, palomas we listen to as they nest in the eaves of the house.) Her long hair, front pieces pulled behind into a miniature ponytail that sits atop the back of her head, waves up and down with each hop, like the curved neck of a preening flamingo, her flopping dress a swish of color, the bird's bright tail feathers. I am the mama bird watching her leave the nest, one empty hand, one lift of the stroller, one crooked little hop, one little flutter of wings at a time.

Piel canela mía

Isabel Cerero

Que chistoso es odiarte ahora.
De niña nunca supe lo hermosa que eras:
besada por el calor del sol,
con poderes de princesas Aztecas,
sensualidad de diosas.
¿Pero como pude ver lo preciosa que eras,
sí era pecado enamorarme de la prietura?
¡Esa niña se merecía todas las disculpas del mundo!
O por lo menos alguien que le hubiera dicho
que no tenía tenerle miedo a su piel,
que brillaba más que nadie bajo los rayos,
que la vida no es para esconderse de la luz.

When I Wince
Xochitl-Julisa Bermejo

"You are tattooed on the soft/round/parts of me"
— Sonia Sanchez

In the late lamp light, you ask me
to pose. "Look here," you say,
lens pointed my way. I picture rolls
folded over rolls, but I roll
into a position anyway.
You look at the image in your hand
and mumble something like,

"I can't believe how beautiful —"
You don't finish the thought
and drop the phone so fast, I think
I must be ugly. This is what it's like
to love the tender parts of me,
a sharp point dragging hot across skin.
How long can you (or I) stand it?

After we make love, I flip on my phone
to find you sent me the image.
A six-second video of a woman soft
and round in yellow light, her smile
innocent as brown tendrils fawning
over shoulders. How do you touch
what I mean to keep hidden?

La Bailarina

Elisabeth Contreras-Moran

Her short curvy body knows how to move. Innately, purely, from deep within. Her shoulders sway, shimmy, satisfy. Her hips grind, gyrate, groove. Her feet kick, flick, trick. Her whole body twists, thrusts and twirls. She dances in the kitchen, obviously. She ay yi yis when cooking — remembering to sing, not cry, while chopping onions, all while her legs cha cha cha and slow, slow, quick, quick, two step beats. She also dances elsewhere: In grocery aisles, while choosing the perfect pepper. While walking the dog, who circles around her feet, eager to dance alongside. She stops to dance when out on a run, the bouncing beats in her ears compel her body to choreograph sounds into movement. Anywhere. Anywhere. She stops to dance when the tempo beats in her soul, blooms in her mood. She salsas her happiness, fouettes her frustrations, merengues her madness and arabesques her achievements. Her brown hands move to invisible rhythms, cradling and slithering into shapes of her cuentista spirit. Her dark, guerrera hair flips patterns around her round face whipping its frenzied, frizzied curls into the opposite of submission. Sí, she can dance her Latina. And she does. Anywhere. Everywhere.

Washing My Rebozo by Hand
Sandra Cisneros

I wash my silk *rebozo* in the shower
against my naked skin
to keep the fringe from knotting.
Fuchsia cloth draped over my shoulder,
one Amazon breast exposed.

Even folded in half, the shawl
is longer than I am tall,
fringe work grazing the floor.

For an instant, the water
spills out hot as August
when I turn on the tap,
and I regret my reckless idea
to wash the cloth myself.
bougainvillea darkens to cranberry,
but, thankfully, the color doesn't run.
Fibers slick as corn silk when rinsed.

The wet *rebozo* conforms to my skin
like dough draped over my empanada belly,
eggplant breasts, Coatlicue ass.
I admire myself in the mirror.
Some ancient memory approves.

And I think of that fool William Frawley,
of *I Love Lucy*, who said of co-star Vivian Vance,
"She has a body like a sack of doorknobs."

At fifty-six
my Buddha body
bows to gravity.
A life lived.

I am not a sack of doorknobs.

At these heights,
I like myself enough to pose
in this poem just as I am,
solid as Teotihuacán.

A woman of an age
she doesn't give a damn

what's said
by a sack of *pitos*
posing as a man.

Delta Drought
Aideed Medina

Orange-yellow moon
over the valley, over me. I left the sun
        choking on smoke.
Don't fight the tears, it is a privilege
        to have sadness to spend.

To make acid rain,
        there must be ash and water.
To love,
        there must be ash and water.

There is a drought. Reservoir dried up.
The ground clasps all its water
to the center of the lake bed.

Drive blind.
Numb.
Pull the car over on the curve
        of the mountain,
 slide down into the reservoir bed
        to reach the edge of the water.

I am tired this morning.
Aware of every single breath
        as it comes,
        as it goes.

One more day. Soon enough.
For rain,
for news that you are well,
sipping beer with pretty strangers.

I cannot breathe
      in this fire haze,
      in this grief haze.

But we do.

Making Amends to Myself for Letting Men Use Me
Xochitl-Julisa Bermejo

I apologize for not believing
        I was more than my body.

I forgive myself for not believing
        I was more than my body.

I apologize for believing
        I was ugly. For hating my belly

and big nose. My big butt and curly hair.
        I apologize

for not valuing my big butt and curly hair
        until a man deemed them desirable.

I apologize for believing all I had to offer
        was a big butt and curly hair.

I forgive myself for wanting my big butt
        and curly hair to be enough.

You, Me, We
Angela Trudell Vasquez

Circles come back
ancient rivers pour
gather movement/sway us
divine a new path
through sandstone and loam
prairie grass and rich meadows
from mountain pine tops to estuaries
the waters cleaner
no litter, no trash   floating
all people have shelter.

Thoughts river past/paths
collective wisdom
mapped in blood song baths
sounds of rushing
sisters and brothers
splash through courtrooms, classes
libraries and parks
a future laid out for the ones
who need it most,
monarch butterflies and bees
lead their best lives
human hands come together
plant edible forests
we weave we change
honor the ancestors
the animals, the wolves, the plants,
the trees   everything that sings
the sea, all living creatures with a beat
          and we breathe   we all just breathe.

Tulips
Alma Luz Villanueva

The Sacred Sixth Sun rises
Beautifully ***milagros***

Sacred Birds sing so
Sweetly ***milagros***

Sacred Eagles, White Cranes, Ravens,
Sparrows, Rainbow Butterflies, Sacred Bees
Fill Sacred Air, Sacred Sky
Flight ***milagros***

Sacred Madre Tierra Hills 7,000 feet
Hold Shadow Light Rainbow
Prophecies ***milagros***

My blooming pink-purple tulips shed
Petals, change impermanence the
Beauty of existence ***milagros***

They remind me, comfort me as
Russia invades Ukraine human
Suffering these centuries of power
Conquest the cruelties of genocide
War stored in our human DNA
Generation after generation,

One thousand years may the Rainbow
Tribes that survive these centuries of
Cruelties have no memory no DNA SUFFERING,
May they know experience change impermanence the
Beauty of
Existence ***milagros***

My wish, blessing as your ancestor, April 2022
San Miguel de Allende, México

Ancestral Song
Natalia Rivas

my heart sings
songs of tribal
sway and stomp
my feet ready
hips catching the heat
nostrils flared
my ancestors roar fierce
lions shake my soul

power wild
into the hour of groove and swirl
orishas crack the night as aztec warriors chant
rains in spain cast a somber flood
across africa and las americas
dna wrapped through the centuries
stripped from my body
glistening
hues of brown to black
branches on the tree of life

forgotten songs explode
thickly tendrils of ancestral knowledge
grasp me gratefully i surrender
as the sweet scent of smokey incense
hangs in the air

the drums
the chants
the joyful howls

i embrace each howl and feed it to my unborn children
nahual seeds a fruitful meal
youthful giggles bounce tap sway bursting

oh first mother, goddess warrior
beautiful savage buried
beneath colliding worlds
i
follow the footprints
in this ancestral journey
muddled by colonizers
plucked from the garden
in disregard staining the world
with tribal bloods for eternal forevers
shackled and stamped
chattel in brown and black

the
burning of my histories
of my gods
incantations flood my consciousness
as i howl at the moon

drums alert
drums awaken
my heart

oh, let music pour
and soak me with its lushness

celebrate my many deaths
and dance like sloppy colors
bubbling up bursting in frivolity

truths like origami
folded into birds
decided in so many words
reveal the questions
of an exiled soul
as they fly into surrender… awaken

Once Upon a Time the Future
Melinda Palacio

When her human legs turned gelatinous from non-use
and her mind found a new place to roam, the mermaid
didn't complain about the warm sea or how
sunstroke precedes death.

Rain fell but disappeared before reaching a white petal,
a green stalk, a weed, a tree. No flowers or food.
Only a screen, call it a telephone, a computer, an iPad.

Wasn't it yesterday the enviable devices provided food?
The electric mess zaps all our energy, washes it unclean.

When all else fails, remember Joni's words:
You are stardust, you are golden, and you've got to get back to the garden.[24]

24 Joni Mitchell. "Woodstock." *Ladies of the Canyon*, Joni Mitchell, Reservoir
   Media Music o/b/o Crazy Crow Music, New York, 1970.

De-Indigenized

Rosalilia M. Mendoza

Forgive me, for not knowing my native tongue.
For not practicing the thousand-year-old rituals
my grandmothers recognized like their own heartbeats.
Dirt was replaced by marble and concrete sidewalks;
my steps forgot the earth, I wish I could remember.
Seeds of wisdom fell through the drains of colonization.
Dark brown hair now dyed with golden hues of erasure.
Forgive me, for embracing alien ways as if they were my own.
Red, white, and blue cannot tuck me in at night.
Red, white, and green cannot sun-kiss me in the morning.
But I am not orphaned; I know who my mother is;
my bones have not forgotten.

Mictecacihuatl
Shavone A. Otero

Like a cloud
Neither born
Nor dead
Impermanent
Yet continuous

I swallow stars
And plant bones
Crown of obsidian butterflies
And skirt of serpents
Through wind and mountains

To Opochcalocan
Queen of Mictlan
And souls eternal

Ometeotl

Spirit World
Dulciana Rosario Corral

The hummingbird that visits me
In the east
When Tonatiuh rises
Affirming the start
Of another sacred day,
The sacredness of my ancient
Warrior ancestors,
The colors of their chimalli
Plasters the hummingbird's wings,
Fluttering with the speed of light
Using its beak to consume
The sacred substance of the
Honeysuckle
In beautiful reciprocity with Tonantzin.
I can see the energy
In perfect harmony,
Flowing between the aire
The heat radiating from the sun,
The corn of my ancestors,
The water that gives it power,
Los animales sagrados
That surround my home.

With this sacred
Energy around me,
I am rooted in Tonantzin,
I can feel the reciprocal
Energy between her and me,
I can feel the sustenance
She provides to iconehuan, her children
I see my warrior danzante ancestor
Walking with me in my journey,
Guiding me, loving me,

With the power of my people.
My ancestor
Brings me to a deep
Knowing of who I am
And reconnects me
To my purpose,
As I walk in this
Temporary human form,
That my spirit is nestled in,
Carrying the legend of
My lineage with me.

The other day I went to the beach...
Michelle Mojica

Y un llanto tan alto
Me alcanzó.
Como un huracán
Mi pecho saltaba.
Dolía tanto
Que ni podía respirar.

Alcancé mi respiro
Poco a poco
And I allowed the waves
To wash away the pain.

Porque Madre Tierra hiere,
Porque la madrecita nos quiere.
Y, aun así
Tú la hieres.

So much hurt,
So much grief:
De lxs Ancestres,
De Tonantzin.

I feel it in my throat:
Como un nudo mi garganta.

I feel it in my crown:
La presión que me aplasta.

I feel it in my chest:
So much pressure.

I feel it in my womb:
Un dolor que circula.

I feel it in my bones:
Como se me congelan.

I feel it in my Heart:
Un chingo de lamento.

I feel it in my Spirit:
Con firmeza y paciencia.

I return to be grounded
Con mis pies en la arena.
El mar sabe a sal
Y el viento me abraza.

I return to center
Entre Chalchiutlicue
Y mi hombligo.
Creating spaciousness
In this vast darkness.

Water Memory Mosaic

Angela Trudell Vasquez

Body of water
          boundary waters
                    lace the landscape.

People moved up and down the mouths
          found themselves
among the reeds, the fish, wild rice.

Mound dweller remains.

Here, see rocks stacked
how they stood   on boulder dams
speared our ancestors laying eggs,
spiraling back to their birth place.

Celebrants smoke flesh at night
sing songs of praise   prayers answered,
sustenance for the next season.
Fins ford the way home.

History in bones.

Our *cuerpos* remember I tell her
liquid memory
DNA swims in our blood
when we drink —

she, beautiful child blinks
believes me
stops running the sink.
Precious,   I say
humans over seventy percent *agua*,
water is life,

all the wet that ever was
here now *for all*, and we walk
enter the lake
splash and race
this summer day
when school is out.

How vast are we in our veins?

Pages from the Journal of La Mexicana
Loretta Carpio Carr

Valley of the Moon, California

Me llamo Augustina Juarez. Soy de Guanajuato, Mexico, pero ahora vivo en el Valle de la Luna en California. My boss doesn't like me to speak Spanish, pero no me importa. I don't care. I need to speak before I run out of time. My life has been one of servitude, but gracias a Dios, I've also ridden to the top of the mountain. I work as a maid for rich Americans. Who knows what they do for work or where they get their money, but as long as they pay me, I cook and clean and occasionally sing for centavos at la cantina.

August 1898

Mi Papá tends the animals at the Home for the Feeble Minded, the big, red brick hospital at the base of the valley en el pueblito de Glen Ellen. Probrecitos. Some residents need so much help just to survive while others seem inexplicably abandoned because of poverty or merely being pronounced undesirable by the state. Many seek refuge in the naturaleza of the fruit orchards or animal stables. Probably los animales help them feel less trapped — in their bodies, in that place.

I know the horses give me my freedom.

"Augustina, venga aquí." Mi Papá trusts me to exercise the horses. We worked together on our rancho near León where I learned as a muchachita how to approach the horses, talk to them quietly, stroke them gently, and eventually saddle them. Mi tío Miguel was a master saddle maker who took much pride in his beautiful, intricately carved saddles. I remember wanting my brown skin to have the same sculpted swirls running down my legs, so I would look like an extension of the leather seat.

I usually ride by myself on the wooded trails behind the hospital, but today Papi wants me to show one of the horses to an American woman who may be interested in buying it. I saddle the vigorous grey colt and ride at a brisk pace down the dirt road towards the village. As I approach the bridge over the creek, two white women dressed in puffy skirts stare at me in disbelief.

"Excuse me. Do you always ride like that?" one called out.

I couldn't tell if she was asking a serious question or making fun of me.

La blanca persisted. "Do you always ride like a man?"

I had never thought about it. This is the way Papi taught me to ride. I mean I've seen las americanas ride with both legs hanging over one side of the animal, but that makes no sense. Balancing acts are for the circus. No estoy con el circo, y no soy estupida.

Later that day, the curious lady bought the horse, and I soon saw her riding on the trails like a man, como yo. La señora created a big sensation, claiming to be the first female to revolutionize the traditional female sidesaddle, but she needs to trade that skirt for some pantalones.

March 1906

I've been feeling unsettled lately — not sure what it is. I wouldn't say I'm psychic, but my intuition is very strong. There are some things I just know. Even as a child I was connected to a different consciousness. Papá was a restless man, always thinking about his next move, but it was my young spirit that directed our eventual course.

I knew when it was time for us to leave Mexico because it came to me in a dream. Papá and I were walking through the fields when a cloud of dust appeared in the distance. As we stared in curiosity, the cloud grew ominously larger and darker, moving relentlessly towards us. Afraid of being trapped in the threatening haze, we turned and ran, holding hands as we fled for our lives. When I told Papi about my dream, he explained its meaning in one concise sentence.

"Keep your eye on the horizon and always have an escape plan."

He said it was time to leave for California.

That was long ago, and since then we have made our home en el Norte. I am no longer a child but a mystical woman usually at peace with myself, but today I have decided to visit la curandera Mari to treat mis nervios. She lives high in the Mayacamas Mountains, so I will spend the night at her camp among the redwoods. I have been there before, sleeping on the ground to get centered and listening to los coyotes' song to clear my ears. Mari is always calm, and she extends that stillness to me as she smudges away any bad energy with the smell of copal and a shot of mezcal.

As the saying goes, "Para todo mal, mezcal, y para todo bien, también." I needed it now for something very bad. Mi amiga, this weathered, wise woman with the hazel eyes and black braids, understands that mi dolor foretells of tragedy.

"¿Cuál es su tristeza, mija?"

"No sé, Mari. I don't know why I'm sad. I feel nervous, like something terrible is going to happen."

"Tiene susto. Vamos a hacer una limpia." A cleansing was recommended to treat my fear.

Silently, la curandera picked up several fronds of romero, rosemary as the Americans called it, and tied them together with red thread. She dipped them in a clay container of water to sweep the aura first. Sprinkling the water around me, pressing it on top of my head, my brow, my ears, stomach, feet, and lower back, she finally spoke.

"Cierra tus ojos."

Closing my eyes as the healer directed, I breathed in the warm, pungent aroma of the herbs while the smoke encircled my head. I recognized the smell of the copal incense carrying its power to ease my depression.

As the spiritual cleansing proceeded, my awareness slowly shifted from the solid, pebbled ground to the temperamental winds circling high in the air. Much like a hawk in flight observes the panorama of wooded mountains above flowing streams and deep valleys, I witnessed the tops of the trees shaking, and monuments, both natural and man-made, crumbling to the ground.

Surprisingly, I wasn't frightened because I had long ago accepted that the course of fate could not be changed. I actually felt relieved that the gravity of my apprehension had been confirmed. I inhaled a deep breath, then another.

When I opened my eyes, la curandera Mari had her hands placed firmly on top of my shoulders, anchoring me to earth.

She whispered, "Terremoto. Gran terremoto."

"Ya entiendo." I understood that soon the ground would shake with more power than man had to resist.

April 1906

My main memory of the great earthquake is that it changed more than the profile of buildings and tierra. Thousands of people without homes en San Francisco moved north, leaving city ruins behind. They crossed the choppy bay in steamer boats to make a new start but were met with tents and suspicion.

Many residents in the North did not welcome these migrantes because they were strangers who needed too much — too much food, too much water, too much help. It happens over and over again. I remember when the Chinese vineyard workers from Buena Vista had to stay off the streets of Sonoma at night or be arrested. However, they were industrious people and somehow built underground tunnels to get around this restriction to do their business and socialize for a time, but they were eventually expelled.

It took a decade for la bahía to recover from the earth's strained energy, but my spirit was still struggling to achieve dignity in this place. I continued cooking nopales and making tortillas for los americanos, and Papá kept feeding los caballos and cleaning up the mierda. But I was getting tired of the arrogance of the blondes.

August 1916

Whenever I finish wiping the dust and mopping the floor of the house de una señora, she can manage to say, "Gracias, Augustina," so I know she knows my name, but when many of them are together dressed in fancy clothes at a dinner party or barbacoa, they only look upon me as a piece of furniture or a kitchen tool.

Because I am not white and have little money, I am regarded as a lesser person. Es una tormenta de injusticia. Land of the free? This country persists in its practice of unofficial slavery. The slaves just changed from los africanos to los mexicanos. They have forgotten that this land was part of Mexico not that long ago. They are the newcomers!

Tranquilo, Augustina. I am not a patient woman, but I must calm my thoughts and conduct myself in a manner worthy of my ancestors. What would la curandera advise me to do? I close my eyes, so I can be receptive to her spiritual counsel. Eventually, my heartbeat slows, and my breathing deepens until my body and mind coexist in a timeless union. The ancient wisdom transports me through the past battles and conquests de nuestra gente into the time yet to come. A prophetic sense tells me that this struggle with the Anglos will persist until California is reclaimed by los mexicanos. It may take another 100 years or more, but this is one of those things I just know.

November 1918

After so many years of enduring insults from both nature and man, I wish I still had the strength to fight back, but as I lay here delirious, reliving experiences from my life, it's hard to distinguish the real from the unreal.

The fiebre is devouring my body, the same fever that killed Papá. Soldiers from the Great War have taken lives with their diseases as well as their bullets, and our small valley did not escape. The sickness arrived at the hospital where it spread quickly from room to room to patio to stable. This unmerciful influenza did not care what color you were or how much money you had, whether you were a disabled patient or an educated doctor. Over twenty people from the hospital have died so far.

Now my legs that once rode proudly astride stallions are weak, and my hair is matted with sweat. What I would give to be young and strong and beautiful, singing with the mariachi again. In desperation, I sob to myself, "No quiero morir asi."

The vibrating light surrounding me is growing brighter. Despite blinking, I dry my eyes several times trying to clear the image, the persistent illumination gently envelops me until I understand that it is time to rest, not to fight. Nestling my head on the clammy wool blanket, my consciousness drifts into the rolling hills, green in the spring, golden in the fall, sensing the cool splash of Sonoma Creek, and hearing the quail calling to its young. My soul feels the pounding of hooves on the dusty trail as I ride el caballo up the mountain for the last time. With a determined kick to the horse's flanks and a quick snap of the reins, I will myself to enter this beautiful vision, unafraid and finally free.

My Total Sum
Andrea Hernández Holm

My elders transition peacefully
with prayers of God willing on their lips
and our songs carrying their hearts.
The stories of how we came to be go with them.
The last embrace of the bisabuelos,
Chihuahua on their skin,
and words, and songs, and laughter that built us —
these ways of us go with them.
We can only keep what we make room for.
Hundred-year old photos of family;
the Rio Bravo--
both sides, in it, on it, with it;
long memories;
rural desert landscapes;
tortillas and nopales;
just snippets.

I struggle.

Who are you? Where do you come from?

Always the same questions.

I try to find my way through
fragments, dreams, and longings
for ways to navigate
these questions.
Are you, am I
north west south east?
Are you, am I
in the homelands?
Are you, am I
the homelands?
Am I
Chicana? Latina? Mexicana?
(add x, @, e to everything;
insert remove insert a hyphen;
silence the visibly invisible accent; align
Rarámuri or Mexica or *other;*
layer the Arizona earth
and the monsoon scent,
carry the generations
x y z;
multiply parent, spouse, child, and sibling
and divide it all by home;
add home, subtract home;
arrive at zero,
the ancestral center
where I am everything
and nothing?)

And what does that mean?
What does any of it mean?
The same fears
the same dreams
water dreams
abuela dreams
language dreams
snake dreams;
the same longing
to remember
to replace
to restore
to tell you that
my ancestors wove me into being,
pulled my story
from yarns reaching back through time,
across milpas,
and deserts,
and canyons,
and dry dusty roads between
cotton fields and cottonwoods,
through stars and mud
to give me light.
To love me
To love me
To love me.

That's it.
That's all I am.

First appeared in *Not Enough, Too Much*, Andrea Hernandez Holm,
FlowerSong Press, 2004.

it's the old hunger to grow wild

and sprout poems to make
composted earth of my flesh and my breath   earth turned relentlessly
and simmered slowly with the weight of memory and desire and the deep
deep clench of muscle and yearning

i ate the seeds i ate all the seeds bit them chewed
them let them rest on my tongue tasted their sweet their bitter their salt
i gathered the roots gossamer and rough knotted things and branching
masses in my hands and shoved them into my hair

the earth must think us flowers   flowers of meat
and air flowers that grunt and weep and laugh slow flowers that uncurl
and reach for the sun and bloom and seed and darken and wither and fall
flowers that crumble like all flowers that will feed her

i will give you more flowers than you can eat push
them into your mouth with my mouth lick them into you   thrust them
into the hollow of your chest curl them beneath your eyelids whisper
them over your skin until they dissolve into you

i am eating flowers and the petals are spilling out
of my mouth out of my eyes out of me spilling and spilling i am
birthing flowers devouring devoured blooming bursting i am eating
flowers life eating life death eating death my flesh   flowers

ire'ne lara silva

First published in *the eater's of flowers*, ire'ne lara silva, Saddle Road Press, 2004.
(Reprinted with permission from Saddle Road Press)

Autumn
Jen Yáñez-Alaniz

Stems curve, sprawling
& revealing

an intimate bud. It's a rosy thing,
it moistens as she anticipates

October's brisk morning.
Delirious & dumb, nocturnal creatures spin.

Emerald moths take in sweet nectar & drift
into the haze of harvest's moon as it wanes.
In my dream of flowering & fireflies

October comes to me as a bird, its soft wings,
the azure warmth of Texas skies.

Clamped in its beak, soft pods dangle.
My tongue unravels to touch the furred
surface of fruit

yearning to be born.

First appeared in *there is so much I want to tell you: a Corazón Collective anthology*, Mouthfeel Press, March 2024.

learning to peel a pomegranate
jo reyes-boitel

Between two knuckled tree branches, one foot at the trunk,
the other along the top of the fence, I managed
to wedge myself in.

I reach up for the pomegranates, my dress scooped up,
place them in carefully until I have a half dozen or more.
Each with their own intact crowns.

My father, seeing me there, calls from across the empty lot.
My brother comes running ahead of him. The him that was
still inquisitive. My father too, for that matter.

I want to eat as many of these as I can. I jump down,
my skirt still hiked up to my thighs. I hand a piece of fruit
to my brother. He hands it to my father.

I hold one in my hand, try to balance it in my palm.
Larger than my whole mouth — larger than my heart,
I'll bet — I try to bite it. *No*, he says, *here is how.*

And from his pocket a knife I knew nothing about.
He scores the splotched skin then edges the knife
into the crown and peels its skin away — his skin, its skin,

the knife — held in one space for a moment. Juice
runs down his fingers, pools in his palm. He laughs.
Another unexpected thing. He is full smile and

he sucks at the seeds, nestled tight together
like candy-stained teeth. His teeth too.
Red and jubilant.

Bordado
Dhalia Aguilar

Your mother taught me
end in the same hole where you began
It was more than my own mother taught me

Scolded like a dog
For my stray hair, muddy mouth and
almost sending plaster Virgencita smashing to the ground

Your mother clothed me
In what you'd outgrown,
What you wore into treasure

I remember your mother
When I broke the lanceolate leaf of aloe vera
Snapping it, its pulp about to stain my shirt and her carpet

She pulled me close
Took the sacred salve onto her finger tips
Taught me how it could heal my burns, scars and scratches

She taught me
There is no harm in pushing the needle
back from its crooked line

Especially for what could become beautiful
Unstitch or unravel altogether
It's how a peacock became peyote

How I became yours
Leaving behind marbles swirled Aegean and slate
For the threaded design of sisterhood

Ode for Aurora Reyes Flores
Aideed Medina

We will resurrect
all our sisters,
call their names,
out of the wilderness,
open the doors of Mictlán,
City of the Dead,
pull sinews, spirit, and legacy
through the walls
of old buildings,
thick with paint.

We will build their cathedrals
on the unfinished roads
of an unfinished revolution.
Graffiti sidewalks, smash windows,
entice the Angel of Revolution
to turn into a wailing angel.
Announcing Angel.

We will only
leave the murals untouched,
imprints of soul.

Painted desert landscapes
with windows into the blood,
saguaros haunt us
from Chihuahua to Tenochtlitalán.
The First Encounter.

All of my goddesses live
in Mexico City
in the underworld,
beneath the stone of Coyolxauhqui
and Christian churches.

We make them whole,
speaking their names.
We will finish the revolution
 they were born of.
Woman of War

Aurora Reyes,
mother of murals,
her name invokes
royalty
and the rising of the sun,
makes us inheritors
of her dawn.
Feminism.

A call to fight for the marginalized.

With her paintbrush, life force,
and
cactus woman ways,
brought forth
a battalion of artists.

The great revolutionary generals
never meant to liberate us,
from kitchen fires, laundry
lines, and the marriage bed.

So, she lifted herself
out of a mule cart
to finish the job.
Liberation seeped into Aurora's belly,
and invoked a voracious appetite
for women's rights, for the poor.

We have not finished
the movement quickened
in her visions.

Aurora Reyes, poet, painter,
mounted battles on the walls,
gave rural town teachers
a war-cry
in reds, browns, and stucco.

The naked woman stepped out
of the shelter of the conch.
Brave new world.
Aurora Reyes, naked in paint,
dressed Frida as Death, and
Concha as the eternal muñeca.

Aurora Reyes, we say your name,
Sirena Coronado. Transform us
into mermaids, embroider our tongues
in the poems of
Human Landscapes.

First!
Muralist mother.

We found you in a collection
 of wild women, savage poets, sculptors,
and painters.

Found you, and marveled at
breast exposed,
bare bodies weaponized
by the
sisterhood of 100 years.

Resurrection,
¡Qué viva Aurora Reyes Flores!
No final death
for the artist,
or
her art.

I am All in a Line

Lorna Dee Cervantes

My life condensed into poetry
and coffee, my grandmother
holding my hand in the half-
light mornings as I write. The pen
pulling the curtains back — where
I see her, and right her, turn her
back to her place, she, who never
had one. Here was what she
built herself. Her workman's shovel
making an exact line across
the yard. Her measured depth,
my future. The present tense
pours into these lines, mornings
weather in my hands. In this
I drink from, color de café, pushing
her back to where she belongs:
the line that wrote me, what I speak
now.

The Mountain Lion
Ada Limón

I watched the video clip over and over,
night vision cameras flickering her eyes
an unholy green, the way she looked
the six-foot fence up and down
like it was nothing but a speed bump,
and cleared the man-made border
in one impressive leap. A glance
over the shoulder, an annoyance,
an "as if you could keep me out, or
keep me in." I don't know what it
was that made me press replay and
replay. It wasn't fear, though I'd be
terrified if I was face to face with
her, or heard her prowling in the night,
it was just that I don't think I've
ever made anything look so easy. Never
looked behind me and grinned or
grimaced because nothing could stop
me. I like the idea of it though, felt
like a dream you could will into being:
See a fence? Jump it.

Sureños Salvajes
Shavone A. Otero

Generations deep
in the mountains

Escabosa
Chilili
Tajique
Yrisarri

Sureños salvajes

Pliers for
my aching tooth
Ahí está

To the earth we eat
Volveremos

And my bones become dust
to daredevil their way
through the canyon
down the valley
over seashells
across mesas
up volcanoes
And back

Notes on the Holy Ghost and Her Atheist Daughter
Sonia Gutiérrez

"Amá — promise me when you die you will return and talk to me,"
I request months before a tall Sequoia tree with long emaciated branches
elongates her last breaths.

I.

When I am finally ready,
I call out, *Mamá,*
and the laptop turns on.
I talk with you, floating electrical current,
who flickers lights.

We talk for about ten minutes —
I say my goodbyes.
Gracias Mamá por tomarte el tiempo
para hablar conmigo.
Mother always on point the laptop turns off.

II.

You are looming, emitting soft gentle tinkers
above the glass bulb holders.
Who knew your presence could make
such sweet sounds even in spirit?

How do you do that? Are you holding an invisible fork?

III.

You are already in the room
when Father returns
to celebrate you.

He opens the guest room,
and you turn off the lights on a whim.
I tease Dad, "Es mi Amá.
¿Qué hiciste pa' que te apagara la luz?"

IV.

Queen of the Cempasúchil, on your day,
family comes from distant places
to be with you, our Holy Ghost.

The tamales and champurrado are ready.
*Come and eat. Oh, please don't hide behind
the white columns.* We are all here waiting
with our bony faces.

V.

Around here, in front of your bedroom window,
your green thumb is still present in the earth.
Outside, a thorny rose bush blooms the heaviest of reds.
Mother, you look so majestic dressed in deep green foliage.

> In dreams, wearing a crown of flowers and an obsidian face,
> you tell me, your atheist daughter, Dios te ilumine, Mija.

First appeared in *La Bloga: Chicana, Chicano, Latina, Latino, & More.
Literature, Writers, Children's Literature, News, Views & Reviews*, 1 Nov. 2016.

Reprinted in "Best Poems of 2016" *La Bloga: Chicana, Chicano, Latina, Latino,
& More. Literature, Writers, Children's Literature, News, Views & Reviews*, 7 Jan.
2017.

Ode to "The Resurrection of Mayahuel"

Ekphrastic poem in five movements inspired by
"The Resurrection of Mayahuel" by Rick Ortega
Brenda Vaca

i

Allow me to take you
on a spiritual trip
Allow me to remind you
it's okay to die
and be born again

Allow your thick leathery leaves
to burst through the verdant tierra
Learn to fly again
and be full of joy   wonder and laughter
Allow me to blow
a gentle whisper into your ear
Beloved, do not fear
Mi aguamiel flows   pure and clear

It unlocks the truth

ii

I almost stayed silent
I almost stayed dead
Almost gave way to
the desperate voices
inside my head

In the chrysalis of the earth
Madre Tierra held me tight
She whispered:
Mija, it's okay to fall apart
Mija, it's okay to give up this fight

In the dankest dark
in the womb that is our mother
Tlaloc poured out his waters
to accompany my tears
My old self disintegrated
I dissolved
into the amniotic fluid of the womb
My Spirit danced with the
shadows and gloom

It was then I remembered my celestial home
Winter circle of the sky still swam in me

I locked myself in the story chamber
for what felt like forever
I remembered how carefree
and promising life seemed for a moment

Then I remembered the brood of vipers
in my own household   in the church
the predators   lurking in the shadows
The stares and whispers that made me cross the street
The wolves in sheep's clothing
who know nothing about   No!
Stop!   Please!   Don't put it in!

So, I fell down to my knees and asked for mercy
and a new life came calling for me

iii

My beloved and I
plumed serpent
fly high
in the midnight sky

Ehécatl brushes my cheek
with his lips
a serpent's sweet kiss
It's divine love that creates
and resuscitates this

diosa desmembrada
hueso y polvo
se convierte en agave
una madrugada

vivas se fueron
         vivas las queremos

iv

We're tired of saying ME TOO
We're tired of having to stand before you
and shout out what's true

Tired of holding the shame within
the anger too
What would you do?
Would you speak your truth?

Las hijas de Mayahuel
we rise like smoke
Our power   it burns your throat
We hold you accountable
for what you've done
Generation upon generation
not just one mother's son

A legion of demons have violated
even little ones

We're tired of saying ME TOO

The truth is we just want to live
to rise in the morning
with the heaviness of eyelids
not our hearts   not these bodies
hear Centzontle sing Their song
feel plumed serpent's kiss
again and again
as Ehécatl carries us to shelter

Isn't that our birthright?

V

My sacred rage runs through these veins
My sacred rage discards these chains
Coatlicue rising Tonantzin fighting
All through these days
you feel our pain

My daughters are now unleashed
polvo of our bones will speak

mujer desmembrada
resucitada
mujer fructífera y poderosa
vámonos del camino doloroso
aguamiel corre por nuestras venas

You cannot stop our resurrection
Great Spirit is our protection
There is power in the words we say
We burn Palo Santo and Grandfather Sage
We whisper one to another:
Mija, vuelva a tu sombra
Mija, speak your own name

Your power
    Your light
        Your dark
            Your beauty
                Your fight
                    are here to stay

ABOUT THE AUTHORS

Angela Acosta, Ph.D. is an Assistant Professor of Spanish at the University of South Carolina. Her Rhysling and Utopia Award nominated writing has appeared in *Somos en Escrito, Apparition Lit, Radon Journal,* and *Space & Time.* She is author of *Summoning Space Travelers* (Hiraeth Publishing) and *A Belief in Cosmic Dailiness* (Red Ogre Review).

Dahlia Aguilar, a mother and emergent writer from Texas lives in Washington, D.C. She's an alum of Under the Volcano and her manuscript *Tidal Range* was a finalist for the Louise Bogan Poetry Award 2024. Her poems appear in *Naugatuck River Review, Boundless 2024, Write Until You Cry* and *The Skinny Journal.*

Axolotita is a first-generation Xicana who survived Y2K and a world plague, and now wields the power of the pen to document/explore chaos and to dream. Warning: side effects of reading may include laughter, tears, and the strong desire to question everything.

Rosanna Alvarez is a braided storyteller, artist, and poet. She is the author of *Braided [Un]Be-Longing,* co-founder of *EASTSIDE Magazine,* and co-editor of *The Early Works of Luis Miguel Valdez in El Excentrico Magazine.* Her work appears in various journals, and she proudly embraces her role as a multifaceted *rezongona.*

Juliana Aragón Fatula, Corn Mother, author of: *Crazy Chicana in Catholic City, Red Canyon Falling on Churches*, High Plains Book Award for Poetry 2016, member of Colorado Alliance of Latino Mentors and Authors, and Macondo Writers Foundation, lives in Southern Colorado, home of her ancestors.

Erika Ayón emigrated from Mexico when she was five years old and grew up in South Central Los Angeles. She is a former PEN Emerging Voices Fellow. She has taught poetry to middle and high school students across Los Angeles. Her debut poetry collection *Orange Lady* was published by World Stage Press.

Carmen Baca is the author of six books and a variety of short publications in diverse genres. She received New Mexico Magazine's 2023 True Hero award for celebrating and preserving her culture through story telling. Two of her short works were nominated to Best of the Net and the Pushcart Prize also in 2023.

Victoria Ballesteros Ramírez is a writer from Los Angeles. The daughter of Mexican immigrants, her stories reflect her bicultural upbringing and experiences. Her work was selected for Best Small Fictions 2024, and has appeared in trampset, Your Impossible Voice, Cutleaf Journal, LatineLit, Latin@ Literatures, and elsewhere. She is enrolled in the creative writing certificate program at UCLA Extension.

Dr. Victoria Bañales is a Chicanx educator, writer, and founding editor of *Xinachtli Journal — Journal X —* a social justice literary arts magazine. Her writing has been published in various journals and anthologies. She has received two poetry awards, a teaching excellence award, and several writing fellowships. More at vickybanales.com.

Xochitl-Julisa Bermejo is the author of *Incantation: Love Poems for Battle Sites* (Mouthfeel Press) and *Posada: Offerings of Witness and Refuge* (Sundress Publications). A former Steinbeck Fellow and *Poets & Writers* California Writers Exchange winner, Bermejo›s writings can be found at *Acentos Review, Huizache, The Offing*, and others. She is the director of Women Who Submit.

Irene I. Blea, 1st female President of the National Association of Chicano Studies, began her career as a poet in the early days of the Movement. Blea has a Ph.D. in Sociology, wrote 7 textbooks, *Toward a Chicano Social Science* and *La Chicana* are classics. She retired from California State University-Los Angeles as a Full Professor and Chairperson then wrote 4 novels and her autobiography.

Vanessa Marie Bustamante, Ph.D., (a.k.a. Homegirl Doctora) born and raised in the San Fernando Valley, CA, is a self-identified first-generation, bilingual, queer Xicana sCHOLAr, with a deep-rooted appreciation for community involvement and grassroots organizing. As the First Queer/

Muxer Chair of el Partido Nacional La Raza Unida, she cohosts Radio La Raza KPFK 90.7FM Los Angeles.

Xánath Caraza is a traveler, educator, award winning poet, short story writer, and translator. She is the author of 20 books of poetry and two short story collections. In 2018, she received First Place for *Sin preámbulos / Without Preamble* for "Best Book of Bilingual Poetry" in the International Latino Book Awards.

Elvira Carrizal-Dukes is a Xicana, native New Mexican and graphic novelist. She earned a Doctor of Philosophy in Rhetoric and Composition, a Master of Fine Arts in Film, and a Bachelor of Arts in Journalism and Chicano Studies and a minor in Theatre Arts. She produced *Cholx counterstory* to center Cholo and Chola culture.

Loretta Carpio Carr was raised in Selma, California, the daughter of a Mexican mother and Anglo father. She has taught English, ESL, and citizenship classes in Sonoma. Her writing has been published in the Sonoma Valley Sun newspaper, Sonoma State University's 2017 fire anthology *Dear Sonoma*, and San Joaquin Valley Writers' anthology *Great Valley Stories*.

Ana Castillo is a distinguished poet, novelist, short story writer, essayist, editor, and playwright, translator, independent researcher and visual artist. She has published over 24 books of poetry, fiction, nonfiction, translation, and theater, many of them classics in Xicanisma literature. Her book *Masacre de los Sonadores: Essays on Xicanisma*, is considered a foundational text in feminist studies.

Erica Castro is a Xicana English high school teacher who has taught for twenty-seven years. She has dedicated herself to publishing student work. She published the Oracle school anthology, and she has recently launched Daxson Publishing to publish marginalized voices.

Isabel Cerero, born and raised in Chicago to two first generation Mexican parents, she graduated with a B.A. in teaching Spanish from UIC. Presently, she teaches at Little Village Lawndale High School.

Isabel was drawn to explore the arts in Mexican folkloric dance, as a way to interpret the Xicana experience, which led her to explore poetry.

Lorna Dee Cervantes, awarded NEA Fellowships, Pushcart Prizes, a Lila Wallace/Readers Digest Award, state arts grants, and Best Book awards for 6 books of poetry including her first, EMPLUMADA, and APRIL ON OLYMPIA, the former Professor and Director of Creative Writing at CU Boulder now writes in Seattle.

Jesenia Chavéz is a proud Chicana, 18-year veteran public school teacher, storyteller and writer. Her poetry collection, *This Poem Might Save You (me)* is a journey through the streets of Los Angeles that explores intersectionality and the rituals of survival. She has an MFA from UCR. Find her at www.jeseniachavez.com. IG @chabemucho

Sandra Cisneros is a widely published, highly decorated Chicana trailblazer from Chicago, and author of classics like *The House on Mango Street*, and *Caramelo*. She is founder of the Macondo Foundation and the Alfredo Cisneros Del Moral Foundation. Her latest poetry collection is titled *Mujer Sin Vergüenza* (2022).

Elisabeth Contreras-Moran is an environmental scientist turned poet. She has degrees from Princeton University and John Jay College of Criminal Justice, CUNY. Currently living in England, she creates at night, when the house is quiet. A newly emerging voice, her poetry has been in Litro Magazine and The Ascentos Review.

Candi Cipactli Corral, Ph.D., (she, her, ella), is a Xicanx indígena (Cahita, Tahues, Mexica), Brown Beret, 1st generation, Temachtianih who teaches courses on Proletarian Femme, Hip Hop, CRT, Intersectional Movements, and Decolonialism. She publishes on Marxism and political economy of extractivism. She is a practitioner of curanderismo and cultivates her semillas de maíz.

Dulciana Rosario Corral (she/her/ella) is an indigenous Xicana activist, Brown Beret, artist, and (song)writer who promotes revolutionary healing ways for youth as an alternative to mainstream healing. She is an undergraduate, double majoring in Biomedical Science and Music. She is decolonizing her life by growing corn and working with curanderismo.

Liz Coronado Castillo, originally from West Texas, is a Chicana higher education professional, playwright and poet with a BA in Theatre from SRSU and an MFA in playwriting from TTU. She is a performer, a writer, an educator and an advocate. Her works include *Little Girls Don't Do That, Casa De Muñeca, Aye, No!,* and *Moises: A Modern-Day Tragedy.*

Marissa Cueva is a Chicana screenwriter born and raised in Los Angeles, California. She is a student at Loyola Marymount University, where she is a double major in Screenwriting and Chicano/Latino Studies. She is pursuing a career in writing for the film industry and also has a prominent interest in writing poetry and prose.

Gloria (Calvillo) Delgado, born in San Francisco's Haight-Ashbury district, daughter of a Mexican father and a Hawaii-born Puerto Rican mother; formerly of Albany, CA, now living near Santa Fe, NM. Has published in Berkeley Community Memoir Project, also five stories for Somos en escrito, including "El Parbulito," first-place winner of our 2019 Extra Fiction Contest.

Laura Díaz Tovar is a poet, visual artist, and community educator. Her work explores cultura, family, and justice, weaving narratives of personal and collective love that heals and transforms. Published in *Journal X, La Libreta for Women in Creative Rebellion*, and *La Raiz Magazine*, her poetry supports healing and connection.

María Elena Fernández, born and raised in L.A. and the daughter of Mexico City migrants, is a writer, performer and professor. Her work has been published in the anthologies *Voices from the Ancestors, Waking Up American* and *Remembering Frida*. Her full-length solo shows include *Confessions of a Cha Cha Feminist* and *Ancestral Body Navegante*. She teaches in the Chicana/o Studies Department at CSUN.

Anel I. Flores, an award-winning visual artist and writer, is the author of *Emapanda and Curtains of Rain*. A Mellow Foundations Fellow and founder of La Otra Taller Nepantla, Flores exhibits internationally, creating sanctuary for Latina/e, BiPOC, and 2SLGBTQIA+ communities through writing, art, and teaching. Visit: Anelflores.com @aneliflores.

Consuelo Gallegos is an aspiring Chicana writer from New Mexico, working towards combining her love for science, and Latine history to craft compelling fiction and non-fiction stories that educate and entertain. When she's not working as a professional healthcare worker or being a mom, Consuelo is busy volunteering, researching science, Chicano history, or studying languages and art.

Esther Garcia is a proud daughter of New Mexico. Esther emphasizes preserving oral histories and has utilized writing, photography, art, and short films to document local culture and practices. Her art comes from her heart, her life experiences, expressions of home, and the community where she feels nurtured and safe.

Elisa A. Garza is a poet, editor, and former writing and literature teacher. Her full-length collection, *Regalos* (Lamar University Literary Press) was a finalist for the National Poetry Series. She has also written three chapbooks, including *Between the Light / entre la claridad*, and *The Body, Cancerous*, forthcoming in 2025 (both from Mouthfeel Press).

Inez González Perezhica, born and raised in Tijuana, México, is the Executive Director of MANA de S.D. and founding director of the Latino Communications Institute at Cal State Fullerton. Dr. González Perezhica gained her media expertise during her nine-year tenure at the National Hispanic Media Coalition (NHMC). She currently serves on the EJE Academies Charter School Advisory Board and is proud to be a binational citizen.

Sonia Gutiérrez is author of *Spider Woman / La Mujer Araña* and the recipient of the Tomás Rivera Book Award 2021 and the International Latino Book Awards 2022 for her novel, *Dreaming with Mariposas* (FlowerSong Press, 2020), and she is the winner of the ILBA Book into Movie Awards 2023. Her bilingual poetry collection, *Paper Birds: Feather by Feather / Pájaros de papel: Pluma por pluma* was published with El Martillo Press in April 2024.

Andrea Hernández Holm is from Arizona. Relationships with land, community, and family are integral in her writing. Her poetry has appeared in numerous venues. She has forthcoming publications in *Beyond Borders Literary Review* and *Teaching for Change*. Andrea's first book, *Not Enough, Too Much*, is available through Flowersong Press.

Carmen Jackie writes about Hispanic characters who live and thrive in Southern California. Carmen is part of a large Mexican American family that loves to celebrate all of life's big moments. In addition to being a writer, she is also a college instructor with an MFA from UCR.

Elizabeth Jiménez Montelongo is a poet and visual artist — an Indigenous Mexican Chicana whose poetry appears in journals and anthologies. She earned a BFA in Pictorial Art and BA in French from SJSU; received a Creative Corps Initiative grant from California Arts Council and YBCA; founded *La Raíz Magazine*. www.ejmontelongo.com.

ire'ne lara silva, 2023 Texas State Poet Laureate, is the author of five poetry collections, furia, Blood Sugar Canto, *CUICACALLI/House of Song, FirstPoems*, and *the eaters of flowers*, two chapbooks, *Enduring Azucares* and *Hibiscus Tacos*, a comic book, *VENDAVAL*, and a short story collection, *flesh to bone*, which won the Premio Aztlán.

Ada Limón is the current Poet Laureate of the United States and the author of six books of poetry, including *The Carrying*, which won the National Book Critics Circle Award for Poetry. Her most recent book of poetry, *The Hurting Kind*, was shortlisted for the Griffin Poetry Prize. She is the recipient of a MacArthur Fellowship, and a *TIME* magazine woman of the year. As the Poet Laureate, her signature project is called *You Are Here* and focuses on how poetry can help connect us to the natural world.

Norma G. López nació en San Antonio, Texas. Se formó en Literatura Comparativa, enfocándose en literatura escrita en Español, Portugués, y Francés. Tiene una maestría en Español y otra en Educación. Se ha dedicado a la enseñanza de idiomas. Su poesía suele emerger en español a pesar de que su primera lengua es el inglés. zepolgn40@hotmail.com

Guadalupe T. Luna is an internationally recognized scholar who teaches property law, agriculture law, and remedies. She has authored dozens of law review articles including an extensive bibliography on the Treaty of Guadalupe Hidalgo, published by Oxford University Press. Professor Luna's career is marked by her advocacy for social justice and the rights of marginalized communities.

Maria Miranda Maloney is a writer, editor, and founder of Mouthfeel Press. Her poetry and essays have appeared in the *Bellevue Literary Review, Huizache, Acentos Review, La Bloga,* and others. Maria has an MFA in Creative Writing from UTEP and an MPS in Publishing from George Washington University in D.C.

Carolina Martinez is a Chicana writer and first-generation college graduate with a BA in Communication, currently pursuing an MBA in music business. She honors Chicano and Latino resilience through her writing and her role as creator of Voices From Detention, a project that amplifies voices often unheard within the community.

Aideed Medina's work has appeared in various publications, theatrical and musical productions, and municipal mural projects. She is the author of 31 Hummingbird, Editorial Xingao, a full-length poetry collection, Segmented Bodies, Prickly Pear Publishing, and Nopalli Press, and a forthcoming binational chapbook, selected poems from Segmented Bodies published by Universidad Autónoma de Nuevo León.

Aimée Medina Carr's debut novel, *River of Love,* received The Rudolfo Anaya Award at the International Latino Book Awards (2020). A native daughter of Southern Colorado; a Coyota (Indian/Spanish) with ancestral ties to Native American and Hispano/Chicano communities. Her homeland is Southern Colorado/Northern Nuevo Mexíco—our history/antepasados live through us. aimeemedinacarr.com

Rosalilia M. Mendoza was born and raised in the San Fernando Valley/ Tataviam lands, a daughter of migrants from Zacatecas and Michoacan. As a former therapist, teacher, community & political activist, Rosalilia shares her healing journey facing sexism, colonialism, and discrimination. Rosalilia envisions creating a world for her sun Chalchihuitl to thrive.

Claudia Meléndez Salinas is an award-winning journalist, poet and author. She is the co-founder of Voices of Monterey Bay, an online magazine in California's central coast. Her poem "Transitioning" was the recipient of the 2022 Red Wheelbarrow Poetry Award. Her first book, "A Fighting Chance," was published by Arte Público Press.

Kelsey Milian Lopez was raised in Miami, Florida. With a strong sense of cultural identity, she has been able to connect and trace her heritage to her Mexican, Guatemalan, Aztec, Zapotec, K'iche Maya, Spanish, and Japanese ancestry. She now resides in New York City as she pursues a Ph.D. in Ethnomusicology at CUNY Graduate Center.

Michelle Mojica is a first-generation detribalized Xicana Indígena, with 12 years of experience working in the mental health field & 18 years of Indigenous Spiritual Healing Practices. Michelle is a Ceremonialist, Ancestral Practitioner, Writer, & she creates gatherings for BIPOC that teach how to connect & heal with their ancestors using ancestral healing practices.

Carolina Monsivais is a poet and historian originally from El Paso. She is a founding organizing member of Poets Against Walls and is also a member of the Macondo Writers Workshop. She is the author of the poetry collections *Somewhere Between Houston and El Paso* (Wings Press) and *Descent* (Mouthfeel Press). Monsivais is a graduate of NMSU (MFA) and the UTEP (Ph.D.). She is Assistant Professor at UTRGV.

Gaby Moreno is an overall creative, who goes by the artistic name 7 Octoberz to honor her abuelita's legacy. She is a poet, artist (music and painter), journalist, podcaster, writer and more. She was born and raised in San Diego, CA and is always representing her love for her city. She has dropped two Hip Hop EP's and has gone to open mics to share some of her poetry via spoken word. She is proud of her Mexican and Chicana roots and always tries to incorporate it in her art.

Briana Muñoz is a poet from Southern California. She is the author of two books of poetry, *Loose Lips* (Prickly Pear Publishing) and *Everything is Returned to the Soil* (FlowerSong Press). Her work has been published in the anthology *How to Reimagine America, Cultural Daily,* the *Beat*

Not Beat Anthology, the *Oakland Arts Review,* the *Dryland Literary Journal,* and several other publications.

Reyna Muñoz is an Associate Professor at El Paso Community College and co-host for the *Literally Literary* podcast. She is a board member for the Association of Women in the Community College, and has served on the Las Americas Immigrant Advocacy Center board. She is a proud daughter of immigrants.

Shavone A. Otero's writing explores Xicanisma and ancestral memory has been featured in the New Mexico Poetry Anthology. Born and raised in Albuquerque, New Mexico, she holds a BA in English with a minor in Chicano Studies and dual master's degrees in Community and Regional Planning and Latin American Studies.

Amber Ortega (MFA, BFA) is a Queer Xicana-Tejana, choreographer, educator, and dance scholar researching dance in community, embodiment, and technology. Ortega is engaged in exploring embodied writing practices; her *Body As Land* project brings the body closer to the earth to incite, generate, and derive language from an embodied relationship to the land.

Amalia Ortiz is a spoken word performer and playwright. She was awarded the 2020 American Book Award for Oral Literature. She appeared on three seasons of *Russell Simmons Presents Def Poetry* on HBO and the NAACP Image Awards on FOX. Amalia received her MFA in Creative Writing from The University of Texas Rio Grande Valley.

Melinda Palacio is Santa Barbara's first Chicana Poet Laureate. Author of Ocotillo Dreams, her poetry collection, *How Fire Is a Story, Waiting,* won first prize at the 2013 International Latino Book Awards. In 2015, her work was featured by the Academy of American Poets. Her latest book is titled *Bird Forgiveness.*

Diana Pando is a Chicago writer, poeta, and storyteller with roots in Chihuahua, MX and Mexico City. Recently, her poem *Mythology of Flesh* *and Turquoise Serpents* was included in the *Mujeres de Maiz* Anthology published by the University of Arizona Press. Thankful to *Somos Xicanas* contributors for their creativity and beautiful palabra medicine.

jo reyes-boitel is a poet and playwright pursuing a Ph.D. at Texas Tech University. Their publications include *the matchstick litanies* (Next Page Press) and *the impracticality of silk* (Gnashing Teeth Press). jo also wrote "she wears bells," a hybrid opera which was a finalist in Guerilla Opera's 2021 virtual festival.

Martha Rivas Maravilla, mother, profa, artist y peleonera, was born in Mexico but raised en Califas. Dr. Martha holds four degrees from UCLA, and is known for her *critical-poetic* voice. She weaves scholarship, intuition y facultad en esta vida de escritora. Dr. Martha lives in L.A., with her daughters: Alicia-Ixchel y Sol-Inez.

Natalia Rivas is a Chicana writer in her 70's from California who has worn many hats in life. She was part of a group of poets, in the early 70's, that helped create murals in the Mission District of San Francisco. Natalia is a retired drug counselor who plays with words to create atmosphere through storytelling.

Amanda Rosas is a poet who draws strength and creativity from the Mexican women in her family, and from her husband and three daughters. Her work has been published by *The Latino Book Review, CALYX, The MockingHeart Review* among many others. She dreams of becoming a fulltime writer and storyteller.

Angelina Sáenz, an award-winning Chicana educator and author, has been honored by La Opinión and President Obama's Advisory Commission. She's written the children's book *Waiting for Luna* and two poetry collections. Her latest collaboration, *Escaramuza: The Poetics of Home*, is currently displayed at the National Cowgirl Museum in Texas.

Petra Salazar is an educator and artist from Northern New Mexico, rooted in embodied, land-based practices. In their work, they explore the sacred dynamic between artist, art, and audience, drawing inspiration from Indohispano knowledge traditions related to environmental activism, medicine, philosophy, and art. Learn more at www.petrasalazar.com.

Cecilia Sanchez is a Mujerista, poet, professor and activist from Orange County, California. She comes from a multi ethnic background and she reclaims her roots by writing about her identity crisis and constant state of nepantla as a Mexican & Salvadorian woman in the United States.

Angela M. Sánchez (they/she) is a Mexican American writer from Los Angeles. They write for animation, including Disney's *Primos* and Nick Jr.'s *Paw Patrol*. In 2018, the LA Times featured Angela's picture book, *Scruffy and the Egg*, about family homelessness. Angela is co-editing the upcoming comics anthology, *From Cocinas to Lucha Libre Ringsides*.

Irene Sanchez, Ph.D. is an award-winning educator, poet and writer. Born in Southeast L.A., she was raised in the Inland Empire. She taught high school Chicano/Latino studies for six years. She has published in numerous publications including CNN, *Huffington Post*, Zócalo Public Square and more. Dr. Sanchez is also the author of the blog *Xicana Ph.D.* She is currently an Assistant Professor of Ethnic Studies at SBVC. www.irenesanchezphd.com.

Isabella Santana is a 20-year-old poet from Los Angeles, California. She is the proud daughter of Ecuadorian and Guatemalan immigrants. She is the author of *Abuela Lore* (2024, Somos En Escrito Press), her debut chapbook. She studies English and Latin American & Caribbean Studies at the University of Michigan, Ann Arbor.

Sandy Shakes is a spoken truth artist bloomed from Boyle Heights pavement. She has hosted and performed on mics along California's coast. Her dream is to set readers free, especially those life has caged. Her first chapbook *Scribble Scrabbles* was birthed in 2024; an ode and intro to spoken palabra.

Elena Solano is from Southwest Detroit, has a bachelor's in bilingual education, a masters in counseling and a post masters in school counseling. Ms. Solano is a writer, mentor, educator, activist, mother and tía. She is one of fourteen children of Juan and Rosa Solano.

Carmen Tafolla is a multi-award-winning Chicana literary trailblazer, first City Poet Laureate of San Antonio, 2015 State Poet Laureate of Texas and first Latina to be elected President of the Texas Institute of Letters. Author of more than 40 books, including the classic, *Get Your Tortillas Together*, her latest, *Warrior Girl* (Penguin, 2023), is a novel-in-verse set in her home barrio of San Antonio. She is at work on the full biography of 1930s activist Emma Tenayuca.

Sendy Tapia is a mesmerizing daydreamer in the world of storytelling. With over 15 years of experience in storytelling, Sendy has evolved from a seasonal farmworker to a first-generation college graduate to bridge opportunities to her community so they, too, can turn daydreams into reality. Follow her journey @sunlightbysailynn

Laura Díaz Tovar (ella/she), born in Guadalajara, Jalisco, México, is a poet, mixed media visual artist, creative educator, and co-founder of Colibrí Collective living on occupied Ohlone land in San José, CA. Her poetry and art, have appeared in *Journal X, La Libreta Women in Creative Rebellion Poetry Journal,* and *La Raíz Magazine.*

Blanca Torres, a native of Washington state, now calls the San Francisco Bay Area home. She earned a B.A. from Vanderbilt University and an M.F.A. on from Mills College. She writes short stories, personal essays, and is working on a memoir about her mother's childhood in Mexico.

Brenda Vaca is a Xicana poet, author, and independent publisher from Sejatnga, Unceded Tongva Territory, known as South Whittier, CA. She earned her B.A. in English at U.C. Berkeley with a Minor in Creative Writing and later earned a Master of Divinity and Master of Arts in Biblical Languages at the Pacific School of Religion/Graduate Theological Union. *Riot of Roses* is her debut collection of poetry published by her indie house, Riot of Roses Publishing House.

Angela (Angie) Trudell Vasquez, a second and third generation Mexican-American originally from Iowa, served as the city of Madison, Wisconsin Poet Laureate from 2020 to early 2024. She earned her MFA from the Institute of American Indian Arts. Her fourth poetry collection, *My People Redux,* was published in January 2022. Angietrudellvasquez.com.

Erika Vallejo is a Doctoral Candidate (ABD) in the Department of Political Science at Michigan State University, and obtained certificates in Chicano/Latino and Women's & Gender Studies. She earned a BA in political science and philosophy from the University of Texas Rio Grande Valley, and an MA in political science from Michigan State University.

Katarina Xóchitl Vargas' (she/her) poetry collection *The Half That Runs* was runner-up for the 2024 Andrés Montoya Poetry Prize, selected by Juan Felipe Herrera, and first runner up for the 2023 Wilder Prize. Xóchitl is the first-place recipient of the Mulberry Literary Fresh Voices Award. She was raised in Mexico-Tenochtitlan.

Alma Luz Villanueva is the author of four novels, most recently *Song of the Golden Scorpion*, and eight books of poetry, most recently *Gracias*. She's published poetry, fiction and non-fiction in magazines, anthologies, textbooks. Alma taught in MFA in creative writing program for twenty years at Antioch University. www.almaluzvillanueva.com

Christiane Williams-Vigil is a Xicana writer from El Paso, Texas. Her work has been published in various literary magazines such as Marias at Sampaguitas, Fatal Flaw Literary Magazine, The Write Launch, La Raiz Magazine, and Latinx Literatures. Christianewilliamsvigil.com @christyvigilwriter

Diosa Xochiquetzalcóatl is a spoken word poetiza and seasoned language arts educator with a B.A. in English and M.Ed. in Cross-Cultural Teaching who has been published on both sides of the US-Mexico border. Diosa X is the author of six poetry collections, with more still to come. Learn more about her at www.diosax.net.

Jennifer Yáñez-Alaniz is a dynamic ChicanaMestiza activist, educator, and poet, pursuing her PhD in Culture, Literacy, and Language at UTSA. She is author of a poetry chapbook *Surrogate Eater*, a critical biography of Carmen Tafolla in Chicana Portraits and a contributor to Corazón Collective poetry anthology. Yáñez-Alaniz is a co-founder of Welcome: A Poetry Declaration.

ABOUT THE EDITORS

Luz Schweig (she/ella) is the chief editor of the *Somos Xicanas* anthology, and a former staff member at Somos en escrito Literary Foundation. She ran an international women's poetry journal for ten years, through which she edited and produced five anthologies and a posthumous poetry collection. She writes autobiographical poetry under a pen name and grew up in La Ciudad de México.

Jenny Irizary co-edited *El Porvenir, ¡Ya!, Our Creative Realidades,* and other books published by Somos en escrito, while working there in various capacities as a volunteer staff member for six years. Their/ her work has been published in *CERASUS, Squalorly, HInchas de Poesía, Communion, Snapping Twig,* and other journals. Jenny has a B.A. in Ethnic Studies and M.A. in literature from Mills College.

Scott Russell Duncan, a Xicano writer, was editor on the first Chicano sci-fi anthology, *El Porvenir, ¡Ya!,* which was a finalist in the Next Generation Indie Book Awards. He is the lead editor on *Chicanofuturism Now!! Chicanofuturuism* and director of Palabras del Pueblo. In 2016 his story "How My Hide Got Color" won San Francisco Litquake's Short Story Contest, and in 2019, his nonfiction piece "Mexican American Psycho is in Your Dreams" won first place in the Solstice Literary Magazine Annual Literary Contest. He is the author of *Old California Strikes Back*, (FlowerSong Press, 2024) and is currently working on a collection of short stories called *Plurality*. www.scottrussellduncan.com.

Armando B. Rendón, born in 1939 in San Antonio, Texas, authored *Chicano Manifesto* (latest edition, Somos en escrito Press, 2021), the first book written by a Chicano about the Chicano Movement. In 2009, Rendón founded Somos en escrito Magazine and in 2016 established the Somos en escrito Literary Foundation, which operates the Magazine and Press. In 2019, his essay titled "Blueprint for the Next 50 Years," led to the creation of MeXicanos 2070, a national organization dedicated to preserving and advancing Mexican American culture.

Rendón is also the author of an award-winning four-part series for Young Adults titled *The Adventures of Noldo and His Magical Scooter* and a sequel, *The Wizard of the Blue Hole*. He lives in the San Francisco Bay Area. Contact him at abrendon39@gmail.com.

ACKNOWLEDGEMENTS

I would like extend my heartfelt gratitude to the following people who offered their support, assistance and encouragement as we worked together to bring *Somos Xicanas* to fruition and take it out into the contributor's local barriors:

My deep appreciation to Reyna Grande, Norma Elia Cantú, Rosa Martha Villareal, Carlos Cumpián, David Bowles and Estella González who kindly took precious time out of their busy schedules to offer *Somos Xicanas* glowing advanced praise.

To queer, Chicana and Cuban poet, playwright and scholar jo reyes-boitel for recommending *Somos Xicanas* to the Letras Latinas Blog 2 of The Institute of Latino Studies at the University of Notre Dame who named it one of its "most anticipated books of 2024."

To Chicana [Mestiza] poet activist, scholar and educator, Jen Yáñez-Alaniz, for writing such a very thoughtful, scholarly and yet poetic Foreword, eloquently illuminating the contents so beautifully!

Author Aimée Medina Carr, for her valuable review referrals, her support from one anthology curator to another, overall enthusiasm surrounding the book, and help getting the word out.

To the 2023 Texas State Poet Laureate, ire'ne lara silva, who catalyzed the book launch event in San Antonio, Texas, along with Jennifer Yáñez-Alaniz.

Much appreciation to Dulce Stein, for offering to host our Los Angeles book launch event at her beautifully curated XICANA art exhibit held at the Experimentally Structured Museum of Art (ESMoA), in El Camino College, Torrance, California.

To Jenny Irizary, my friend, a talented writer, and former colleague at Somos en escrito Magazine & Press, who applied very nuanced ethnolinguistic and content sensitivity editorial skills to material throughout this volume, offering much appreciated insights and suggestions. Jenny was also instrumental as an editor of the anthology in the delicate processes of vetting and editing submissions early on.

To my friend, and former colleague author Scott Russell Ducan, for first championing my book proposal at Somos en escrito Literary Foundation Press—where we both volunteered together at the time—and helping *Somos Xicanas* reach the production phase after a long year and nine months of waiting for it to be approved. Thanks to Scott, for additionally acting as one of the editors for this anthology, helping with vetting decisions and organizing our *Somos Xicanas* "Enduring & New Mujer" panel at the 2024 Lit Crawl Festival in San Francisco—an event which he also emceed.

To my hardworking and inspiring publisher, Brenda Vaca, who, upon hearing that the *Somos Xicanas* manuscript was looking for a new home, promptly invited me to publish it at her Xicana-run, revolutionary press, Riot of Roses Publishing House. Since then, Brenda made miracles happen so that we would have a 2024 release, as originally planned . . . and so much more!

To Emily Anne Evans, Riot of Roses' in-house skilled book designer who worked swiftly and meticulously to produce a beautiful interior layout and back cover design.

To all the contributors who kindly agreed to have their images grace the book's front cover, and those who enthusiastically offered to organize book readings at their local bookstores, and other venues.

Respectfully, to Armando B. Rendón, author of *Chicano Manifesto*—the seminal book on Chicanismo and the Chicano Movement—founder and Executive Director of Somos en escrito Literary Foundation Press, for originally accepting my manuscript, for the subsequent and careful work he put into vetting submissions and editing content, and for the amistad we cultivated around it and the other projects we worked on together.

ACKNOWLEDGMENTS

A mi querida amiga and publisher extraordinaire, Alice Maldonado Gallardo, who very generously offered to publish the *Somos Xicanas* manuscript via her bilingual imprint, Ediciones Océanicas, before I had decided on a press. Mil gracias, always, for continually championing my dreams.

My gratitude to poet Carolyn Chilton Casas, my dear Reiki sister, for her eagle-eyed proofreading, detailed copyediting, and for being one of my main cheerleaders.

To my youngest, Nishi, and their partner, my sweet daughter-in-law, Auzy, con mucho amor y cariño, for their very helpful editorial suggestions and continued emotional support through the bumpy and long road that has led to the publication of this book.

Graham, mi amor, for the countless ways your love for me acts like the wind in my sails, in the pursuit of making all my wild project ideas come true.

A very special tlazocamati to the 80 Xicanas who entrusted me with their valuable palabras. It is due to their generosity and enthusiasm to share their writings that *Somos Xicanas* was born. I am so grateful to each and every one of these hermanas, whom I've gotten to know to various degrees, and grown to admire, during the course of this project.

My appreciation, de todo corazón, to all the talented Xicanas whose work didn't make it into this anthology for length constraints, etc. Thank you for receiving the news so gracefully. This is a testament to Xicanas' dedication to solidarity. ¡Juntas, sí se puede! Your voices are valuable and also belong to the intricate tapestry of our Xicana literature.

And, mil gracias, dearest reader, for giving yourself to these beautiful, powerful Xicana voices. I invite you to explore other wonderful publications that many of our contributors appear in.

Lastly, I offer this book to the well-being of the Xicana community, in hopes that it will inspire more Xicanas to share their voices.

ABOUT THE PUBLISHER

Riot of Roses Publishing House was founded in 2021 specifically to amplify the stories of historically silenced voices.

Xicana owned. Mujerista focused. For the people.

We publish books that heal and liberate.

Read our rebellion.

Find & follow us @riotofrosespublishing

Visit us at www.riotofrosespublishinghouse.com